HEART OF A
CHAMPION

Other Heart of a Champion™ Books from Steve Riach:

Passion for the Game
Inspire a Dream
Above the Rim
The Drive to Win

Heart of a Champion™ Videos Available:

Spirit of the Game
Give Me the Rock
Driving Force
Sammy Sosa: Making History
Joe Gibbs: Fourth and One

WRITTEN AND COMPILED BY STEVE RIACH
WITH JOHN HUMPHREY

COMMENTARY BY

Clark Kellogg

HEART OF A
CHAMPION

Profiles in Character
including the stories of Kurt Warner,
David Robinson, Michelle Akers,
Jeff Gordon, Alex Rodriguez, and
many more.

BROADMAN
&HOLMAN
PUBLISHERS

Nashville, Tennessee

0-8054-2419-9 (pb)

Published by Broadman & Holman Publishers, Nashville, Tennessee

Dewey Decimal Classification: 796
Subject Heading: ATHLETES
Library of Congress Card Catalog Number: 00-048582

This book is the result of the cumulative efforts of several researchers, over many years, securing information on thousands of sports personalities. In the writing and editing of the book, each person involved in the research process throughout the years has added value to the underlying factual material herein through one or more of the following: unique and original selection, coordination, expression, arrangement, classification of the information, and original text.

Unless otherwise stated all Scripture citation is from the Holy Bible, New International Version, © 1973, 1978, 1984 by International Bible Society. Scriptures marked NKJV are from the New King James Version, © 1979, 1980, 1982, Thomas Nelson, Inc., Publishers; and TLB from The Living Bible, © Tyndale House Publishers, Wheaton, Ill., 1971, used by permission.

Library of Congress Cataloging-in-Publication Data
Heart of a champion : profiles in character / Steve Riach
    with John Humphrey.
        p. cm.
    ISBN 0-8054-2419-9 (pb)
    1. Athletes—United States—Biography. 2. Athletes—United
States—Conduct of life. 3. Character. I. Riach, Steve, 1961– .
II. Humphrey, John, 1959– .

GV697.A1 H3679   2000
796'.092'273—dc21   00-048582
                                                            CIP

1 2 3 4 5 6 7 8 9 10 05 04 03 02 01

This book is dedicated to
the life and example of Bob Briner, the original Roaring Lamb,
who set a standard, inspired great dreams,
and showed so many of us the way.

And to our wives,
Wendy Riach, Rosie Kellogg, and Kathleen Humphrey,
who have been profiles of character for each of us,
as our greatest human form of support and encouragement.

Additionally, we choose to dedicate this work to
the men and women from the world of sports
who possess the heart of a champion—
who, in demonstrating lives and careers driven by faith and virtue,
have become wonderful examples to the world.

CONTENTS

FOREWORD

When I think of the phrase *heart of a champion,* what immediately comes to mind are the character traits that I believe are embodied by a true champion. I think of men and women who participate in their sports for reasons beyond money and fame. Rather, they have a passion to fulfill their destiny. They are living out a significant part of the very thing for which they were created. Those possessing the heart of a champion are driven to become all that they were meant to be. Win or lose, in personal acclaim or individual failure, they never waver in their sense of purpose.

This is because those with a true heart of a champion are steered by commitment, compassion, and courage. They are committed to the pursuit of excellence in each and every aspect of life and competition. They are committed to live and work to a higher standard than the norm. They understand that they can never reach their goals without the discipline or the sense of priorities necessary to be willing to pay the price to become a champion. As well, they will never compromise personal convictions for the sake of temporary success.

True champions also possess depth of compassion—a sensitivity and tenderness toward others, and a willingness to place the needs of those around them above their own. They will never gain personally at the expense of causing harm or embarrassment to another, either friend or foe. They know success cannot be achieved without teamwork, and within the structure of a team, winning the prize itself is usually secondary to experiencing the journey of becoming winners. They also understand the most fundamental principle of leadership: the best and most effective leaders are those who serve rather than those who impose their will on others.

Courage is also a hallmark of a true champion. Courage can be defined as doing what's right even when it's not the easiest thing to do . . . or when no one is around to see you do it. It means doing what's right, simply because it is right, regardless of the outcome or consequences. It takes courage to admit failure, to take responsibility for a mistake or error, and to face the critics. Courage is also on display when one overcomes adversity or perseveres in chasing a dream. After all, it isn't the goal that provides meaning to our lives. It is the struggle to reach the goal—and what we learn through that struggle—that has so much value.

The heart of a champion also engenders thoughts of wisdom, work capacity, and perseverance. Wisdom is the ability to discern between what is best versus what is good. A champion never sacrifices the best for the good. Thus a champion would never use performance enhancing drugs or cheat in any way, knowing that doing so would be settling for less than their true best. Work capacity is the desire and discipline to put forth consistent effort in all endeavors. It is the capacity to work at a level that exceeds expectations from others, knowing that, ultimately, effort is not judged by peers, stopwatches, fans, or media. Rather, it is judged from within. Perseverance is patient, purposeful effort—staying the course and not giving up or giving in despite inevitable roadblocks and obstacles. It is in times of pressure, when one feels trapped in a veritable crucible, that true character becomes evident. When a man or woman is tested, their character speaks ever so loudly, and much more so than any words.

The heart of a champion is also about faith. Faith to hope for what is yet unseen. Faith to believe that the finish line can be reached, the play can be made, the record can be attained, the best can be given. And faith in the Creator, that his plan, purpose, and destiny are what will bring real fulfillment.

The heart of a champion encompasses everything that is good in sports and in our world.

The heart of a champion in those we watch is the reason we stand up and shout or cheer.

The heart of a champion in those whose stories we read about is what draws us to sports' real heroes.

The heart of a champion is not just about what you've won or what you've done. It's an attitude. A way of life. It's how you live and what you stand for. It's the foundation for your whole life and existence.

The heart of a champion is not just something you have. It's something you are.

— Clark Kellogg

ACKNOWLEDGMENTS

The amount of research necessary for a book such as this is almost unmanageable. Sorting through thousands of individual personality files for relevant information, consulting articles, and reviewing transcripts gives new meaning to the phrase *tired eyes*. Yet the task was made easier through the help of some key people.

First, we'd like to thank Mary Ann Van Meter, our trustworthy assistant, for her efforts in scanning, sorting, typing, and generally keeping track of all pertinent and important information and notes. In typical fashion, she put up with last-minute requests and changes from the author, recreated lost information sheets, made countless calls to fill in holes, and did it all with her usual joyful and encouraging spirit.

Next, a big thanks to Kirk Albrecht, who scoured the Internet and other outside sources for additional appropriate information. Kirk asked for "a few" names to research, so we gave him about five hundred. Undaunted, Kirk spent many long nights "surfing the web" for tidbits on the many names listed. He came up with a veritable sports library. We appreciate Kirk's patience and persistence in gathering information as the mountain of information grew and the months passed.

We also want to thank the many individuals who transcribed hundreds of hours of interviews: Lauren Board, Faith Briguglio, Melanie Courtright, Diane Fisher, LeAnn Fisher, Kathryn Flenniken, Alyssa Garrett, Annette Glavan, Jennifer Lewellen, Lori Matheny, and Ruth Menefee.

Thanks also to John Peterson, Dave Koechel, Lance Wubbels, and Tom Henry of Koechel-Peterson & Associates for the photographs they contributed to the book.

For the fine folks at Broadman & Holman, a big thank you to all who have had a part in this work. Special thanks to Gary Terashita for his guidance, encouragement, and patience in the writing process; and to him and Lisa Parnell for their expertise in the editing process and their desire to see a finished work that will influence many. Much gratitude to Ken Stephens and Bucky Rosenbaum, as well, for having a vision for such a book, and trusting us to complete the task.

To all the athletes and coaches we've been blessed to interview over the years—thank you for sharing your lives with us. And thank you for allowing us to share them with the rest of the world. Your examples of virtue in a time when real heroes are so desperately needed have been bright lights in a dimly lit world.

Finally, we would like to express our appreciation and undying respect for our families.

In Steve Riach's case:

To my children, Kristen, Joshua, and Elissa—for understanding during my days and nights of writing when we had less time to do the really fun things—thank you! You continually brought me joy in a process that would have otherwise become arduous. I love you all.

To my parents, Tom and Joan, who have always believed in me, your encouragement and support is beyond what most people could ever deserve or hope to receive.

And to my wonderful wife, Wendy, who never complained about hearing papers ruffling or laptop keys pounding at all hours of the night or early morning; who kept the children occupied on a number of Saturdays; who put up with the phrase "how does this sound . . ." more times than I can count; who read pages until her eyes blurred; and who always said, "You are doing a great job, honey; this will be a great book,"—thank you for always standing by me and supporting my dreams. I love you.

In John Humphrey's case:

A note of personal thanks to my children, Jessica and Lauren, for permitting me the time necessary to work on this book. Your sunny dispositions brought hope to every day.

And a word of deep love and gratitude to my wife, Kathleen, for your understanding and patience as we have navigated the daily uncertainties that come with entrepreneurship. You have been a pillar of reality and encouragement.

> **A champion gives his all
> no matter what the score.**

CHAPTER 1

EXCELLENCE

A challenge we constantly face—no matter what realm or profession we're in—is to not settle for "good" versus "best."

In our society, good sometimes impresses others and is often acceptable. Our best, on the other hand, is a matter of the heart. Unfortunately, we sometimes deceive ourselves into thinking we've given our best when we've simply settled for good.

One thing I learned when I played basketball was that if we settle for anything less than our best effort, we cheat ourselves and our teammates. For instance, a basketball player trying to help a teammate by stopping an opponent from going to the bucket might reach out but fail to move his feet and miss the block. Or when attempting to catch a pass that wasn't quite on target, he reaches for it instead of running for it and misses the ball by mere inches. Because he failed to give his full effort, everyone on the team suffered.

I can think of a particular game during my rookie year. It was late in the season, I had banged up my foot, and probably could have played but decided against it. It was the only game I missed that

excellence: the quality of being excellent, very good, virtue.

1

year. On occasion I remember that and think, *I probably should have played in that game.* I wouldn't have missed a game that whole year.

Excellence is really about giving the highest quality effort you can in every situation. Some days your best effort is going to turn out as 80-85 percent of your capabilities. But your attitude is what matters. You must strive to give your best in concentration and in effort, then allow the results to take care of themselves. The results won't always be the same, but keep the commitment and effort level consistent. That's what you strive for: to be consistent and to do your best.

If you establish that pattern of consistently trying to do your best—in whatever activity—then you are assured of enjoying a level of excellence.

—**C. K.**

"If you can't be a good sport, don't play."
Sam Skinner, Former Radio Sports Announcer

Randy Johnson

Randy Johnson vividly recalls his first experience in organized baseball. He was six years old, attending a Little League tryout in his hometown of Livermore, California.

"I went there by myself because my mom and dad both worked," he recalled. "There I was, with a bunch of other kids, feeling like a lost puppy dog. I didn't know where to go, who to see. I got lost, started crying, and went home."

But Johnson's baseball destiny was saved by a committed mom. Upon arriving home to find her unhappy son, Johnson's mother, Carol, took him by the hand and headed back to the tryouts, where Johnson was placed on a team.

"She knew I wanted to play," Johnson said. "And when I think about it, if she hadn't taken me back, I might not be where I am today."

Where he is today is firmly entrenched—along with Boston's Pedro Martinez—as one of the game's two most dominant pitchers in the current era. His performance has earned him the Cy Young Award as his league's best pitcher in 1995, 1999, and 2000. His one-two punch of a blazing fastball and nasty slider has made hitters fear him.

No one ever doubted Johnson had the ability to intimidate hitters. After all, he was fast. And tall. At the start of his career, the six-foot-ten-inch left-hander used his height, and a hint of wildness, to his advantage. By the time his 98-mph heater left his hand, it looked to the batter as if it was already on top of him. But, by Johnson's own admission, it took years of searching before he became a pitcher, not a thrower.

Ironically, it was his boyhood hero, and major-league foe, Nolan Ryan, who played a key role in Johnson's coming-of-age process. During the 1992 season, Ryan's Rangers and the Mariners were both out of playoff contention early, so Ryan thought nothing of helping an opposing pitcher—especially Johnson, in whom Ryan saw much of himself from his own early years.

Gene Clines, Seattle's hitting coach at the time, asked Ryan to consider helping Johnson, who was struggling through an 11-game stretch in which he'd gone 2-9 with a 5.63 ERA, and more walks than Central Park. Ryan invited Johnson to shadow him through a forty-five-minute workout with pitching coach Tom House hours before the game in the emptiness of the Seattle Kingdome. Then the three men talked pitching.

"He couldn't have been better," Johnson said. "He was very helpful, and I came away with a lot of confidence. For Nolan, I think it was his way of passing things on. It was very special for me. . . . It helped me realize that pitching is more than going out there and throwing a baseball. It's going out there with a purpose of trying to keep your team in the game as long as you can, even when you don't have your best stuff."

"I was just trying to help a fellow pitcher, but my role wasn't that large," Ryan said. "Mostly when I'm asked to talk to other pitchers, it's like a five-minute conversation. They come with questions, but they have their own answers. They hear me, but they aren't listening. Randy was totally different. He truly wanted a different point of view."

From Tom House, Johnson discovered a mechanical flaw and fixed it. "My control improved almost overnight," he says.

Johnson's next start was a three-hit, ten-strikeout masterpiece against Kansas City. A month later, he struck out eighteen in eight innings at Texas before taking himself out of the game. He was well on his way to dominance.

The transformation in his pitching came at a time Johnson was experiencing personal changes as well. He was hit by a twenty-four-month emotional meteor shower of death, marriage, birth, and spiritual rebirth.

Randy's father, Bud, suffered an aortic aneurysm while Randy was flying from Washington to California to spend Christmas 1992 with his parents. By the time Randy made it to the hospital, his father had died. He laid his head on his father's chest and wept.

Distraught, Johnson told his mother, "I don't know if I want to pitch anymore. I'm thinking of quitting."

Once again, it was Johnson's mom who played the key role. She strongly advised him to keep pitching. Randy eventually agreed. Searching for meaning, he also became a Christian and drew a cross and the word *Dad* on the palm of his glove. To this day, he often glances at the markings when he feels a need for inspiration while on the mound.

"Yes, changing my mechanics was a key," Johnson says of his turn-around. "But that's just a small part of it. My heart got bigger. Determination can take you a long way.

"After my dad died, I was convinced I could get through anything. I don't use the word *pressure* anymore. That's for what he went through—life or death. I use the word *challenge*. And I'll never again say, 'I can't handle it.' I just dig down deeper."

Since the start of the 1993 season, Johnson has had Hall-of-Fame numbers: nearly 130 wins, an ERA title, four 300-strikeout seasons, and Cy Young Awards in each league. He has gone from Seattle to Houston to Arizona in the high-stakes free-agent game, but through it all has kept things in perspective, in the midst of a marvelous career that almost never was.

"I can look you in the eye and tell you I have never enjoyed playing baseball more than I do now," Johnson says. "Not in Little League, not in high school, not in college. The word *potential* used to hang over me like a cloud. People would say, 'What kind of game are we going to get today?' Now I'm content. Right now I'm enjoying every aspect of my life."

"The quality of a man's life is in direct proportion to his commitment to excellence, regardless of his chosen field of endeavor."
Vince Lombardi, Green Bay Packers Hall of Fame Coach

Kevin Malone

For most men who hold the job, the life of a Major League Baseball general manager is like a short-lived stint at the front lines of a battlefield. Making trades, wooing free agents, negotiating with agents, overseeing the farm system, juggling payroll, conducting interviews, dealing with fan and media perception, and putting up with the whims of owners can quickly leave these men battle weary and burned out. The glare of the spotlight and the pressure to "win now" has caused many general managers to bounce from team to team, or even call it quits. The emotional strain is immense.

The life of Los Angeles Dodgers General Manager Kevin Malone is no exception. After serving as general manager or assistant general manager in both Montreal and Baltimore, Malone has been charged with bringing the Dodgers back to the heights of their former glory days. To do so means long days, constant travel, and huge cell phone bills. There is no normal day for Malone, just a new round of problems and public critique. The overarching challenge is to maintain sanity and a sense of perspective.

"I've always looked at it that I'm accountable, I'm responsible, that's why I take it so personally," Malone said. "I'm going to do the best I can to make this a championship team and a winning organization. All I can control is my effort; I can't control the outcome."

The challenges are diverse. With agents, it's a simple game of cat and mouse. The agents want Malone to pay his player more; Malone wants to pay less. Normally they meet somewhere in between with the press and fans knowing every move, like a public chess game. As a large market, well-heeled team, the Dodgers can afford to pay more than most of their rivals. So Malone is quite popular among agents. How much to pay to whom is the big question. Make a mistake and the scrutiny never ends. Malone understands the stakes.

"I think most of the agents know my forte is player evaluation," Malone says. "I'm a former player, coach, and scout. I think there is a respect factor I get there. Ask them what they're dealing with in Kevin Malone, and I think most of the time they'll tell you that I tell them the truth. They know it's business. You try to keep it from being personal."

Malone's approach with the media and fans is similar. He speaks openly and intelligently.

"I do that for three reasons—one, for the fans," he says. "I think the fans have a right to know as much about the team as possible. Two, because the members of the media have a job to do, and they are part of the game. They are promoting the game. Three, I want to be an example of the love of God. I want to show these guys that I'm here to help them, and I want them to know I'm different because of Jesus Christ. So I think nurturing and developing relationships is important. I think we should help them be the best they can be, and the more accurate information they have, the better they'll be.

"I can't tell them everything, and I can't always tell them at the time they want me to, but I do as much as I can."

Beyond all this, Malone also oversees a large organization. Managing a franchise presents a unique set of challenges. Still, Malone knows the key is to focus on people.

"I think the GM job is a very difficult job because of the diversity that is needed to be successful," he says. "A major part is relationships. I think I've improved in that area over the years because of my relationship with God. I've become a better listener. I have more compassion. I wouldn't ask anyone in the organization to do anything I wouldn't do, or that I haven't done. I must recognize that I'm not any more important than any other part of this organization."

Malone's caring and humble approach grows out of his desire to excel in putting people first and staying focused on what matters most.

"I can't do this job without Christ," he says. "There are so many demands on my time and so many opportunities to make the wrong decision and go down the wrong path. I need wisdom. I need so many things that only he can provide."

> **"Where have you gone Joe DiMaggio;**
> **a nation turns it's lonely eyes to you."**
> **Paul Simon, Singer, "Mrs. Robinson"**

Ritchie McKay

Ritchie McKay went to Portland State University in 1995 to restart a college basketball program that was dropped sixteen years earlier due to financial problems. When the coach arrived at the school gym, the only signs of the past he found were a couple of moldy uniform shorts that reminded him of another sport. "You know those Speedo swimsuits?" asks McKay, who had been an assistant at the University of Washington before coming to the Vikings. "That's what those shorts reminded me of."

On recruiting visits with prospects, McKay had no highlight tapes to play, no fancy brochures to show. He couldn't even dangle the prospect of an NCAA tournament bid because Portland State wasn't eligible for one until 1999. "I had to find kids with very high character and sell them a dream," says McKay.

But McKay did find players who shared his dream. In the fall of 1995, he took his team on the road for the school's first game since the program's cancellation. They played the University of Mississippi, a strong national contender. With just 3.3 seconds left in the game, PSU was on the verge of upsetting the Rebels and creating a historic moment.

"At this point, I'm literally shocked," McKay says, reliving the final seconds of the game. "We're leading 54-53. We've got a Christian at the free-throw line who once made forty in a row in high school. He misses. Ole Miss passes the ball up to half court. The red light comes on; the buzzer goes off; a guy throws up a shot from thirty-six feet—a heave. The shot goes in. The buzzer has gone off. Our guys are celebrating. But one of the refs counts the basket. I thought to myself, *How would God take that from us?* The replay clearly showed the shot shouldn't count."

McKay soon came to understand, and accept, a larger purpose for that outcome—not for his own squad, but for the Old Miss team.

"If Ole Miss had lost that game to a team that had not had basketball in sixteen years, their confidence might have been shot. But they learned they had to prepare for every team. They had a great season, ended up 21-8, and their coach, Rob Evans—who is a Christian—got his contract extended.

"Life is based upon principles, not circumstances. Sometimes we have to get past our circumstances to see what the real point of the situation was."

The same is true for McKay, who resurrected the PSU program to competitiveness by focusing on excellence. The nation noticed. In 1999, McKay was hired by Colorado State, then in 2000 by Oregon State where he continues his rise as one of the nation's most promising young coaches.

> "The prospect who does what is required of him is a player;
> when he does <u>more</u>, he becomes an athlete."
> **Anonymous Coach**

Dr. James Naismith

At nine years old, James Naismith became acquainted with personal tragedy. It was then a series of events unfolded that would help shape the young man's life.

First, he witnessed the death of both of his parents from typhoid. Shortly thereafter, his brother, Robbie, also suffering from typhoid, begged Naismith to end the suffering by helping him take his life. "You wouldn't let a rabbit suffer like this," he screamed at Jim on the night he would eventually die.

Later, while Naismith was teaching gym class, one of his students flipped, landed on his head, and died. Then, Naismith's wife, Maude, was also hit with typhoid and became deaf from the disease.

Yet Naismith didn't despair. To him, these events fell within God's control. He recognized his personal experiences as a small role in a much bigger struggle between good and evil. It was this philosophy that compelled him to choose a life's work that would help reduce the growing evil in the world.

As a college student in his midtwenties, Naismith was recruited by several athletic teams. He turned them all down, reasoning that academics came first. Later, solidifying his education, he participated in rugby, fencing, and gymnastics. Following college, he pursued graduate studies at Presbyterian Seminary in 1887.

While studying theology, he served the Montreal YMCA and McGill University as a physical education instructor. But Naismith never completed his formal seminary training. In 1890, after joining future sports legends Luther Gutlick and Amos Alonzo Stagg at the YMCA training school in Springfield, Massachusetts, he found his true calling. He saw that, as a Christian, he could use sports as a means of influence. He would never truly recognize the enormous impact of that decision.

Early on, Naismith was faced with a simple challenge: How could he create a new game that would also be a means to educate people about moral values? He wanted an activity that would be recreational and appeal to athletic instincts but would also educate athletes in certain values. Naismith felt that all play and game activity was part of a larger experience—a part of the balance between stimulating the body and mind. The new game, Naismith felt, should be self-instructional—a key part of the YMCA heritage—rather than one in which the coach was the center of focus.

One day, before class, Naismith asked James (Pop) Stebbins, the Y's janitor, to find him two large boxes. Instead, Stebbins returned from the storeroom with peach baskets, which Naismith nailed to the balconies at either end of the gym. When the students arrived, Naismith divided them into two groups of nine players. After selecting a center for each team, he tossed up a soccer ball to begin the game. The rules were simple. Players tried to throw the ball into the basket and could bat, pass, or bounce the ball, but couldn't run with it. William R. Chase scored the historic contest's only point on a twenty-foot shot. The ball nestled into the basket, and Stebbins had to climb a ladder to retrieve it.

Over the next several months, Naismith and his students fiddled with the rules, and the new sport found a name: basketball.

Ever the teacher, Naismith wrote, lectured, and taught coaches during the developmental years of the game. Not only did he pass along the techniques and rules of the game, but he attempted to instill in coaches the importance of sports as a way of communicating values to children. The character traits gained from discipline, hard work, teamwork, and responsibility were important to Naismith and his basketball disciples. From the YMCA, he was able to continue his devotion to meeting the needs of others, as well as sharing the timeless truths of God in local communities.

Little did he know that his game, needing only a ball and a hoop, would be adopted by people worldwide—and that future participants would share the love of God from the platform of their successful careers and/or touring teams. The little part of God's bigger picture had a much larger role than Naismith could ever have imagined.

**"To improve, you must make your
weaknesses your strengths."**

Pat Summitt, University of Tennessee Women's Basketball Coach

Nolan Ryan

Nolan Ryan's credentials are familiar to those who followed his remarkable career with the New York Mets, California Angels, Houston Astros, and Texas Rangers. He is baseball's all-time record holder, with 5,714 strikeouts and 7 no-hitters. His 324 career victories is tied for twelfth all time. He owns more than four-dozen Major League records and was a physical phenomenon over his twenty-seven seasons. He was also a shining example of character, who never complained while performing at a level of excellence that routinely exceeded that of the teams for which he played.

It was in high school that Ryan first gained a dedication to excellence. As a senior at Alvin (Texas) High, Ryan completely dominated the competition, posting a record of 19-3 and carrying the Alvin Yellow Jackets to the state finals. Over the 32 games in the 1965 season, Ryan pitched in 27 of them, starting 20. He finished the year with 12 complete games, 211 strikeouts, and only 61 walks.

But it was Ryan's dedication and durability that amazed those around him. In March of that year, Ryan pitched three innings of relief in a day game, giving up 1 run and striking out 5. Later that night, he started a second game, pitched five innings, giving up only 1 hit and striking out 10 in a 9-2 victory. Two weeks later, Ryan pitched back-to-back complete game victories in the space of just forty-eight hours.

In the postseason, Ryan's lore grew when he pitched a 12-strikeout no-hitter against Brenham High and followed that with a 2-hit shutout against Snyder High five days later in the state semifinals.

The speed of his fastball and his intimidating presence on the mound became storied right there, and Ryan's legend was born.

Some stories from Ryan's senior year have been repeated more than his statistics. After a bout of wildness in the first inning of a game against Deer Park, during which Ryan cracked the batting helmet of the leadoff hitter, then hit and broke the next batter's arm, the third hitter decided he had seen enough and refused to enter the batter's box. His coach finally entreated him into an at bat that produced the season's quickest three-pitch strikeout.

But Ryan's heat caused trepidation for more than just opponents. Once Alvin catcher Jerry Spinks observed a small tear in his mitt, which quickly developed into a sizable hole, caused by the force of Ryan's fastball. He compared the sound of Nolan's heater hitting the glove to a "muffled rifle shot." The "bullet-holed" mitt caused repercussions: "No matter how much padding I put in my glove," Spinks said, "as each game wore on, I had fewer fingers on my left hand capable of gripping a bat."

When baseball scout Red Murff, then of the New York Mets, first caught a glimpse of Ryan, he knew he had stumbled onto someone special.

"He wound up again and threw another pitch that looked like it had come from a rocket launcher, this time on the outside corner of the plate for another strike," Murff would relate later in his book, *The Scout.* "You could hear it sizzle like a thick slab of ham frying on a red-hot griddle as it roared toward the plate.

"That God had richly blessed this young man was blatantly obvious. That fastball of his was unbelievable. It was the fastest I'd ever seen anywhere. . . . And it had life. It jumped off his hand and appeared to hop as it hurtled toward home plate."

Based on that assessment, the Mets selected Ryan in the eighth round of the 1965 amateur draft. Ryan posted a 17-2 record his first season in the minors before making his Major League debut. And, as is commonly said, the rest is history.

The legend of the Ryan Express began in a small Texas town when a young, skinny kid with a once-in-a-lifetime arm set out to become the best pitcher baseball had ever seen. The final chapter concluded fifty-three Major League records later with a spot in the Hall of Fame. What came in between was perhaps the greatest example of a dedication to excellence the sports world has ever seen. Ryan refused to be outworked, which he never was. Because of that, he became a physical marvel, with a fastball that still terrorized hitters well into his forties. And he became a model for athletes of all generations.

Alex Rodriguez

He has all the qualities a man in his position should have.

A strong work ethic. Humility. A sense that you never forget where you come from. Faith. Generosity. Class. Curiosity. An appreciation for people.

He has millions of dollars in the bank, millions of fans in the stands, and millions of admirers who would like to be him.

He is baseball's answer to Tiger Woods, Kobe Bryant, and Jeff Gordon.

He is young, handsome, articulate. And simply the best shortstop in baseball—certainly now, and perhaps ever.

He is Alexander Emmanuel Rodriguez—"A-Rod," as he is known to various parts of the country.

The nation's top high school player became, at seventeen, the Mariner's No. 1 draft pick; at eighteen, the third shortstop to debut in the major leagues so young since 1900 (joining Tony LaRussa and Robin Yount); at twenty, the youngest shortstop ever to make the All-Star team; at twenty-one, the third-youngest batting champ in history, one vote short of MVP; at twenty-three, the third player in Major League history to post a 40-home-run/40-stolen-base season; and at twenty-four, a five-time All-Star and a bona fide superstar—perhaps the best all-around player in the game today. And at twenty-five, the first $200-million athlete, when he signed a ten-year, $252-million contract with the Texas Rangers.

He is the one player most baseball experts say they would select should they ever start a team from scratch. He is the present and future of the great American game.

Hall-of-Famer Ernie Banks, who went to a game once to see for himself this phenom who is in the process of breaking his own records and came away as impressed as everyone else, says, "Alex Rodriguez is going to do things I never came close to doing. He's going to set a new standard for shortstops."

Perhaps he already has.

He is six-foot-three-inches and 215 pounds of skill and grace who routinely leaves baseball people transfixed. He is the rarely found true five-tool player who can hit for average, hit for power, run, throw with the best, and seemingly make all the plays in the field.

He is also a devout Christian and former honor roll student, a sharp dresser who drinks milk instead of beer, calls his mother five times a week, shows respect for his teammates, and signs—even encourages—autographs.

A-Rod is an increasingly rare commodity in sports: a squeaky clean superstar who works tirelessly to improve on the field while embracing the responsibility of serving as a role model. He is a man who lives to a higher standard of excellence—and it shows.

Some marketers have suggested that Alex needs an image that will "give him an edge." But the young man who once held Cal Ripken Jr. and Dale Murphy as his heroes will have nothing of it. He is a rare athlete who understands—and cares—that his every move will be emulated by young fans.

He wears no jewelry other than a wristwatch, saying, "I don't like gold; it's not me."

His minor-league manager, Steve Smith, says Alex has an aura "like a president," yet Rodriguez is ever humble and always respectful of his peers, the fans, and the game itself.

Were he an NBA player, most of the world would know him well by now. There would be A-Rod shoes, A-Rod cologne, A-Rod cereal, or even a movie.

Yet, playing in Seattle for his first seven years, tucked away in the north-west corner of the Pacific time zone, A-Rod has not gained public notice in a way that correlates to his achievements. But those who really know the game have known all about Alex Rodriguez since long before he had a nickname.

In 1995, he was an eighteen-year-old up-and-comer, getting his first taste of the big leagues. When Seattle lost to Cleveland, knocking them from the playoffs, Joey Cora, the Mariners' veteran second baseman, sat in the dugout sobbing in his palms. Alex, the rookie, draped an arm over Cora's shoulder and comforted him.

Those early signs foreshadowed what baseball has now come to realize: A-Rod is special. He has maturity beyond his years and demonstrates rock-solid character attributes many call "intangibles."

Mantle, Mays, DiMaggio, A-Rod. The name association game began dur-ing the 1996 season when Rodriguez was frequently spoken of in the same sentence with the others. It was also the year his name was etched in the baseball history books—and splashed across nearly every sports publica-tion in circulation.

Rodriguez understands he is now forever linked to Banks, Ty Cobb, Mel Ott, Al Kaline, and others whose names echo throughout the game's his-tory. Hitting .358 in 1996, he became the eleventh player to make it to the majors by age twenty and win a batting title at some point in his career. Ten of the eleven—among them Babe Ruth, Lou Gehrig, Ted Williams, Mickey Mantle, and Cobb—are in the Hall of Fame.

A-Rod is awed simply to be mentioned in the same sentence as they. "Especially Ernie Banks, because he was a shortstop," Rodriguez said of the Cubs great. "Most of the names ring a bell . . . as all-time players. I'm only human, so I'm tickled to be mentioned with them, compared to them."

Statistically speaking, Rodriguez's '96 season was at the time the best ever for a Major League shortstop. He set five all-time offensive marks for the position: 215 hits, 54 doubles, 141 runs, 91 extra-base hits, and .631 slugging percentage. He batted an American League-leading .358, becom-ing the first shortstop to win a batting title since Lou Boudreau in 1944. He also became the fifth-youngest player to drive in 100 runs in a season. With his 36 home runs, 123 RBIs, 379 total bases, 15 stolen bases, a 20-game hitting streak, 3 grand slams, and a .977 fielding percentage, at age twenty-one, it made for a mind-boggling season.

There was no sophomore jinx in '97, as A-Rod hit .300 with 23 home runs, 84 RBIs, and 29 stolen bases.

In '98, he bettered most of his '96 numbers, hitting .310, with 213 hits, 42 home runs, 124 RBIs, and 46 stolen bases, in what was easily the greatest season ever for a shortstop—at least until another Alex monster year. He became the first Mariner ever to post a 30/30 season, and the only player other than Jose Canseco and Barry Bonds to reach 40/40.

He was sidelined with a knee injury in the second game of the 1999 season, limiting him to just 129 games during the year. Nevertheless, he pounded 42 home runs, scored 100 runs, and knocked in 100 runners. He carried on in 2000, hitting .316 with 41 home runs and 132 RBIs, a .420 on-base percentage, a .606 slugging average, and only 10 errors, in what may have been yet another greatest season ever.

A-Rod's records and numbers continue to grow each year. By the time he is finished, he may own them all. But what tells it all about Rodriguez is not statistics and accolades; rather, it's the way he lives his life.

He hangs with his brother, Joe, at home and on the road, and remains close with his sister, Susy. He lived in his mother's house until a couple of years ago when he bought his own, on the next street over in their South Miami neighborhood. His house is not the fanciest and not the biggest he could have afforded. He lives there because it is close to his mom.

"Why not?" he asks. "My mom is my best friend."

Lourdes Navarro, a single parent, has given her son balance and heart. "My mom says fame and money mean nothing if you don't stay the same person you were," Rodriguez said. "I won't ever forget when she was working two jobs to support us—Susy, Joe, and me. You forget these things, you forget who you are."

"I haven't seen anybody as polished all the way around as he is," says Mariners' manager Lou Piniella. "His tools, his personality, the person . . . he's a great kid."

It is evident Alex Rodriguez has much—health and wealth, film-star looks, charisma, fame, and good fortune galore. All this, so young.

But he doesn't have it all.

Alex Rodriguez doesn't have a father.

At the core of his very being, the love of his mother, sister, and brother, and fans around the nation notwithstanding, there is an empty place in A-Rod.

"Dad left us when I was nine," Rodriguez said. "What did I know back then? I thought he was coming back. I thought he had gone to the store or something. But he never came back. . . . It still hurts."

Victor Rodriguez left his family in Miami. He had been a successful business man, operating a busy shoe store in Manhattan and creating enough financial security that he and his wife, Lourdes, returned to their native Dominican Republic to retire with their three children, Susy, Joe, and baby Alex.

But the relatives Victor left running the store started running it down. Forced back to work, the Rodriguez family moved to Miami and opened another store.

"From talking with Mom, I found out that Miami wasn't fast-paced enough for Dad, that he wanted to go back to New York and Mom didn't," Rodriguez said. "They talked but couldn't agree. So he split."

Rodriguez did not hear from his father for nine years, until the day the Mariners made him the first player taken in the June 1993 amateur draft.

"To this day, I still don't really know how a man could do that to his family, to turn his back."

If Alex's mother felt the same way, she never showed it. With a family to support, she hardly had time. She immediately got a day job as a secretary in a Miami immigration office. At night, she waited tables.

She wound up owning an immigration office, as well as a Latin-American restaurant.

When you see Rodriguez create memorable moments on offense or defense, it could be with talents inherited from his father, whom he remembers as a good athlete.

But when you see him dig hard to first base on a simple ground ball or observe him sweating out on the field as the sun peeks over the Camelback Mountains of Arizona during spring training, it is with the indomitable spirit and pure work ethic of his mother.

Lourdes Navarro instilled this heart in all of her children. Susy earned her law degree. Joe went into business.

But Joe and Susy had already graduated from high school when their father walked out. With Alex, so much younger, it was harder.

He threw himself into baseball. Joe would pitch to him, always letting Alex win up until the end of the game, then beating him. It made Alex cry, but it also birthed in him an intense desire to get better. His aunt would come to take him to the movies on Sunday afternoons, but baseball won out over popcorn and Alex would instead play the game every day until dark.

Immersed in athletics, and gifted at them, he was still keenly aware that other kids had both of their parents at the games. With Victor gone, Lourdes was working. Alex went solo.

"After a while, I lied to myself," Rodriguez said. "I tried to tell myself that it didn't matter, that I didn't care. But times I was alone, I often cried. Where was my father?"

Others became father figures to him: Joe Arieto, a Miami business-man and family friend who has often counseled Alex and helped him sign with Seattle; and Rich Hoffman, the coach who helped mold him at Westminster Christian High School, where A-Rod came of age as a player.

When Alex enrolled at Westminster in 1990, Hoffman figured he had a slick-fielding shortstop with little power. But during the summer between his sophomore and junior years, Rodriguez blossomed to a six-foot-three, 190-pound superstar in the making. He began to hit the ball hard and far, leading to the inevitable comparisons to his hero, Cal Ripken Jr. In 100 games at Westminster over three years, often playing in front of some 100 pro scouts, Rodriguez hit .417 with 17 home runs, 70 RBI, and 90 stolen bases. The team went 86-13-1. In 1992, Westminster won the national high school baseball championship, and Alex became baseball's No. 1 draft pick.

Still, Rodriguez maintains a commitment to education. He has taken junior-college classes, with a long-term desire to teach. He actively partici-pates in his Grand Slam for Kids education program in Seattle schools and has helped write a short book for teens, *Hit a Grand Slam with Alex*, that emphasizes the positive attitude that drives him, on and off the field.

"I want to help kids; I want to impress on them the importance of edu-cation," he said. "I want to have a long and successful baseball career. But when it's done, I want to have another career, teaching civics and coaching basketball."

Knowing his attitude, friends told him a couple of years back about a gifted athlete at a Miami high school who was not reaching his potential in class. "This kid, Javier, was acting like a jerk, a real knucklehead in classes," Rodriguez said. "I met him. I told him he was screwing up and blowing his chance. I promised him one of my bats if he made the honor roll."

Javier made the honor roll and got the bat. Then Alex pushed him to go even higher.

"Athletics can be a big part of kids' lives, but they shouldn't be the biggest," Rodriguez said. "Education comes first. With an education, all things are possible to kids."

Some say it's too early to tell if fame will change Alex. But both those who have known him since his youth, and those who observe him on a daily basis say if anyone can be a superstar *and* a great guy, it'll be Alex.

"The way he plays the game sets him apart from every other player," says former teammate David Segui. "He plays the game with the intensity of a fringe player, which is a compliment. He plays the game the way it's supposed to be played, plays to win. Let me put it this way: Most superstars wouldn't do the things that he does. He's the best in the game today."

But A-Rod doesn't let his achievements determine where he is among the game's elite. He continues to strive for more. He hired a personal trainer following the 1997 season and works out five to six times a week in the off-season.

"I really feel like I've been given this gift, that I've been blessed," says Alex. "I thank the Lord for that, but I have to remember that it can be taken away too.

"I just want to be a good person. That's the most important thing to me. . . . I want people to look at me and say, 'He's a good person.'"

**A champion sees every
challenge as an opportunity.**

CHAPTER 2

OVERCOMING ADVERSITY

Overcoming adversity starts with attitude, recognizing that your adversity isn't the only adversity in the world. It means having a broader perspective so that you can move forward and deal with whatever it is you are facing in a healthy and a persistent manner.

Adversity tests you. It tests your ability to persevere. It tests your willingness to go that extra step. It tests your patience.

There are all types of adversity, and typically the resolution—working through it—is a process. It forces you to continue to chip away and realize that you have to keep your eye on the big picture. You can't be overwhelmed by the seeming lack of progress.

At twenty-six years old, I was in the prime of an NBA career that was starting to flourish when it abruptly ended due to injuries. To have basketball taken away and yet through that process discover a personal relationship with God through Christ has fortified, strengthened, and blessed me beyond what I ever imagined. Sure, my playing days were over, but at some point that was going to happen anyway and I was going to have to continue to live. So my attitude was to go in another direction and try to apply the things I

adversity: hard times; misfortune

learned while playing basketball—discipline, hard work, sacrifice, team-work, and all of those things—in another avenue. It turned out to be broad-casting.

Adversity is an inevitable part of life. To overcome I must have the right attitude. For me it is simply a matter of knowing that my future belongs to God. My relationship with God through Christ enhances and fortifies every other aspect of my life. That has really given me a sense of gratitude, a sense of purpose, a sense of significance. Even though basketball gave me a lot as a player, I didn't have those other elements in place. Quite hon-estly, as much as I dream of being on the court again, if I could rewind the clock, I don't think I would change a thing based on what's come out of that period.   —**C. K.**

> **"You can learn a lot from adversity. Adversity can make you stronger."**
> **Mark Brunell, Jacksonville Jaguars Quarterback**

Paul Azinger

Paul Azinger's success on the PGA tour is remarkable considering what he has overcome.

For years, Azinger played in golf's biggest events with severe pain in his right shoulder. In 1993 the source of the discomfort was diagnosed as lym-phoma, a form of cancer. Azinger never complained or used his plight as an excuse. He merely pressed on.

Today "Zinger" is both pain and cancer free. Yet the experience is still a constant reminder of his own mortality and a lens through which he views his priorities.

"It was a life-changing experience in a lot of ways," he said. "You feel pretty bulletproof when you're thirty-three. I look at life a lot differently now."

Azinger first noticed shoulder pain in 1991. A biopsy was negative, but the pain never completely left. At the '93 U.S. Open, he had a bone scan of the shoulder blade and another biopsy. An MRI was suggested but he refused.

The pain persisted, so Azinger had another bone scan. Dr. Frank Jobe, PGA Tour medical director, called following the tests to again request an MRI because of abnormalities that showed up.

"I said, 'Look, Doc, I'm playing pretty good right now. The pain usually comes at night, and I can handle it,'" Azinger remembers. "With the help of antibiotics, I just played through the pain.

"I never talked about it. My wife knew. My caddie knew. But it's hard to complain when you're number one on the money list and leading a major championship. It was an arc pain and didn't affect my swing."

Playing through pain, he beat Greg Norman in a playoff at the PGA Championship that year for his first major championship.

But after hurting his back before the Skins Game late in the year, Azinger finally agreed to another bone scan and MRI. This time lymphoma appeared.

"I sensed something was wrong," he said. "But you still didn't expect anybody to tell you when you're thirty-three, you've got cancer."

Surgery, chemotherapy, and radiation provided a difficult course for Azinger. His weight dropped from 178 to 158 pounds. At one point, he said, his right arm became so weak from the radiation that the only way he could lift it was with the help of his left arm. In his worst moments, Azinger leaned heavily on his wife, Toni, and his faith.

"That first chemo session was a doozy," he says. "I suffered intractable nausea and got so dehydrated that I had to be rushed back to the hospital for emergency treatment. But after a few days Toni and I flew home. Coming home is always a relief to a professional athlete, the real reward at the end of the game. This time it was even more so.

"Then one morning while I was getting ready for the day, something happened. I was standing in my bedroom praying, wondering in the back of my mind what would happen if I didn't get better. The sun was forcing its way through the blinds when suddenly a powerful feeling swelled over me like a huge, gently rolling wave lifting my feet off the sandy bottom of the seas. I stopped everything I was doing and experienced an incredible peace-giving sensation. I knew that God was with me. I felt absolutely assured that I would be OK. It wasn't that God told me what would happen next, or that the cancer would go away. I simply felt positive I was in his complete and loving care, no matter what."

While ensuing treatments took Azinger's hair, they couldn't stop his infectious smile.

"What I've learned from this is that I'm not bulletproof. I'm as vulnerable as the next guy, and now I'm grateful for every blessing I have.

"If my doctor told me I couldn't play golf again, I'd be all right. If you have your health, you've got it all. I probably took that for granted, but I'll never take it for granted again."

Azinger has attended the PGA Tour's weekly Bible study meetings for years and was always known as a man of deep faith. Following his ordeal, however, he seemed to have a stronger sense of responsibility to share his experience, to try to help and encourage others affected by the deadly disease.

"Obviously, I'm a much higher profile player than I ever would have been if I'd have won five major championships because of cancer," he says. "I would have to say that probably 95 percent of the people in this country have been affected by cancer at one time or another, in one way or another. So I know people are really going to be interested in what I'm doing. I've had people tell me that I've been an inspiration.

"I feel as secure and happy as I've ever been. I'm on the backside now, and, honestly, it went pretty fast. It was a wonderful time at home with my wife and kids. Now I know where my happiness really comes from."

"The opera's not over until the fat lady sings."
Dick Motta, Former NBA Coach

Mark Brunell

Mark Brunell is considered one of pro football's top quarterbacks. He has led the NFL in passing, been selected to three Pro Bowls, led the Jacksonville Jaguars to become a consistent playoff contender, and has gained a reputation around the league as one of the game's most gifted leaders. He's also known for his courage and toughness.

In 1997, Brunell went down after being hit while attempting to pass in a preseason game against the New York Giants.

The diagnosis was a partially torn anterior cruciate ligament and a completely torn medial collateral ligament in his right knee. Surgery was planned. With all due respect, Brunell begged to differ with the doctors' opinions.

"I knew it wasn't completely torn because I had that injury on the same knee in college," Brunell says. "When they opened me up and saw it wasn't torn, I knew God had healed my knee."

Forty-five days later, to a thunderous ovation that shook ALLTEL stadium, Brunell trotted onto the field to play a Monday night game against AFC Central rival Pittsburgh.

Wearing a bulky knee brace, Brunell was tentative, but he completed 24 of 42 passes for 306 yards and a touchdown in a 30-21 victory.

Such is the growing reputation of Brunell—the guy with the not-so-big body but amazingly large heart.

Brunell is six-foot-one, small by NFL quarterback standards. But he is incredibly athletic—he once ran the 40 in 4.58 seconds—and strong, in the mold of Steve Young. His toughness has never been questioned.

Brunell is a solid family man, father of two young children, and a Christian who takes his role model duties seriously. Mature, mellow, but with a prankish sense of humor, he is the clean-cut all-American hero straight from the pages of a Chip Hilton book.

That kind of character kept Brunell throwing missiles though he went down with a wounded right knee as a college sophomore in 1991. It was a severe injury that would have forced many to quit. But after an incredibly difficult road to recovery, two seasons later, Brunell led the University of Washington to the Rose Bowl. That grit would later set him apart as a quarterback in the NFL.

"You can learn a lot from adversity," Brunell says. "Adversity can make you stronger. It is at those times that I find my strength in the Lord. I realize that he has a plan for my life. Even though I go through such rough times, he is going to bring me through them. They are times I really need to go through."

"You can't be a good leader without good character," says Jags offensive tackle Tony Boselli, Brunell's closest friend. "Mark's a man of his word, a man of integrity. When he says he'll do something, you know it's going to get done. That's what you need in a quarterback."

"Football is very temporary," says Brunell. "You can't put your faith into something that is so temporal because it could end so soon. [Christ] is who I draw strength from. I need him every day. I count on him to take care of me, to look after me, to protect me, and to lead me in the right direction."

"If you can't accept losing, you can't win."
Vince Lombardi, Former Coach, Green Bay Packers

Tony Jones and Mark Schlereth

Tony Jones and Mark Schlereth are two-fifths of the smallest offensive line in the NFL. They are also stalwarts who paved the way for the successes of NFL superstars Terrell Davis and John Elway on the way to back-to-back Super Bowl championships in 1998 and 1999.

"At times it can be a very miserable profession," says Schlereth of being a lineman. "There's a lot of pressure, a lot of pain."

The two men are linked in many ways beyond Super Bowl rings. They play beside each other on the line—Schlereth at right guard, Jones at right tackle. They are close friends. They share a common faith. And they both understand the meaning of pain and adversity.

"Overcoming adversity," Jones says, referring to his teammate. "You've got the right man there. When I'm hurting, I look at him and say, 'Well, I know this guy's gotta be hurting worse than me.' If he can go, I can go."

Schlereth, by his mere presence on the field, does nothing to discourage the comments of his teammate. Right knee, left knee, back, kidney, elbow, you name it, it's been cut on. But the spiritual leader of the Broncos views his twenty-nine (and counting) surgeries as events that have built character and perspective.

"People are always saying to me, 'Mark, what are you going to do when you're forty? You're going to be in pain,'" he says. "My thinking is, you know I could pull out of here tomorrow morning on my way to work and get hit by a bus and that could be it. So, I'm going to live for right now. Now I can sit here and tell you I'm not happy that right now my back hurts. I'm not happy that I've got about 90-degree range of motion in my knee. But you know what? I've got a wife that loves me. I've got three wonderful children who love me. I know Jesus loves me. And I know that when I leave this planet—whether it's tomorrow, or whether it's twenty or thirty or forty years from now—I'm going to heaven. I've got a spot in eternity. So I have joy in my heart about that.

"A lot of times when we really learn things about ourselves is during those tough times, during the times of adversity."

Such was the case with Schlereth's blocking buddy, Jones. In 1994, he went into a Cleveland hospital for routine arthroscopic surgery on his elbow. An allergic reaction to the anesthetic triggered a massive heart attack. Jones flat-lined. He was dead. As in D-E-A-D. Doctors administered an injection into his heart to bring him back to life.

After about a week in the hospital, including some frightening days in intensive care when he was unable to speak, Jones pieced together the facts about what had happened. His thoughts were dominated by his death experience.

"A lot of people asked me, 'What did you see?' I saw a total blackness. I didn't see any light. If I would have actually died, I was definitely going straight to hell, with a Do Not Pass Go sign. I'm glad it happened when it happened, because it really changed my life and put everything into perspective.

"I sat there and said, 'God . . . I don't care if I ever play football again. I don't care what happens to me. I just want to be able to see my son being born.'"

Jones survived not only to see his son born, but eventually a set of twins as well.

Jones' doctors concluded there was no heart damage and cleared him to play football again. Three years later, he was traded from the Browns to the Broncos, where he became a cornerstone of the Super Bowl champions and a Pro Bowler. His thankfulness for a second chance gave Jones a new fire inside to get more out of himself.

"Every time I step on that field, I say, 'Lord, one thing I'm going to do today. I'm going to go out here and play this game as hard as I can for you—thanking you for my talent and abilities. And when I get through playing, I'll kneel down and praise you, and leave it at that.'"

Adversity has served to mold Jones and Schlereth into true examples of courage, overcomers who have stood tall in the face of their own personal struggles.

> **"When you're a professional, you come back,
> no matter what happened the day before."**
> **Billy Martin, Former Manager, New York Yankees**

Jerry LeVias

Growing up in Beaumont, Texas, Jerry LeVias didn't know much about college football's Southwest Conference (SWC). And why should he? After all,

LeVias is black. And through 1965, when he was a high school senior, the conference was all white. And all wrong.

No black athlete had ever been offered a scholarship by a SWC school. Even traditional college football powers Texas, Arkansas, and Texas A&M were made up entirely of white players. Until LeVias came along.

Just as baseball had Jackie Robinson and Branch Rickey working for integration in the 1940s, the SWC had Jerry LeVias and Hayden Fry. Fry, the maverick coach at Southern Methodist University (SMU), was committed to seeing the conference's unspoken form of racism broken. He had a plan much the same way Rickey had twenty years earlier. He was convinced LeVias, a fleet runner and receiver, was the young man who could make the plan a reality. All he had to do was convince the player.

Fry was persuasive, and LeVias agreed to break the SWC's color line by becoming its first black scholarship athlete.

But being a pioneer wasn't met with fanfare. On the contrary, it was brutal. On the field, LeVias said when opponents got him under a pile after tackling him, they kicked him, tried to gouge his eyes, spit in his face, and cursed him with racial slurs. He was even subjected to death threats. At SMU, it was equally rough. Often, LeVias would have a whole row of seats in the classroom to himself.

But just as Robinson did when he broke baseball's color line in 1947, LeVias answered the hate with remarkable personal restraint and dazzling performances on the field, becoming a three-time all-SWC receiver and earning all-American honors in 1968.

In a game at Texas Christian University in 1968, the abuse nearly pushed LeVias over the edge when an opponent spit in LeVias' face. The score was tied 14-14 with about thirteen minutes left. The receiver went to the sideline and told Fry he'd had enough and wouldn't endure any more. Fry ignored the game and sat down to talk with his pupil.

"He said, 'Levi, just go in one more time and run this punt back and you don't have to play anymore,'" recalls LeVias.

Forgetting his helmet, LeVias walked out onto the field and pointed to the scoreboard for all to see. Fry tossed the helmet to him. LeVias took the punt, slashed to the right sideline, and went 89 yards for the game-winning touchdown.

"I think the racism was a motivation," said LeVias who still holds eight

SMU records, more than thirty years after he played his last game for the Mustangs.

In the end, LeVias not only opened the door for other black athletes to excel in the SWC; he also made it easier for them.

"I did not disgrace myself or the black race," he said. "I graduated from college. I wasn't in any trouble. I made all-American and was all-SWC for three years. But as far as the education I received at SMU is concerned, I should have paid them."

LeVias, who went on to a productive NFL career with the Houston Oilers, said the most important thing he gained from his experience is perspective.

"I just feel that if a person respects himself and those around him and has faith in the Lord, we can all get along together."

> **"Don't look back,**
> **something might be gaining on you."**
> **Satchel Paige, Hall of Fame Pitcher**

Dan Reeves

In November 1999, four days after quadruple-bypass heart surgery, Atlanta Falcons coach Dan Reeves was released from the hospital, saying through tears that he had undergone a "life-changing experience."

"I'm blessed," Reeves said in an emotional news conference that day as he grabbed hold of the hand of his wife, Pam. "I understand how precious life is. You do break down a little bit more. You do cry a little bit more."

The life-changing experience deflected a life-ending experience only because Reeves, contrary to his nature, finally spoke up about how he was feeling.

The Falcons were in the midst of the finest season in franchise history. Much of the team's success was due to the personnel Reeves had brought in under his role as general manager, and the innovation and motivation he had fueled his team with as the Falcons' head coach. They were rolling toward an eventual trip to Super Bowl XXXIII. Reeves wanted nothing to stop the momentum.

Not even his own chest pains.

Although he had been experiencing significant chest pains for some time, Reeves was determined to wait until the final play of the season before mentioning the need for a checkup.

But then what Reeves refers to as "divine intervention" saved him. Following a game against the New Orleans Saints, Reeves pulled his family doctor, Charles Harrison, who happened to be at the game, into a corner of the Falcons' locker room and spilled the beans. Twelve hours later Reeves received an angiogram by team cardiologist Charlie Brown III, which showed one artery to be completely blocked. Reeves needed immediate bypass surgery.

"If Dan hadn't spoken up when he did, it would have been catastrophic," Dr. Harrison now says. "If we'd played a Monday night game that weekend, he would have probably died in his hotel room."

"To have a doctor that doesn't even make your trip normally to be there and he's your family doctor . . ." begins a misty-eyed Reeves. "The only reason I went back to the training room was to talk to Bob Christian, who was injured in the ball game. Dr. Harrison was there, and it was almost like I wanted someone to verify to me that I was being smart, that I was OK by waiting till the season was over. Dr. Harrison looked like the ideal one to talk to. And I called him over and I said to him, 'I've had these symptoms they say you'll have if you have a heart problem. Am I being smart by going ahead and waiting till the season is over to get something done?' He said, 'No, you're the dumbest guy I've ever heard of. It's dumb; we need to get it checked out tonight.

"So then when we did check it out we went right into the open-heart surgery. It shook me up because, in fact, at the time that he told me, in my mind I'm going, 'Why in the world didn't I wait?' But then when you find out when they went in and saw the blockage . . . all those things are miracles. Why God did what he did, why those people were in place, you just feel very fortunate."

It was double jeopardy for Reeves who felt the circumstances would spoil what was a very special season and affect his family.

"Bypass hits you right in the head and keeps ringing in your ears," Reeves says. "Your team is in a great position, and you're worried you'll be a distraction. I'd waited forever to get to this point, to have fun coaching football again, and I wondered if this would have an adverse effect on the players.

"Then I went through more personal feelings. I knew I could handle open heart surgery, but what about everybody else? My wife, the kids, the grandchildren, my brothers and sisters, my parents . . . ."

"Something dramatic happened to Dan, not only physically, but emotionally and spiritually, in this surgical procedure," says Harrison. "The fact that he acknowledged that is the key to the whole story. Here's a big jock, who happens to be the winningest active coach in the Tough Guy League. He's so competitive he wouldn't let his mama win at checkers. Now he's showing the cameras the deeply religious, sensitive, and substantial man that lies within.

"The real miracle in Dan's life is his own self-realization of how precious life is."

Reeves, himself, confesses his outlook is entirely different. He is still enjoying football and still focused on winning. But he is also taking time for family like never before. He is still driven, yet driven in a different way—not so much to influence the outcome on the field, but to touch the lives of others. He now realizes how much of life is made up of things that truly are temporary.

"Going through that . . . made [me] more aware of the things you assume or the things you take for granted," he says. "You know how precious your friends are. That people really care about you.

"I'm not afraid of dying. As a Christian you know and understand that there is life after death. That's not something you have to be afraid of. From a loved one's standpoint, you want to spend more time with them. See your grandchildren grow up and all those things that we all want to do.

"You just really put your trust in God. You know he knows what he's doing . . . and that he has your best interest in mind.

"I just felt very fortunate to know for some reason he does want me to stay around. He's not ready to call me home."

"When the going gets tough, the tough get going."
John Wooden, Hall of Fame UCLA Basketball Coach

Michelle Akers

The road to athletic glory is littered with tales of tragedy. Obstacles often become large enough to derail dreams. The best have learned how to turn their challenges into opportunities.

Michelle Akers' story is not unlike many world-class athletes. She started at the bottom and worked hard to make it to the top. In between, there have been a number of ups and downs—struggles that helped define her career and mold her character.

But the difference for Akers, the U.S. women's soccer icon, is that her highs have been like Mount Everest and her lows like Death Valley.

A member of the original U.S. women's national team, Akers was the world's first superstar in the sport. Fifteen years later, she has an Olympic gold medal and a World Cup championship, along with hundreds of individual honors.

At the highest of highs, she's captained the greatest team in the world and been called the world's greatest player.

And the lows? Well, she has suffered through a painful divorce, numerous injuries, which include thirteen knee surgeries, and a debilitating bout with Chronic Fatigue Syndrome that for a time left her bedridden and nearly suicidal.

The desire to be the best is what initially drove Akers in her childhood. It's also what would nearly drive her to destruction.

Raised in Seattle, Washington, she became a standout in soccer, basketball, and softball for four years at Shorecrest High School, earning three-time all-American status. From there, she went on to Central Florida University, where she earned all-American honors all four years and won the inaugural Hermann Award—women's collegiate soccer's version of the Heisman Trophy—in 1988. She graduated as the school's all-time leader in scoring and assists; even her uniform number was retired.

She joined the U.S. Women's National Team in 1985, during her freshman year at UCF, and scored the first goal in National team history. In '89, she became a full-time member of the team and rapidly gained recognition as the world's best player, though hardly anyone on domestic shores knew.

When Akers flew back from the inaugural Women's World Cup, held in China in 1991, an elderly lady sitting next to her on the plane asked where Michelle had been. She explained that she had just played in the world championship soccer tournament, where she scored an unheard of ten goals in five games and was selected the tournament's Most Valuable Player.

"How'd you do?" the woman asked.

"We won," said Akers.

"That's nice," the woman said.

It was more than just nice. The 2-1 win over Norway gave U.S. soccer its first world championship since 1862. But the brief interchange showed Akers how much further she needed to go to bring the team and the sport into the American mainstream.

With each challenge, Akers went into attack mode. Relentless in her preparation and her play on the field, she built upon her World Cup success. Later that year, she was named the FIFA World Cup Golden Boot Winner and the U.S. Olympic Committee Athlete of the Year. She was literally on top of the world. But to get there Akers had consistently run on full throttle using all cylinders. Burnout was lurking, and Akers had nowhere to go but down.

From such tall heights, the falls can be devastating.

In the aftermath of the World Cup, Akers struggled for two years with unexplained fatigue and injuries, eventually collapsing on the field at the Olympic Sports Festival. She was diagnosed with Chronic Fatigue Immune Dysfunction Syndrome (CFIDS), a disease that saps strength and energy to the point it is difficult to get through a normal daily routine, much less compete as an athlete at the world-class level.

"On the very bad day, it is all I can do to survive," Akers said in her testimony at a Congressional hearing on the disease in 1996. "I walk off— drag myself off the field, my legs and body like lead . . . . My breathing is labored. It is all I can do to get to the locker room, change my clothes, and keep from crying from utter exhaustion. I am light-headed and shaky. My vision is blurred. My teammates ask me if I am OK, and I nod, yes. But my eyes tell the truth. They are hollow, empty. . . . I have no energy to eat, to shower, to call someone for help.

"When it was bad, I couldn't sit up in a chair. All I could do was lie in bed. At night I sweated so much I went through two or three T-shirts. And the migraine headaches pounded. *Boom! Boom! Boom!*

"You don't sleep; your balance and short-term memory are gone. I've gotten lost going to the grocery store."

Her battle with CFIDS brought Michelle's world crashing down. But it also provided the impetus for her search for help.

Akers had always been self-sufficient, an achiever who set goals and accomplished them, no matter how great they seemed. Suddenly she was powerless against this invisible opponent. She had nothing within to draw from. No way to win. So she looked outside and found help.

In her own "death valley," Akers found God.

"Even though I couldn't put it into words at the time, I had this big feeling inside that I needed to get things right with God," she wrote in her autobiography, *Face to Face with Michelle Akers*. "I hadn't spent much time thinking about spiritual things since I was in high school. I still went to church on Easter and Christmas, but I didn't bring religion into my daily life. God was definitely not a part of my marriage, nor my soccer career. I threw up a prayer here and there for help or strength or a team win. But I made my own decisions and dealt with the consequences; and I thought I had done a pretty good job of keeping those things under control. Until now. . . . I was forced to lie there and look at my life. I didn't like what I saw.

"At that point, I was glad to give God anything he wanted. 'You can have this stuff,' I said. 'You can have this body. You can have this life. You can have me, because I've made a mess of everything.'"

Since that heart-to-heart with God in 1994, Akers says her life has been completely different. And while her competitiveness did not diminish, her perspective changed.

"You can only go so far with people in talking about a gold medal, because very few people have had that experience," Akers says. "But everybody goes through some kind of suffering, whether it is physical, emotional, or spiritual. The illness has brought me to my knees in all those areas. It's really broadened my testimony and also allowed me into a lot of peoples' hearts where I wouldn't have had access before."

Akers was once the leading scorer in the world—since surpassed by teammate Mia Hamm. During her 1992 season in Sweden, she scored 43 goals in only 24 games, more than any other player—male or female—in the country. As National Team coach Tony DiCicco says, "She was Mia before there was Mia."

In the late '90s, Akers' goals on the field changed. Unable to run hard for thirty minutes, much less ninety, she transformed herself from the world's best striker into the world's best defensive midfielder. Her energy level had diminished, but her skills and heart had not. She became the team's captain and emotional leader; the one all others looked to when they need to be picked up, inspired, instructed, or even chastised. She held that role until her retirement in 2000.

When she put away her soccer shoes for the final time, Akers closed a career that will show her as a winner. She raised the cup at the World Cup finals in 1991, 1995, and 1999, and wore gold around her neck at the 1996 Olympics in Atlanta. In 1998, she was presented with the FIFA Order of Merit—soccer's highest individual honor—given previously only to Henry Kissinger and Nelson Mandela. She was also selected that year as the CONCACAF Top Woman Player of the Twentieth Century. In 2000, she was honored by FIFA as the female soccer player of the century.

No moment epitomized Akers' career more than her courageous performance in the 1999 World Cup final against China. Just six days after the U.S. celebrated Independence Day, Michelle and her teammates lifted the world cup following a dramatic shoot-out triumph. But it was not without an intense struggle for Michelle.

"I knew that to play my game would take everything I had and more, and, unfortunately, I knew the consequences well," said Akers.

"I found comfort and courage in Luke 22–23, which chronicles the crucifixion and Christ's temptation to evade his call to death. Like Jesus, I am sometimes tempted to take the easy way out. His courage to face the cross gave me courage to face my cross and to be faithful to the challenge and privilege God placed before me. Like Christ, I can endure and overcome whatever comes at me, because in light of what God has for me later, the momentary troubles and challenges of today are simply building blocks to something far greater in the future.

"I walked out onto that field with my teammates and before 90,185 of our closest friends knowing I might get pummeled, take a hit in the head, or have to endure ninety minutes of soccer until I was sick as a dog. It isn't anything heroic or mind-boggling. It is simply exacting preparation, a steadfast faith, and an unswerving commitment to run my race so I can cross my finish line with the pride and satisfaction of knowing I gave the game and my God my all."

For the '99 World Cup final, Akers wrote a Bible Scripture on the ankle tape around her socks. It was Joshua 1:9, a passage that reads, "Have I not commanded you? Be strong and of good courage; do not be afraid, nor be dismayed, for the LORD your God is with you wherever you go" (NKJV).

Akers wanted a reminder that strength and courage both come from God. She was unaware, however, of just how much she would need both.

Before the game, Akers, who was staying in a single room due to her CFIDS difficulties, spent time alone writing in her journal. Before leaving her room for the Rose Bowl, she wrote, "Who will I be when I return to this room after the game and look into the mirror? I don't know. I think the key is I'm willing to put myself on the line to find out."

Her role in the very physical final was to keep China's top scorer from shooting, to control the midfield area, to direct the team on the field, and to control and distribute the ball to her teammates. She gave everything she had until she had no more to give.

For the entire second half Akers was delirious. She was oblivious to the crowd noise. The only thing she was aware of was the pounding in her head and the words going through it with every step she took: *Only twenty more minutes. Don't quit. Only nineteen more minutes. Track that ball. Don't look at the clock. Win this head ball. Only sixteen more minutes. Win this tackle. Get lost in the game. Don't quit. Don't quit. Do not quit.*

"With about fifteen minutes left in regulation time, I started getting a little loopy," she recounts. "The 110-degree heat on the field, combined with the demands of the tournament, finally took its toll on me. In the ninetieth minute, I went up for a head ball when our goalkeeper, Brianna Scurry, who was trying to clear the ball, punched me in the head. I went down in a heap, but not necessarily because of the blow to my head. My body simply said, 'OK, Mich, that is enough of that.' Although I tried to rally, my body was having nothing of it. The doctors took me into the training room to get treatment."

Akers has no recollection of the events that followed. Soccer's ultimate warrior doesn't remember being carried from the field, or the ensuing penalty kicks that would determine the game's outcome. The medical staff began IVs on Michelle and administered oxygen, while trying to determine whether they needed to send her to the emergency room. Michelle was alert enough to see Brandi Chastain's Cup-winning goal.

"I slumped back with relief and joy that we had won and that, in my terms, my mission was accomplished," she says. "Immediately, I told the doctors to get the junk out of my arms so I could join my team to celebrate."

Akers wobbled out of the tunnel and made her way to the medal podium to hug her teammates. She sat and rested while the others enjoyed a victory lap around the Rose Bowl. Soon she heard the cacophonous roar of thousands of fans chanting her name, "Akers! Akers! Akers!"

The moment moved her beyond words. She made her way to the middle of the field to respond to the throng with a wave, a smile, and a panoramic gaze at the unforgettable scene. She searched through the crowd, trying to spot her father. Her body was dead, but the rest of her had never felt more alive.

The morning after the title game at the Rose Bowl, Akers woke up in her single hotel room. She was still a mess, but she felt compelled to write something in her journal. She wrote, "I looked in the mirror last night and saw the weary face of a battle-worn soldier-warrior. But the eyes said it all. Exhausted, but fulfilled, satisfied. We did it."

"It really has been an amazing and miraculous ride," she says. "God has used the past ten years of struggle to prepare me for this moment. The adversity and challenges have shaped my perspective and, most important, my heart. It's easy to get caught up in the hoopla of the moment or get lost in the darkness of a trial, but because God has so demonstrated his grace and power to me, I hold steady to what is most important and crucial in my life: My relationship with God and the privilege of being his kid."

A champion is one who makes all those around him better.

CHAPTER 3

LEADERSHIP

I think leadership is about who you follow.

I lead only as I follow God. My leadership style and my approach to leadership are based on the example laid out in the Bible. There are a lot of dynamics and elements that go into leadership, but the core of it is being humble enough to follow the true Leader.

I've always been, and still am, somebody that typically tries to take charge, not in a heavy-handed way but within reason. To do so, I like to have some sense of the direction in which I'm going and where those that might follow me are going.

Yet to lead really is about serving others. As you lead, you want to equip other people to lead and discover who they are, what they are, and what their potential is. So, to me, leadership is serving and building other people up so that at some point they in turn may be leaders in their own right.

In addition to serving, leaders have an impact that lasts even when they are not around.

The great leaders in sports—like Tom Landry and Joe Gibbs—have done just that. They have served others and in doing so have left a legacy. Their impact has lasted beyond their years of being hands-on.

That is true leadership.   **—C. K.**

"Good fellows are a dime a dozen, but an aggressive leader is priceless."
Red Blaik, Former Army Football Coach

Rick Aguilera

In a day when sports stars are noted for brash sound bites, chest thumping, and look-at-me attitudes, Rick Aguilera seems a breed apart.

Quiet and serious, the bearded relief pitcher has cultivated what those who have coached him call the "quintessential leadership style" among major leaguers.

Says Minnesota Twins tough-guy manager Tom Kelly, whom Aguilera played under from 1989–99, "He conducts himself in a classy manner. He's a professional in every way, and he's dedicated to his job."

Aguilera is a true personification of the overused sports cliché "leader by example." He is a tireless worker who goes about his business in a workmanlike fashion. Often when reporters arrive early at the ballpark, they see the lanky Aguilera running alone in the outfield, hours before the game, with groundskeepers the only others to have set foot on the diamond.

When he stops running long enough to talk, Aguilera says of his leadership style, "I'm not a real vocal person. If there's one way I lead best, it would be by my example. Just trying to show a great work ethic and being prepared."

Aguilera's penchant for preparation has helped him put together a widely respected career. In thirteen years on the mound for the New York Mets, Twins, Boston Red Sox, and Chicago Cubs, the California native has appeared in 732 games. In 2000, he surpassed the 300-career-saves mark with 318 and is now eighth all-time in that category. He has appeared in fifteen postseason games and three all-star contests, and has been a key member of two World Series championships.

Still, with all of his accomplishments, Aguilera remains as driven today as he was when he first broke into the majors as a twenty-three-year-old starting pitcher for the Mets in 1985.

"We've been given this opportunity to play this game, and I think it's something players should appreciate," says Aguilera. "It's easy to take this for granted because of the attention and the salaries we get. But once you start to let that happen, it's a terrible thing. If you appreciate the blessing of the game, the least you can do is prepare yourself the best you possibly can, mentally and physically."

Aguilera not only leads on the field and in the locker room, but he's also been a chapel leader for each team he has been with. Here, too, he wants to do the best he can to build into the lives of this teammates.

"Let's be concerned about one another," he says of his approach to chapels and Bible studies. "Let's try to meet each other's needs. Let's try to be accountable to one another. Let's try to set an example in the clubhouse for the nonbelievers in there. Let's stand tall in our faith. Let's be examples of Jesus. Let's try to show the way by the way we go about our daily work and our daily lives."

> **"I've always believed the greatest form of leadership is through example. You don't talk it. You walk it. You live it."**
> **Bart Starr, Green Bay Packers Hall of Fame Quarterback**

Felipe Alou

It was 1956, nine years after Jackie Robinson broke in with the Brooklyn Dodgers and integrated baseball. Felipe Alou dozed restlessly as the bus in which he was riding made its way east through the Louisiana night. Alou was sitting in the back of the bus because in that day that was where a person sat if he was black and traveling in a public vehicle from a place like Lake Charles, Louisiana, to a destination like Cocoa Beach, Florida.

Alou, who was about to turn twenty-one, had only recently discovered he was black. His father, Don Abundio, was black. His mother, Dona Virginia, whose father had emigrated from Spain, was white. Felipe had never thought much about his skin color until he came to the United States from Santo Domingo in the Dominican Republic. Now he was forced to confront it.

In his first professional baseball season in the States, he had just nine at bats in five games before officials of his Lake Charles team realized that discrimination laws in other Evangeline League cities prohibited Alou and two other blacks on the team from playing there. That was why Alou was packed into the rear of a bus on his way to the Florida State League, where the legacy of the Alou family first began.

Felipe, now manager of the Montreal Expos, was the first of three brothers brought to the U.S. He arrived a year earlier than middle brother Mateo and three years before the youngest sibling, Jesus. They would become the first set of three brothers in major-league history to play in the same outfield together, which they did for the San Francisco Giants in 1963.

Felipe's son, Moises, has followed his father's path. He has been in the majors since 1992, when he played for his father in Montreal. Felipe had two other ball-playing sons and namesakes: the first Felipe, who died in 1976 at sixteen, and the second Felipe, who was a highly sought after teenage talent in the mid-90s. A fourth son, Jose, was a minor league prospect until a bum shoulder turned him into a patrolman on the Delray Beach, Florida, police force.

There are also Alou's nephews, the Rojas brothers: relief pitcher Mel, who has bounced around the majors since 1990; and outfielders Francisco, who played in the Giants' system in 1977 and wound up in the Mexican leagues, and Jose, who was signed by the Detroit Tigers in 1988 and released the next year.

Finally there is Jay Alou, Jesus's son, who as a youth played more violin than baseball and desired to become a doctor. Still, in 1994, he went to the Expos minor-league camp instead of pursuing his medical education.

Just as it appears to be inevitable that one day all Kennedys find themselves in politics, sooner or later, it seems, all Alous will play baseball.

"Alou," says Jay, "means baseball."

Felipe's mother had plans for all six of her children—Felipe, Maria, Matty, Jesus, Virginia, and Juan. She wanted them to be professionals, and baseball was only a game. To her fishing seemed a way to earn a good living.

But the family's destiny kept tugging them in another direction.

Baseball quickly became the family business. Matty forgot the sea and decided to follow in his brother's footsteps, signing with the Giants two years after Felipe. He was grateful his brother had cleared the way because when he took the bus from the spring training complex in Sanford,

Florida, to play Class D ball in Michigan City, Maryland, he knew precisely which rest rooms were meant for him. Jesus would soon follow.

Felipe made the Giants during the 1958 season, becoming the second Dominican-born player in the major leagues (the Giants had called up Ozzie Virgil two years earlier, but Virgil had grown up in New York).

Five years later, on September 10, 1963, San Francisco was playing the New York Mets at the Polo Grounds. Felipe was the Giants' starting right fielder. Matty and Jesus entered the game as pinch hitters and stayed in to play center field and left field, respectively. For the only time in the history of baseball, three brothers were playing on the same team in the same major-league game.

"We weren't aware we were making history," Jesus says. "I don't even remember it exactly. It was like my second or third day in the majors. There was a thrill, but it was the thrill of the game, of finally getting to all these beautiful ballparks filled with all these people. We had played hundreds of games together for Escogido [of the Dominican Winter League]."

Felipe, however, has always been the leader, a role that has come naturally to him. Today, he has solidified his reputation as one of the top managers in baseball. In nine seasons in Montreal, Alou has set franchise records with 603 wins and maintained a winning percentage above .500. More than that, he has consistently taken young, inexperienced teams and turned them into competitive groups while also developing individuals, just like one big family. For Felipe, to coach means to treat each player as if he were his own son. For that reason—relationships—Alou turned down millions to manage the Los Angeles Dodgers in 1999, to stay in Montreal.

"The bottom line of why we believe we have been successful with the development of players—and of men—is because of love; trying to follow the words of the Lord about loving your neighbor," says Alou. "And we have shown people we believe in love and respect. It doesn't take them long to understand that even though I'm their manager, I'm not a whip. So they can develop without fear.

"We bring people here; we make the atmosphere respectful, loving. We're working hard, projecting for the future. We care about their baseball career; we care about their personal life, about their domestic life, about their spiritual life. When you come into an atmosphere like that, I believe

41

chances are that you are going to believe what they teach you . . . you're going to obey everything that they tell you.

"We've always had that vision of teaching, not only baseball, but teaching men, so that when they leave here to go to another team, they can be an example for young people."

"No coach sure of himself and his team constantly bawls out the athletes."
Jock Sutherland, Former University of Pittsburgh Football Coach

Brad Smith

For two decades, Brad Smith was one of the most successful high school basketball coaches in America. In his twenty years coaching girls teams at Oregon City High in Oregon City, Oregon, Smith led the Pioneers to a 479-71 record and won six state championships and three national titles. The team gained national recognition from ABC, *USA Today*, and *Sports Illustrated*.

Sports Illustrated senior basketball writer Jack McCallum went to watch the team play in 1997 for a story for the magazine and was amazed at what he saw.

"I'm overwhelmed," said McCallum. "They're fantastic. They may be the best high school girls team ever."

Such were the accolades for Smith, who became the most acclaimed girls high school coach in the country, a position he kept until 1998, when he accepted an assistant coaching position at Vanderbilt University, where his daughter, Ashley, was a star guard. Since, Smith has come back to Oregon City and the high school game.

Smith remembers a turning point in his coaching career, when his perspective changed dramatically and set success in motion. It came in 1988 when he had lost his second-straight state championship—both by one-point losses.

"I remember going to my bedroom and crying out to God, asking him why I couldn't win a state championship," Smith recalled. "I told God how he knew I would have given him credit and praise and how I tried to live a good Christian life. I wrestled with God for most of the remaining night until the answer came the next morning about 6 A.M. It was as if God said, 'Brad, I didn't put you in that coaching position to win state championships. I put you where you are to serve and obey me. What happens while you are doing that doesn't matter.'"

From that moment on, Smith says he was a different man, and his coaching reflected it. "I really started loving the kids more and not putting so much pressure on myself," he recalls.

Smith believes coaching is not a job—it's a way of life. As such, his instruction often takes on the essence of higher principles.

"Love your kids more than you love the game," says Smith, stating his most important principle of good coaching. "Having an attitude of being there for them makes them be there for you. It isn't about winning or losing. It's about being teammates. It's about being part of a group and trying hard. It's the little things."

The "little things" may consist of time off from practice for family activities, church camps, and driver's education class. Practice is even canceled on prom day so the girls have time to get their hair and nails done. The atmosphere is jovial and informal—Coach Smith is just "Brad" to the girls—lessening the stress of the daily routine.

As a part of commitment—to the sport and to the team—each year the players are required by Smith to give up something they love. Red meat, candy, fast food, and movies are a few things players have offered up as a symbol of their sacrificial love toward one another and to the success of the team as a whole. This, says Smith, is a key to success.

"If you want to find a great coach, all you have to do is look at God's characteristics," says Smith. "All God cares about is the team, yet in the same sense all he cares about is the individual. Everything that happens in my life as a Christian is to make me a better team player and to make me a better person."

> **"There are two kinds of people.**
> **There are leaders and there are followers."**
> **Mickey Mantle, New York Yankees Hall of Famer**

Mary Lee Tracy

In 1996, the gymnastics world discovered Mary Lee Tracy when she helped lead the U.S. women's gymnastics team to the gold medal at the 1996 Summer Olympics in Atlanta.

As assistant coach of the "Magnificent Seven," Tracy had the responsibility of turning seven highly talented girls into a championship team. For Tracy, working with two of the girls would be easy—she had served as longtime coach for both Amanda Borden and Jaycie Phelps. But taking five other girls from different backgrounds and coaches and getting all seven to gel as a unit was quite an undertaking.

"These girls had always competed against each other. They came from different parts of the country, and they didn't train together," says Tracy. "I was selected to motivate them to work together. It was an important role that I took seriously. I think that's what helped add to what we did in 1996.

"We had only two weeks together as the USA national team before the Olympics would begin. This close to the Games, we decided to rely on the girls' strengths instead of looking at things we didn't have time to correct. When we would have coaches' meetings or lineups with the girls, we would always focus on what we were going to do, not on where we were weak.

"We recognized that our best shot at gold was as a team—not as individuals. To accomplish this, the girls and the coaches had to make individual sacrifices for the ultimate good of the team. These seven girls also had to believe they were not only the best in the USA but also the best in the world. That's pretty big stuff to believe. You cannot believe in success until you believe in yourself. We had to get rid of all their doubts."

Tracy and the other coaches decorated the house where the team stayed in Atlanta with posters to create a positive environment. They wrote a theme for the day on the outside of a jar and then filled the jar with related quotes and Bible verses.

"The really strong sports psychology words like *believe, perseverance,* and *confidence* are biblical," Tracy says. "Because of the positive role my Christian faith has had in my life, whenever I teach something, I always make sure it's based on Scripture."

And that method hasn't changed for Tracy since Atlanta. She is still turning out champions, as evidenced by her work with Morgan White, who was a top hope for gold at the 2000 Olympics in Sydney before a broken foot caused her to miss the games entirely. Seeing that White needed hope beyond her immediate circumstances was further proof for Tracy that her positive approach was the right one.

"This was a philosophy I took in helping a team win Olympic gold [in '96]," she says, "and it's the philosophy my staff and I continue to follow in coaching our athletes."

> **"A good leader is someone who the people around him will be better with when he's around—whatever that takes. Hopefully, when they look in my eyes, they see something solid there, that's going to be there for them through thick and through thin."**
> **Danny Wuerffel, Green Bay Packers Quarterback**

J.C. Watts

On January 1, 1980, J. C. Watts was leading the University of Oklahoma Sooners football team on a comeback drive against Florida State University as the final seconds ticked away at the Orange Bowl. Today, Julius Caesar Watts is focused on leading the Republican party on a comeback drive as the party of the people.

The former Sooners star quarterback is now a rising star in the House of Representatives, representing the Sooner state in Congress.

Watts was raised in Eufala, Oklahoma, the fifth of six children of a Baptist minister. After a successful high school career, he went to the University of Oklahoma as a wishbone quarterback, leading the Sooners to consecutive Big 8 conference titles in 1979 and 1980, and Orange Bowl championships in 1980 and 1981, where he received game MVP honors.

"J. C. was a great player and a great leader," says Barry Switzer, his coach at Oklahoma. "He was a leader on the field and a leader off it. He was as respected as any player I've coached. I sensed the day he entered politics that he would be the first black governor of Oklahoma. He was a tough, tough kid that stood up and said what he believed in. He's always been his own man."

Following his run at OU, Watts was drafted by the New York Jets as a running back. But he wanted to play quarterback in the pros, so it was off to the Canadian Football League for Watts, where he played six seasons for Ottawa and Toronto, and was voted the MVP of the Grey Cup in his rookie season.

In 1986, Watts says he felt "called" away from football to something new. By 1990, he was headed into the political arena, where he experienced a whirlwind climb to his current post. On November 8, 1994, Watts became the first black Republican from a Southern state to win a seat in congress since Reconstruction. Watts knew the election of a black conservative from the South might not go over well with some groups, yet he was prepared for the fallout.

"My athletic experience was a very good teacher," he says. "It taught me endurance, patience, delayed gratification. And being a quarterback teaches you to have tough skin. Regardless of what people are saying, if you stay focused, things will work out. Athletics teaches you that you can lose without being a loser. When you lose the game, people are booing . . . my faith says, 'Lord, I don't know what you're trying to teach me, but I trust your heart.'

"I have gotten booed by fans in the student section at Oklahoma, and I've been booed in the political arena. You have to have tough skin and understand you will have critics regardless of what you do.

"I got my values growing up in a poor black neighborhood on the east side of the tracks, where money was scarce but dreams were plentiful and love was all around," Watts told the nation in his State of the Union response in 1997. "I got my values from a strong family, strong church, and strong neighborhood."

Bobby Bowden

Bowden.

It is clearly the preeminent name in college football today.

While the second generation of Bowdens—Terry, Tommy, and Jeff—are among the most respected young coaches in America, the reason the name inspires such awe is because of the standard set by the family patriarch.

Now a seventy-something grandfather, Bobby Bowden is the most revered coach in all of college football. His successful leadership of the young men who have come through the Florida State program since 1976 has made him a coaching legend.

The Seminoles have won at least ten games and been ranked no lower than fifth every season since 1987. During the decade of the '90s, Bowden's teams compiled an amazing 109-13-1 record. He took his troops to national championships in 1993 and 1999, and at the end of the 2000

47

season, he stood just a handful of wins away from passing Paul "Bear" Bryant's record for career victories at the Division-I level. This is the closest thing to a true dynasty as there has been in modern college football.

Bowden is also the only coach ever good enough and old enough to be a contemporary of his son, or *sons*. Both Terry and Tommy have walked the sidelines across from their dad in games that caused quite a dilemma for Bowden's wife, Anne.

While Bowden has yet to give in to the passage of time, he has compromised. More than a decade ago, he began watching practices from a berth in a tall tower instead of pacing the field. A couple of years ago, he started using a golf cart to go back and forth between his office and the practice field instead of walking. He now brings tape home to view rather than enduring those marathon planning sessions at the office.

"As you get to be my age, you look for new ways every year to hang on as long as you can," says Bowden. "I'm trying to prolong my career because I love it so much."

No one can say exactly when "Saint Bobby," as he is commonly known in north Florida, transcended his status as a mere regional celebrity. But a change was noticed around 1991 by Charlie Barnes, executive director of Seminole Boosters Inc., whose members accompany the coach each spring on the six-week Bobby Bowden Tour. This pilgrimage to speak before scattered groups of the Florida State faithful once covered only the South, but now it makes stops in Washington, D.C., Dallas, and Los Angeles.

"It used to be just me and Coach driving around in a van," says Barnes. "Now he's mobbed wherever we go. It's 'Bobby, could you sign this?' 'Bobby, we love you!' 'Bobby, take my child and raise him as your own.'"

Why do they love Bowden? Because he is a good man and a great coach who makes the game fun for nearly everyone. In doing so, has he ever drawn a following in Tallahassee. From television networks to bowl games to area fans, everyone, it seems, wants to watch the Seminoles. What they see is Bowden's mix of pro-style sophistication and seat-of-the-pants innovation marked by a gambler's daring. At Florida State, football is fun.

Winning *and* enjoying the game. It is a simple formula, yet more than for any other coach in the nation, the combo is Bowden's signature. He gives his kids the full palate of what college football should be all about. And he gives them so much more—like the father figure many of them have never had.

While there are many things this septuagenarian no longer is, there are many things Bowden still embodies. Ever the coach at heart, dedicated to systematically destroying the opponent, he is also a father of sorts to the kids he recruits. He embraces his players much in the same way as a devoted dad to six children he and Anne have shed tears of joy and sorrow over for forty-plus years.

He is a master motivator, who it seems was born to stand at a podium and inspire a large crowd with a lifetime of experiences, or to sit in a small living room and assure a mama he will take good care of her eighteen-year-old boy. He is preacher, teacher, counselor, father, and showman all rolled into one. Genuine in each. And no one in the game does it better.

"I studied the great coaches," Bowden says. "I studied the way they handled the kids and what they thought you had to do to win. Not so much what strategy they were using in games, but how they were going about their jobs."

He discovered early on in his coaching career what those men had also learned—that no one is totally impervious to the slings and arrows a college coach fields, yet withstanding criticism is a job requirement.

Coaching at West Virginia in 1974, Bowden drew on internal fortitude to survive a 4-7 campaign that got ugly off the field. He was hung in effigy and For Sale signs were placed in his yard.

"Oh, it drove me crazy when the dummies came out hanging from the trees with my beautiful name on them," Bowden remembers. "It's kinda hard to explain to your children: 'Hey children, look at me hanging up there from that ol' maple tree.' My kids would come home at night and say, 'Daddy is still up there in that ol' tree.' It got kind of embarrassing to have to say, 'OK, son, go cut Daddy down now.'

"I lay awake at night wondering 'Why me? Why am I being persecuted like this?' I prayed that things would get better quickly. And they did."

Bowden decided then to leave West Virginia at the first opportunity. The next season he orchestrated a major turnaround, posting a 9-3 record and a Peach Bowl victory that attracted Florida State to his doorstep.

The Seminoles were in ruin, having won just four games during the previous three seasons. Rumors circulated that the program might be terminated. Seeing its potential, however, Bowden took the job with FSU at its darkest hour. He later joked, "When I was at West Virginia, all I heard was 'Beat Pitt.' When I got to FSU, their bumper stickers read, 'Beat Anybody.'"

He quickly scheduled away games against some of the nation's top teams. While most head coaches are hesitant to play the powerful teams away from home without some sort of reciprocal arrangement, Bowden's lack of hesitancy infused the program with confidence. The confidence spawned early success. From the success came exposure. From the exposure, greater recruiting opportunities. From there, better players. And so it went.

The final hurdle, once FSU became a perennial contender, was to beat nemesis Miami, whose Hurricanes seemed to have Florida State's number. When the Seminoles finally won in 1993, the way was paved to the first national championship in school history.

For the past few years, some have quietly questioned how much longer Bowden can still do his job effectively. The coach who began this career almost a half-century ago—who as a twenty-six-year-old assistant at Georgia College grew his crew cut out to look older than his players—has, on occasion, asked himself the very same question.

"I was always too young to be a coach," he says. "Now I'm too old. You say to yourself, 'Am I pushing this too far? Should I get out and let younger people take over?' About the time I get ready to give it up, my conscience tells me, 'Nah, you can still kick 'em all on Saturdays.'"

While he still does kick 'em on Saturdays, Bowden's leadership style has changed over the years as he has changed. Talk exists that Bowden now does little real coaching himself—statements Bowden does nothing to discourage. The fact is he is still very much involved in every aspect of the team. Weekday afternoons he oversees the entire practice from his spot on the tower, carefully scrutinizing every play, every drill, and scribbling in a notebook where he keeps careful notes for correction. If a player makes a mistake in a drill or scrimmage, he will undoubtedly hear about it.

Asked to explain the foundational elements of his program, Bowden cites two points he insists on in assembling a coaching staff.

"Number one, I demand loyalty," he explains. "I want you to be loyal to me, and I'm going to be loyal to you. I want us to be loyal to the athletic director, loyal to the [college] president, and loyal to the university. Loyalty is a big issue. You don't say anything bad about me in public, and I won't say anything bad about you.

"The second rule is: We're not going to cheat. All your assistant coaches are coming together for the first time and they're going to do what the head coach says. You can go back and look at my notes from 1970. They say, 'I will not defend you if you cheat.' If I find out you're cheating, you're gone. We're going to build this program right. We took some lickings early, but it finally began to come together in the '80s. Now we've got a real solid program."

Part of the reason for that, Bowden is convinced, is the stability of his staff, whose average length of tenure is a remarkable 10.8 years.

"We hardly ever lose a coach," he says. "That's big. Kids like to know if they go to a school if the coach is going to stay or is he going to leave. Look at some of these coaches [at other schools]. Every four years they get another job."

One of Bowden's strengths is his ability to see his own weaknesses and delegate accordingly. He has surrounded himself with a superb staff, each of whom he gives maximum freedom and responsibility. He doesn't want to be surrounded by "yes" men.

"If I had to tell you how to do it," he tells them, "I didn't need you."

This approach grows out of an experience he once had as an assistant. "The head coach wanted to tell me how to tie my shoes," he remembers. "I wanted to tie them my own way and I couldn't. I think a coach has more initiative when you let him do it his way. You can give suggestions."

"In this profession where there's such inconsistency, he makes his staff a family," says longtime assistant coach Ronnie Cottrell. "I think we've all had opportunities to leave, make more money, but nothing can take away from that family and the security of knowing his heart. You always know where you stand with him."

In 1996, Bowden relinquished the play-calling duties to offensive coordinator Mark Richt. It was a difficult move for the man who had established his reputation as an offensive "genius."

By no means, however, is Bowden a hands-off coach. He frequently gives Richt "suggestions," as he calls them, and is often overheard asking defensive coordinator Mickey Andrews, "Are you sure you've got the right people on the field?"

On the eve of each game, around midnight, Bowden assembles his staff in his hotel room and begins his weekly "What if?" meeting: What if our quarterback breaks his arm on the first play? What if we score a touchdown and want to go for two—what's the play? What if they tackle us for a safety—do we kick off or punt? Only after each scenario has been satisfactorily addressed are the coaches allowed sleep.

"He's a very high-energy man," says Richt. "He still gets into it. He doesn't ever look like he's drudging through it."

Bowden may not be able to assume the fullness of the role as he once did. But make no mistake about it, this is the man who makes the program go at FSU. He is the man the finest high school athletes from around the country dream of playing for. From Texas to California to Michigan, and throughout the state of Florida, they come to Tallahassee—a tiny panhandle city where only Bowden is more popular than country music and grits—to be a part of something special.

"I like to visit kids, like to talk with them and talk with their families," he says.

Bowden is without peer in the dens and living rooms of the schoolboy stars who often end up on his roster. He has a folksiness and sincerity that win over parents. He is charming and homespun. He calls his players "boys" and uses words like *dadgum* and *doggone* in casual conversation.

"I just try to let parents see what I am and what I'm like," Bowden says. "I let them know I have to be the parent when their son goes off to school, and I can make promises to them that mean more coming from me than our assistants. I can assure them that a one-year scholarship will be renewed each year until graduation, and I can assure them I will take care of their son."

"When he looks parents in the eye and tells them, 'I'll take care of your son,' they believe him," says Cottrell.

"He wasn't just persuasive," says Bob Bentley, a Notre Dame alumnus who was initially opposed to having his son Scott, a former Seminole kicker, attend Florida State. "He was mesmerizing. He didn't talk about how our son could help Florida State, but about how Florida State could help our son."

The stories of Bowden's days and nights visiting with top prospects has become legendary. NFL defensive back LeRoy Butler tells of the time Bowden came into the Jacksonville projects in 1986 and turned a threatening environment into the Bobby Bowden Show simply by pointing to the Seminole logo on his shirt pocket and saying, "We came to see LeRoy."

In 1991, Bowden went to visit Derrick Brooks, now a star linebacker with the Tampa Bay Buccaneers, and ended up holding Brooks' five-year-old sister on his lap until she fell asleep. When Brooks' mother started to move the child, Bowden said, "Don't you move this gal; you let her stay here until I leave."

How could mothers not be won over?

In keeping his promise to all moms, Bowden takes a keen interest in what his players do off the field—and in the classroom. He pushes his troops to spend as much time scouring their textbooks as they do the playbook. And not just for the sake of keeping them eligible to play on Saturdays.

Examples? Heisman Trophy-winning quarterback Charlie Ward was an Atlantic Coast Conference all-academic selection in 1992 and 1993, an honor all-American linebacker Derrick Brooks earned in 1992, 1993, and 1994. Quarterback Danny Kanell was awarded a postgraduate scholarship in 1995. Others have followed.

Bowden himself owns an honorary degree in pedagogy (the science of teaching) from Samford University in Birmingham. Although he is not a professor, he says he definitely feels like a teacher, and not just of football. To be a coach, he says, "you better be a teacher in how to live. I want my players not only to graduate, but to play at their highest potential, to be prepared for the future, and to come out of school with a higher standard of life, a life of honesty and integrity."

His caring extends beyond FSU. Bowden is a devout Southern Baptist who is eager to speak to groups about the faith lessons he's learned over his years in sports. His truest leadership, though, is centered on his own family, which has been called "the first family" of college football.

"Bobby sets a good example for his children," says Anne. "He was never one to get out and throw the ball a lot or camp out with the kids. But his guidance and spiritual life has probably been the key factor in his role as a husband and father. The heart's where it's at, and Bobby has a very sensitive heart."

For the soft-hearted Bowden, the appeal in coaching, as in fathering, is in feeling like an insurance salesman or minister, who is focused on long-range returns.

"Football is not my number one priority in life. It's a priority, a big one. It's the ability God has given me to make a living," he says. "Somebody asked me why I'm in coaching. . . . He just led me into it. I think God's got a plan for everybody.

"I'm interested in knowing that ten years from now those players will know I was more concerned about the relationship I had with them.

"When I coach these players and try to build them into a champion, even if we're not a champion on the field, one player might come back to me ten, twenty, thirty years later and say, 'Coach, I'm glad you didn't let me do this.'

"Those are our dividends that come down the road and make you love coaching in college and working with these young men."

"When the man speaks, it is pure inspiration," says Marcus Outzen, a Seminole quarterback from 1996–2000.

While it's true Bowden inspires thousands beyond his team, he spends some thirty Sundays a year in churches across Florida connecting with young and old alike. It is Outzen's response that continues to provide Bowden his reason for staying in the game: to touch the lives of those one hundred kids each year who are fifty years his junior.

"I'm not one of those guys anxious to retire," Bowden says. "I'm still having fun. I still love the whole process of putting it together—trying to recruit the best players, trying to be the best coaches, trying to get the best offense, trying to get the best defense—and then just trying to win 'em all and get that treasured prize.

"When I can't talk to kids, I'll get out."

> **A champion dedicates himself to prepare for success.**

CHAPTER 4
DISCIPLINE

Discipline means doing what you know is right even when you don't feel like it.

Discipline is training, practicing the habit of doing what you know needs to be done even in those moments when you don't feel like doing it. You can't have success without discipline, no matter what area of life you're talking about. It's the hallmark of being successful.

For me, as an athlete, the most difficult aspect of discipline was staying in shape to play. What got me through was recognizing that I couldn't perform at the level I wanted if I didn't do the conditioning and solo work. Still today, that's probably where I struggle with discipline the most—especially when tempted with cakes and pies and cookies.

If an athlete has shown consistency over a long period of time, you know there has been a strong element of discipline in his approach to athletics. A. C. Green is an example of a performer who has maintained consistency for a long time at a high level in the world of sports.

I did radio and some small-scale regional television during the first two years of my broadcasting career. Early on, because I wanted to get better, I disciplined myself to listen to tapes—that weren't very good—of early games that I did. I knew the key was to critique myself in order to further my budding broadcasting career.

That discipline paid off tremendously. My career in broadcasting, although it's been a progression, has advanced fairly rapidly—from radio to local television to regional to national and now to the highest level at CBS covering one of the greatest sporting events of all, the NCAA tournament.

That didn't happen without exercising discipline.

—C. K.

"The only discipline that lasts is self-discipline."
Unknown Football Coach

Orel Hershiser

In 1988, Orel Hershiser rewrote baseball's record books with all of the celebrity of a CPA. He looked like a choirboy but pitched with the heart of a lion. His amazing run thrust Hershiser into the national spotlight as one of the top pitchers in baseball as he led the Los Angeles Dodgers to an improbable World Championship, in what still remains one of the greatest single-season performances by a pitcher in baseball history.

In his last 101²/₃ innings of that season, Hershiser was virtually unhittable, giving up a minuscule five earned runs, all of which came in 42²/₃ innings of postseason play—when he was starting on three days' rest. His victims merely walked away shaking their heads, convinced they could hit him—if given just one more chance.

Maybe it's because he looked so unassuming. Maybe it's because he didn't possess a 95-mph fastball. Maybe it's because those pitches did look hittable until they sank, broke, sliced, or darted at the last moment.

Regardless, he was Cy Young-like all season, winning 23 games and losing 8, with a 2.26 ERA as the Dodgers won the National League West. He surpassed Hall-of-Famer Don Drysdale's mark by ending the regular season with a major-league record 59 consecutive scoreless innings. And he embodied the Dodgers' postseason Cinderella story, pitching and occasionally hitting L. A. to victory over the far superior New York Mets and Oakland Athletics. More than that, he carried himself with remarkable grace and affability. While he was stunning on the mound, he also seemed a little stunned at what he was accomplishing. His humility touched many.

"One thing you have to remember about Orel," said former Dodgers catcher Rick Dempsey, "is his determination. I've never seen anything like it. He wants to succeed so badly that he refuses to give in. He got into this groove, and he wasn't afraid to keep it going. Some guys will walk away from it because of the pressure, but he won't."

Hershiser never seemed to let the pressure rattle him. Through all the hoopla surrounding his achievements in '88, he always kept a sense of peace, which was visible to observers. He knew his role, whether fair or not, and he embraced it and carried the Dodgers.

On the night of the series-clinching game, Hershiser disciplined himself to focus only on the next pitch, the next batter, the next inning—just as he had throughout the scoreless streak—and not what another superb performance could mean to him and his team.

That's how the hymns came about. Television cameras caught Hershiser between innings, sitting on the bench, head back, eyes closed, seemingly meditating. But he wasn't meditating; he was singing. In between innings of the biggest game of his baseball life, Hershiser was singing his favorite hymns.

The two songs he sang were the Doxology ("Praise God from Whom All Blessings Flow") and a contemporary Christian song called "Rushing Wind" by the late Keith Green.

Said Hershiser: "There's a line in that song—'Rushing wind blow through this temple, blowing out the dust within'—that seemed particularly appropriate. I wanted to cleanse my mind of all the clutter in the world at that moment, to block out the pressure and concentrate on the game at hand."

In an appearance with Johnny Carson on "The Tonight Show" the day after the Series finale, Hershiser, at Carson's prodding, proceeded to sing a few bars of the Doxology.

It was pure inspiration.

All of this to-do was over a man who was cut from his high school baseball team, who didn't make the traveling squad of his college team, and who almost quit the game while he was in the minor leagues. His was a classic story, a triumph for everyone who has been told they would never make it. The Dodgers could never win the World Series. Drysdale's record would never be broken. This skinny kid would never become a major-league pitcher.

But once he arrived in L. A. in 1994, he was determined to succeed. Hershiser sat with manager Tommy Lasorda and pitching coach Ron Perranoski, soaking up everything they knew about pitching. His commitment to learn and work was unparalleled. He soon became the Dodgers' ace, going 19-3 with a 2.03 ERA in his second season, setting the stage for his amazing run in '88.

But by 1990, too many sinkers and sliders had taken a toll on Hershiser's pitching shoulder.

Surgery to reconstruct the anterior capsule and tighten the ligaments would end his career they said. Not so, said Orel. After all, this was the "Bulldog," as Lasorda had nicknamed him.

The results of the injury meant he had to become more of a finesse pitcher. To succeed in that role meant even more work and more discipline. It also meant a new outlook.

Before the surgery, Hershiser certainly loved the game, but afterward he learned to celebrate the game anew each day. And work even harder.

"Before the injury, I was a hard worker," he said. "I appreciated this game . . . but . . . it's like people who suffer heart attacks or strokes. The flowers look brighter. The steak smells better on the grill. Everything is heightened when you're given something back."

So, equipped with a new perspective, he went to work again, this time with even more vigor. Following the injury that should have ended his career, Hershiser went on to pitch effectively for ten more seasons, until he retired midway through the 2000 campaign, at forty-one, having become one of the most respected players ever to play the game.

**"Always have a plan, and believe in it.
Nothing good happens by accident."**
Chuck Knox, Former NFL Coach

Cade McNown

It's been said that it's a long road to make it as a quarterback in the NFL, but in the case of Cade McNown of the Chicago Bears, it's possible to be more specific: about six hundred miles up the West Coast on Interstate 5.

In the summer of 1994, after his junior year in high school, McNown packed his life into a Volkswagen Rabbit, put the dusty farming town of Hollister, California, in his rearview mirror, and headed north for West Linn, Oregon, a quiet suburb of Portland. Thus began the unlikely journey that has taken him from a relative unknown to the Bears' quarterback of the future.

After two seasons at Hollister's San Benito High School, quarterbacking a weak, run-oriented team that underused his passing skills, McNown was going nowhere in football. But his disappointing sports career was hardly the most painful issue he was dealing with at the time.

When Cade left Hollister to live with the in-laws of his older brother, Jeff Jr., he did so because his parents' divorce had left him few alternatives. His mother, Vicki, and his two younger sisters were planning a move later that summer to West Linn, and McNown had become so estranged from his father, Jeff Sr., that he hit the road without so much as a good-bye.

Recalling his exodus from Hollister, Cade says, "It was kind of like starting a new life."

Being "born again" might be a better way to put it. In Oregon, McNown found a revival that was both athletic and spiritual.

A stellar senior season at West Linn High School earned McNown a scholarship to UCLA, where over four seasons as the Bruins' starting quarterback he set numerous records and became a Heisman Trophy finalist. Much of his success came—as it does today with the Bears—through his ability to scramble and improvise, to throw on the run and turn a broken play into a touchdown. It's the same thing he has done with his life.

Shortly after moving in with Linda and Dale Ebel, the pastor of Rolling Hills Community Church, Cade was impressed by his brother Jeff Jr.'s renewed devotion to Christianity.

"He had this peace about him I really admired," says Cade. "I had lived my whole life not being accountable to anyone or anything, and I realized there was something missing."

That his older brother would have an influence on Cade is no surprise. Jeff Jr. had spent three seasons as San Benito High's starting quarterback and sparked Cade's interest in playing the position. "Jeff has always been my hero," Cade says.

Inspired and encouraged by Jeff, Cade became a Christian and was baptized in a friend's swimming pool in the spring of his senior year.

"Fatherless kids reach out for guidance," says Cade. "Some find it in MTV, some in gangs. I was lucky enough to be surrounded by godly, Christian men."

Those around him say it's impossible not to be struck by McNown's character.

"What makes him a good athlete is the way he practices, and it's the same with people," says McNown's mom, Vicki. "Cade knows that to be the man he wants to be, it takes practice. That means surrounding himself with the right kind of people, participating in the right kind of activities, even listening to the right kind of music."

His friends agree, attributing his success to the kind of intangibles that aren't measured by college recruiters or NFL scouts: his attitude—"He doesn't get that big brain," says former Bruin teammate Jermaine Lewis—and his work ethic.

"Cade is a voracious learner," says UCLA coach Bob Toledo, who tells of the time shortly after McNown signed with the Bruins, when he persuaded Toledo, then the UCLA offensive coordinator, to send him the Bruins' playbook. "Pretty soon my home phone began ringing off the hook, usually at around eleven at night, because Cade had thought of a new question," says Toledo.

"I don't know if I've ever seen a guy at his age who is as much a student of the game as Cade is," says Troy Aikman, once McNown's hero, now his friend and NFL foe.

"He is one of the fiercest competitors you will ever be around," says Toledo. "But you will never hear a bad word come out of his mouth. He is such a tremendous leader. But as strong of a leader as he is, he is even more of a role model off the field."

To McNown there is no bigger honor.

**"Ability is what you are capable of doing.
Motivation determines what you do. Attitude is how you do it."**
Lou Holtz, South Carolina Football Coach

Scott Simpson

One of Scott Simpson's most thrilling moments in golf, he admits, came when he sank the final putt to win the GTE Byron Nelson Classic in 1993. In a way, Simpson feels a connection with the legendary Nelson, golf's gentle giant.

Each week, it seems, as the bustle of life on the PGA Tour unfolds around him—players huddling with agents, meeting and greeting sponsors, and signing autographs for clamoring fans—Simpson seems relaxed and oblivious to it all. He's more interested in posting the week's Bible study schedule.

Simpson's behavior used to be the reason America loved the gentleman's game. It is called sportsmanship.

Simpson stands out among today's self-centered athletes. He is a champion (1987 U.S. Open) who believes in waiting his turn. In the tradition of Nelson, Simpson is a walking billboard for character and sportsmanship, although few outside of golf's inner circle have even noticed.

That's because, as Nelson once was, Simpson is now golf's finest quiet man. While winning a number of tournaments, he has remained almost invisible among golf's masses. Still, it's hard to find anybody who plays the game with more dignity and grace.

Among his peers, Simpson's work habits are almost legendary—undoubtedly the main reason he frequently seems to be in the hunt for the lead on Sundays. A prominent sports psychologist who has worked with Simpson says he has learned more from his client than the other way around. Yet Simpson has been virtually ignored by the surrounding media.

The reason for such lack of attention is simple: Simpson is too "vanilla" for today's journalists. He is a devoted family man who is only seen with his wife and children. He's a devout Christian intellectual who lives his principles instead of advertising them. He works hard, plays clean, and doesn't talk about himself.

"On the course, Scott is so good he's almost—I hate to say it—boring," says his friend Larry Mize. "He's down the middle of the fairway and almost always putting for birdie. Nothing seems to rattle him one way or another. You play a round with him and you don't seem to notice what he's doing. But later it hits you how awesome he was."

During an exceptional career at the University of Southern California, where he won national collegiate titles in 1976 and 1977, Simpson made a priority of gaining his business degree, figuring "that the chances of making a career out of golf were pretty slim."

After three trips through the Qualifying School, he made it to the Tour in the fall of 1978. But it took two more years and a win at the Western Open to convince him he might make a living playing golf. One ingredient was still missing, however, as Simpson pushed forward—inner peace.

Simpson had spent almost five years debating Christianity with members of the Tour's Bible study group, including Mize, Morris Hatalsky, Don Pooley, and Larry Nelson.

"In many respects, golf was the least of my worries," Simpson says. "The golf was fine. It was fun. I never even suffered a major fall-off. I just wanted an answer to the big questions, and eventually that answer came. . . . There was no crisis or dramatic event that triggered this awareness. It was just a matter of asking a lot of questions."

But the probing provided the answers Simpson was searching for, and, in 1986, he became a Christian.

Some have questioned whether Simpson's faith has hindered him from winning more often by tempering his competitive drive—an inference Simpson remains unfazed by.

"Sometimes I worry about that—that I'm not ambitious enough, that I should be more driven to win," he says. "To me, balance is the key. To be able to win is great. I'm often able to place myself in a position to win, and I'd certainly love to win more tournaments—especially another Open.

"But I also realize that there are no guarantees in this game—not to mention in this life—and we have only a short time to enjoy it. Even when I'm not playing particularly well, I enjoy what I do. I have a great family; the more I read the Bible the more amazing it becomes, and I'm not searching anymore."

> **"There's no love on third down and one.**
> **You need discipline then."**
> Norm Van Brocklin, Former NFL Quarterback and Coach

Aeneas Williams

Ask most NFL fans or media people who is the top cornerback in football and most will quickly throw out the names Deion Sanders and Charles Woodson. But go inside the league's inner circles—ask the top receivers who they feel is the toughest cover man to go up against—and many will tell you it is Aeneas Williams of the Arizona Cardinals.

Williams has been selected to the Pro Bowl nearly every season since 1994. He is nearing 50 career interceptions and is threatening Ken Houston's NFL record of 9 interceptions returned for touchdowns.

Williams' success comes by way of his passion to learn and his staggering dedication to hard work.

Amazingly, Williams has cracked the NFL's elite after playing only two years of football in college—as a walk-on at Southern University in Louisiana. It seems his passion for learning had temporarily preempted his football career.

After performing as an all-city defensive back during high school in New Orleans, he turned down a nonathletic scholarship to Dartmouth to follow his brother to Southern. His first two years there, he hit the books and had no interest in football. But his junior year, a week before the start of the season, he decided to walk-on. Five games into the season, he was starting. Three and a half years later, the Cardinals picked him in the third round of the 1991 draft.

"That's just like Aeneas," says former Cardinals linebacker Eric Hill. "Nothing about this guy is normal."

Amen. Williams is an avowed teetotaler, a fitness fiend, and a devoted student of the game. Several years ago, he cold-called Ken Houston to learn from the Hall of Famer.

"I called him up in Houston, then went to visit him," says Williams. "We talked about techniques, footwork, strategy. When someone has been successful, I have a passion for finding out what made him that way."

Easygoing and mellow at other times, on game days Williams is stubborn and aggressive, refusing to concede what most corners must—the short pass. He prefers to spend the entire game in press coverage, right up in the receiver's face.

"You cannot believe how hard you have to work to get open against him," says Cardinals receiver Rob Moore, who as a New York Jet played against Williams. "And that wears on you. You've got to run thirty, forty routes, and every one of them is a little war."

To get ready for those wars, Williams is like a worker bee on the practice field, never stopping to let his motor idle. While his teammates take a knee during a stoppage on the practice field, Williams works on pass drops or does abdominal crunches. While his fellow defensive backs pinch and slap themselves to remain awake while watching video of practice, Williams scribbles notes and asks questions. His disciplined approach makes him a quick study for others.

"I've told young players who come in here, 'If you're going to pick somebody to follow, watch this guy,'" says Cardinals defensive backs coach Larry Marmie. "Watch him in the meetings, watch him on the practice field and watch him in the game."

Williams' discipline carries over into every area of his life. He rises at five o'clock every morning to pray and read the Bible, and he hosts a weekly Tuesday night Bible study session for teammates and their wives. He says it is his God-given "assignment" to minister to his teammates—all just a part of Williams' devotion to do his best.

"The only question I want to ask myself is this: Did I do my best?" says Williams. "I want to leave the game with no regrets."

Cris Carter

If you had a dime for every pass Cris Carter has caught in his NFL career, you'd be able to cover what it cost the Minnesota Vikings to pick him up, and still have enough left over for a grande cup of coffee.

When Carter was cut by the Philadelphia Eagles in 1990, a cup of coffee was about all he was offered by other NFL teams. A decade later, Carter has amassed more than 1,000 receptions in a career that has seen him become the second-most prolific pass catcher in NFL history. And all it cost the Vikings was a C-note.

Before Minnesota took their one-hundred-dollar gamble, Carter had always been a supremely gifted athlete with hands like Super Glue and the body control of Mikhail Baryshnikov. But he was undisciplined and unmotivated, traits that spread like a bad infection through every area of his life. He was brash and confrontational. He expected those around him to perform to a higher standard—an attitude that got him deeper into trouble.

But a chain of events took place in the early 1990s that brought about change for Cris Carter. This man, born with such talent and an ample mean streak, turned his expectations inward, demanding the higher standard only from himself. To this day few would say the perennial Pro Bowler has lost any of his passion.

"I expect a lot out of myself," says Carter. "I kinda know more about myself than other people do and tend to expect more of myself. Also, I know what I've done as far as training. I know how much ability I have as far as God-given ability. So, that's probably why I'm really so hard on myself. It's because I know what's inside of me. I know what I'm capable of doing."

More than ten years removed from his experience in Philly, Carter is now one of the greatest receivers in NFL history, one who has made a living catching touchdowns and running routes across the middle. In the 1990s, Carter's 835 receptions and 95 touchdown catches ranked second only to the San Francisco 49ers' Jerry Rice, and since 1994, no one has caught as many passes and touchdowns as Carter has. Says Baltimore Ravens coach and former Vikings offensive coordinator Brian Billick, "On Sundays, I'll take Cris over any player at any position."

Carter has become known for his remarkable acrobatic catches—some of them legendary among his peers. Whether it's a lunging one-handed grab; a hug-the-sideline, fully-laid-out, ten-toes-just-in-bounds, fingertip snatch; or a leaping, jump-ball, I'll-take-it-away-from-you snag—he is the master of the circus catch.

"I think he has established himself as the greatest acrobatic receiver of his time," says Vikings coach Dennis Green.

"I believe that almost every ball is catchable," says Carter. "What I try to do is stop the ball, the point of it. Sometimes there's kind of a sweet spot. If I'm able to grab that spot on the football, I feel as if I can control it or bring it in.

"A lot of those catches I make in a game I've made before in my mind and in practice. I practice tough catches. I don't sit around and gawk at my ability. I think about what I can do better."

In 1999, football's Baryshnikov was invited by former teammate Fuad Reveiz to speak at a charity event in Knoxville, Tennessee. Carter talked about his struggles as an alcoholic and a cocaine addict during his days with Philadelphia from 1987 through 1990. The man standing before this group had been an ordained minister since 1996 and a community activist whose work would earn him the NFL's Man of the Year award in 1999. The same man had also flunked three drug tests while with the Eagles.

"I tell people that when they see alcoholics and drug addicts on the streets, they should think about me," he says. "People don't want to believe that's who I am because it's so easy to create another image—NFL Man of the Year, family man, a man who loves God. Yes, all those things are part of the picture, but so are the other things. They're all part of how I got to where I am now."

"Cris has always been an all-or-nothing kind of guy," says Keith Byars, who played with Carter at Ohio State and in Philadelphia. "That's good when it's channeled in the right direction. But when he was doing the wrong things, he was committed to that too. When he was doing drugs and alcohol, I'm sure he was trying to be the best addict out there. Now, after all he's been through, he has priorities."

When the Eagles waived Carter in September 1990, the Vikings picked him up despite his considerable baggage. He remembers then Minnesota receivers coach Dick Rehbein telling him that he wouldn't be starting as long as Anthony Carter and Hassan Jones were healthy. Rehbein, now the quarterbacks coach in New England, thought Carter was smart and talented, but, he says now, "I don't know how much Cris liked to practice or work out back then."

The same conclusion led Philadelphia to cut Carter even though his statistics showed a productive player. In three seasons in Philly, he caught 89 passes for 1,450 yards and 19 touchdowns. His 11 TDs in 1989 were third-most in the league. But Eagles coach Buddy Ryan was irked by Carter's lack of work ethic and his propensity to party. He figured Carter was an attitude problem with on-field limitations. Yes, he had great hands and an uncanny ability to make the spectacular catch, but he also clashed with the quarterback, ran sloppy pass routes, and lived a sloppy lifestyle. The cut went deep.

"I was kind of knocked off my pedestal that I thought I was on," says Carter. "And I really had to reanalyze everything—my career, my life, my situation with my family, and what I wanted out of life.

"For the first time, since I was eight, I wasn't on any type of team. There was no team that I could put my name on. There was no team that Cris Carter could say he was associated with, and that really hurt. Because, for me, I didn't have any other type of identity. So what I did through that process was I said, 'Well Cris, you have to be known for something besides football, and you're gonna have to take this job seriously because you have a wife and a newborn dependent on you.' But the most painful part of the whole thing was that some of the things he [Ryan] said about me were true."

Things began to turn around on September 4, 1990, when the Vikings made one of the best moves in franchise history, quietly plunking down the one hundred dollars to claim Carter off waivers. The New York Giants were also willing to invest one hundred dollars, but no other team in the NFL was interested in taking a chance. Such was the reputation of Carter at the time. As it turned out, Minnesota had acquired a man in the middle of a complete lifestyle overhaul.

Melanie Carter, Cris' Ohio State sweetheart-turned-wife, perhaps had more to do with his turnaround than anyone. She began to talk to Cris about needing grounding, centering, and focus. She spoke about the need for God to be first in their lives.

"I remember my wife telling me, 'I'm going after God. I don't care what you do, but I'm going after God,'" says Carter. "And from a spiritual sense, I was kinda hurt because I always thought that I was more spiritual than her. And then for her to say she's going after God, and as far as our having problems in our relationship, her whole solution was Christ."

Cris listened. He had heard the same message while in Philly, but it never took root. The more he explored, however, the more he opened up. In 1994, following a team chapel service at the Vikings facility, Carter approached the Vikings' chaplain, Keith Johnson, and said he was ready for a total change.

"I was making more money than I ever dreamed of," Carter says, "coming off my first Pro Bowl year. My home was kinda in disarray as far as my spouse and myself, and I said, 'God, I know there has to be more to life than this.' I didn't have any joy. I told him I was sick and tired of running, and I wanted to be happy. I told him that I wanted to serve God and that I wanted to give my life to Christ.

"I finally submitted to that. God has reached out and loved me and done so much for me, it's amazing that I didn't turn to him sooner."

The partying stopped. There were other changes. Less red meat. More prayer. Fasting on Wednesdays. His approach to his profession was 180 degrees different.

"I changed so much, especially as far as my work habits," Carter said. "Earlier in my career I didn't work anywhere near how I work now as far as time and as far as effort that I put into it," says Carter. "But I think getting cut really made me work hard. When I was younger I used to work harder than any high school player. Going through that turmoil in Philadelphia really helped me get back to that.

"I just changed my thought patterns as far as what I was going to do. I dedicated myself to do the best that I could to get the maximum out of what God had given me. That kinda propelled me to go on to a different level that puts me into the position I'm in today. That's the reason why I get up at six in the morning and work out. It allows me to invest in my body, get personal trainers, as far as weights, getting my own running coach and things like that that have helped me."

Carter's off-season regimen had consisted of playing pickup basketball and occasionally running a couple of miles or a series of wind sprints. Now, from April until the start of training camp, he starts a normal day behind Pope John Paul II High School near his home in Boca Raton, Florida, for as much as six hours of torture. Vikings teammates like quarterback Daunte Culpepper and Carter protégé Randy Moss are among about a dozen pro athletes who show up at 8:00 A.M. on a given day to work out with Carter. While many are still wiping the sleep from their eyes, Carter shows up carrying a cooler and looking intensely focused, as if every minute he is going to spend there will be productive.

From there Carter drives to the headquarters of FAST, a speed, agility, quickness, and strength fitness program of which he is part owner, where he launches into ninety minutes of strength training. He ends his workout day with a two-hour-plus session of stretching and sweating with his wife in a workout studio in which the temperature hovers near 100 degrees. Carter follows a similar routine five days a week.

"Work is all I know," Carter says. "There are no tricks . . . I just push my body to the limit. When football season comes around, then I put it all together."

That sense of discipline has become Carter's hallmark.

"Cris came into this thing with his mind made up to be the best he can be," says former Vikings assistant coach Jerry Rhome. "He's a reborn Christian. He has his life going in the direction he wants. And he takes that on the field every day."

The minister takes a missionary approach toward younger players. Carter has taken a number of young teammates under his wing to mentor them in preparing for both the game of football and the game of life.

"I see a lot of myself in them," says Carter. "That's the part that's painful though, when you can see yourself in a young person. You can see the road that he is traveling, that you were on that road. And you got off that road, but you know the end of that road is gonna be a crash course as far as disaster. And that's the part that's really hard to deal with. But you just put that in prayer. You just believe that God can do it. Just like there were a lot of people praying for me before I got off that course."

Former teammate Jake Reed came to the Vikings as a star college receiver out of Grambling. He had loads of talent but little success in his first two seasons in the NFL. He approached Carter before the 1994 season about learning from him. Carter became his mentor, father figure, big brother, and best friend all in one. He even ended up as the best man at Reed's wedding.

"Cris told me to believe in him and what he was telling me," says Reed. "He told me to grab him by the coattails if I had to and he'd pull me through it—whatever it was."

Carter taught Reed how to pay the price to become good. The pupil responded to the tutelage. Reed caught 85 passes in 1994, after snaring only 11 total in his first two seasons.

"One thing about Cris," Reed says. "He's not going to tell you what you want to hear. He'll tell you what you need to hear."

Reed had several productive years in Minnesota—he and Carter combined for 519 catches from '95-'97—before moving on to New Orleans when Moss stepped in.

Moss' arrival in Minneapolis is another testament to the impact of Carter's example.

On draft day in 1998, Green called Carter that morning to discuss the possible addition to the team of the talented receiver with the checkered past. Green told Carter that if Moss was still available when the Vikings' number twenty-one pick in the first round came up, he would take him. Carter agreed.

Then Green asked, "Cris, will you take care of him?"

Carter responded, "Coach, well, you know I'm going to take care of him."

In Moss, Carter sees someone similar to himself at a young age—incredibly gifted but needing direction. Nearly everything Moss had experienced had been endured by Carter earlier, so nothing Moss had been through could either surprise or impress Carter.

He called Moss after the draft to welcome him to the Vikings. But it was Moss who later suggested that he go to Carter's home in Boca Raton to work out with him before the season started.

Again, time spent with the mentor paid off, as Moss blistered NFL secondaries in his rookie season, catching 17 touchdown passes—third most ever in a single season—and became the league's most feared offensive weapon.

"I've talked with him about hundreds of things, but it's better I just live in front of him," Carter says. "We talk about things based upon need, not just to be talking. I don't want to waste his time. But I also want him to be able to come to me if he needs me."

When he exits the game, Carter will leave many wondering what his career would have been like had he always been so focused. Yet he doesn't dwell on what might have been. He's only interested in making the most of the time he has left, and making a difference in the lives of others.

"I'm tired of seeing a news flash come across ESPN—drunk driving, drugs, wife beating," he says. "It's time to make a stand and show we can make good decisions."

Carter's good decisions since his turnaround have resulted in numerous honors for community involvement and his role model status. In 1994, he received the NFL Extra Effort Award for community service. In 1995, it was the Athletes in Action Bart Starr Award for character. And in 1998, Man of the Year.

"We can make an impact if we choose to. We can make a difference. Young people are looking for a role model, for people to be a positive force in their lives.

"There are very few athletes that can be a role model and be a hero. Heroes are people that do things with God-given abilities that we wish we could do. Someone who can sing a song, or someone who can shoot a three-point shot, or someone who can throw a football. Those are heroes in our life. Those aren't necessarily our role models.

"Now I believe that I'm a role model. I believe that God has put me in the position where I should be a role model. I believe that. I believe that my life is under a lot of scrutiny. Can I accept that? Yes. I accept that. Is it unfair? Of course it is, but I still accept it. It's part of the territory that goes along with me sitting in my bed when I was a little boy saying, 'God, I want to be a professional athlete.' That was all part of it. Now that I'm here, I want to accept that. I'm willing to be the part of the community that helps develop our young people."

Cris Carter's remarkable capacity to discipline himself has resulted in him becoming one of the greatest pass catchers in NFL history, and a man of influence. It's also made for one of the great comeback stories in sports.

"Cris was always a sweet person, but there is more of a sense of priority with him now," says wife Melanie. "He's much more at peace."

"When I came into the league, I was a little boy," Carter says. "Now I am a man.

"My favorite verse in the Bible is John 10:10, where Jesus says, 'I came that they might have life, and might have it abundantly.' I had life before, but today I have it far more abundantly.

"Success is not based on how much money you have in the bank. Success is based upon getting the most out of what God has given you."

**A champion may fail,
but he never quits.**

CHAPTER 5

COMMITMENT

Commitment means staying the course.

You establish a game plan. You work your plan, and while it might get altered a bit in midstream, you continue to stay focused on what you're trying to accomplish. You recognize that it's not always going to be smooth. There are going to be some bumps, but you're willing to stay with it to the end.

To go out and do something starts with the thought of doing it. Then you must execute and persist in doing it. When you establish that habit, then it becomes like any other habit—good or bad—and it becomes easier to keep doing it.

There is almost always an opportunity to take a shortcut, or the path of least resistance. However, there's no shortcut to success. Without the commitment to stay the course, to put in the necessary time, you can't maximize your ability or potential. If you're going to put the time in, you've got to be committed to use that time—there's no way around it. Commitment takes effort.

Without commitment I don't think you can have success. Without commitment you'll bail out early, and you might not reap

commitment: to pledge or assign to some particular course or use.

73

the blessing of character development or accomplishment that comes from staying the course.

So many have given up just one step, one play, one race, one game, one day short of reaching their dreams. You have to see the big picture and stay committed to the end.

—C. K.

"Who can ask more of a man than giving all within his span?
Giving all, it seems to me, is not so far from victory."
George Moriarty, Detroit Tigers Former Manager

Jennifer Azzi and Ruthie Bolton-Holifield

It is easy to look at the success of basketball stars Jennifer Azzi and Ruthie Bolton-Holifield and think that it all came easily. Both are physically gifted, have developed great skills, and have solid all-around games equal to the best in the world. Yet, for both women, the road to success held challenges that made quitting seem like the best option. One thing kept both women going. Commitment to a dream.

In high school Holifield was told her skills were not refined enough for the Division-I collegiate level. She was encouraged to attend junior college to work on her game. Holifield politely refused the advice and took her chances at Auburn, to play with older sister Mae Ola Bolton.

It didn't take long for Ruthie to prove her critics wrong. As a freshman, she averaged 9.9 points per game and became a building block for Auburn teams that compiled a 119-13 record during her four years, and finished as NCAA runner-up in 1988 and 1989. In '89 Holifield made all-America teams and earned SEC all-academic honors.

Since then, the five-foot-nine-inch Holifield has been one of international basketball's top guards, displaying her talents all over the world. Her pro career began in Hungary, as the first American ever to play in that country's pro league. Then it was on to Sweden—where she was named USA Basketball's Female Athlete of the Year in 1991—then to Italy and Turkey. In Italy she was unstoppable, averaging 26 points per game in 1993, 28 in 1994, and 25.5 in 1995.

With the USA National Team, Holifield was part of the gold-medal-winning squad at the 1994 Goodwill Games, bronze-medal winners at the 1994 World Championships, and the team that won gold at the 1996 Olympics in Atlanta.

Holifield's never-say-die attitude comes from her upbringing. One of twenty children, she was always competing with her siblings in some kind of sport—even those they made up. But basketball captured the passion of the Bolton kids more than any other sport. And with twenty kids around, they were never lacking for a 5-on-5 game.

Unfortunately for Ruthie, her mother, Leola, who gave birth to all twenty siblings, was not around to see her daughter's golden moment in Atlanta. She died in 1995.

But her mother's model of commitment in raising the Bolton clan fueled Ruthie's own experience and taught her never to give up.

Holifield remembered this when she suffered a severe knee sprain two weeks prior to the start of the Olympics. Team doctors told her the injury most likely wouldn't heal in time for her to play.

Holifield turned to rehabilitation—and prayer. A devout Baptist whose father, Linwood, is a pastor in McLain, Mississippi, Holifield asked God for healing.

Within days, her knee improved dramatically. She ended up starting every game in Atlanta, averaged 13 points a game, and was the floor leader for the gold-medal winners.

"God blessed me to be healthy enough to play," declares Holifield, who is now a WNBA all-star with the Sacramento Monarchs. "Sometimes you doubt . . . but I knew that God wouldn't leave me."

An Olympian again in 2000, she is also now First Lieutenant Ruthie Bolton-Holifield, a member of the Army reserves, committed not only to serving her sport and her God but also her country—in essence, what she's done for more than fifteen years on basketball courts around the world.

Like Holifield, Jennifer Azzi also overcame early doubts to win Olympic gold in 1996.

Although Azzi began playing basketball before she entered kindergarten, as a high schooler in Oak Ridge, Tennessee, she was somewhat overlooked by top colleges. She wound up at Stanford, where she became one of the most celebrated athletes in school history.

She was the backbone of Stanford's NCAA champions in 1990, the same year she won the Naismith National Player of the Year Award. Azzi went on to play professionally in Italy, Sweden, and France before joining Team USA. In Sweden she averaged 31 points a game and became one of the best two-way guards in all international competition.

Despite her vast experience, which included the 1991 Pan-Am Games, Azzi was selected as an alternate to the bronze-medal-winning 1992 Olympic team.

In 1994, she was Holifield's teammate at the Goodwill Games and World Championships. And with the Olympic dream still another two years away, Azzi stuck to her goal, fought through injuries, and was selected to the 1996 team, where she stood atop the gold medal stand next to Holifield.

Azzi also has had success as a pro in the U.S. After four seasons in the now-defunct ABL, she jumped to the WNBA, where she's starred with the Detroit Shock and Utah Starzz.

She is a tireless messenger for the game, running camps and clinics for young hopefuls across America, dedicated to showing girls the values and life lessons that come through basketball.

Azzi and Holifield have both worked hard to help women's basketball gain mainstream acceptance in the U.S. and around the world. They have become models for those who will follow them in the years to come.

> "Remember this your lifetime through—tomorrow, there will be more to do . . .
> and failure waits for all who stay with some success made yesterday . . .
> tomorrow, you must try once more and even harder than before."
> John Wooden, Hall of Fame UCLA Basketball Coach

Dennis Byrd

He never saw it coming.

When Kansas City Chiefs quarterback Dave Krieg sidestepped Dennis Byrd on November 29, 1992, the Jets' defensive end barreled headfirst into teammate Scott Mersereau, who was coming after Krieg from the other side. Having no time to prepare himself for this collision, Byrd instinctively ducked his head just before he slammed into Mersereau's body.

Mersereau fell to the turf—the wind knocked out of him. He was back on his feet within seconds.

Not so with Byrd. Immediately he knew he was seriously hurt.

"I started to get up and the only thing that moved was my neck," he recalls. "My head came off the ground and I felt something crack or crunch, so I put my neck back down. Then the next thing I tried to do was pick my feet up."

But he couldn't. As he lay in front of the silent stadium crowd with team personnel attending to him, Byrd verbalized his realization.

"Kyle Clifton stood over me," Byrd relates, "and he asked me if I was OK and said, 'Get up.' I told him I had broken my neck and was paralyzed."

With one collision, Dennis Byrd's life was forever changed. Instantly he was transformed from a 266-pound, finely tuned, professional football player to a helpless hospital patient who needed assistance with everything. He was indeed paralyzed.

Two weeks after the injury, his neck stabilized by surgery, Byrd began rehabilitation. It was a grueling ordeal in which he spent the majority of the next several months at Mount Sinai Hospital in New York.

After his first day of therapy, the exhausted former football player lay on his back, reflecting on his current state and his wife Angela.

"I could handle feeling pathetic," Byrd recalls about that night. "I was truly prepared to handle anything, with the help of Jesus Christ. But Angela, why should she have to deal with this for the rest of her life? I was determined to walk again. I had no doubt I would. But what if I was wrong? What if the Lord had other plans for me? What if I'd never rise out of a wheelchair? I knew I could live with that, but could Angela?"

When Angela came to visit that night, Byrd's thoughts became words.

"It's not fair for you to have to be with me like this forever," he told her. "It's not fair for you to have to take care of me like this. I'd understand if you wanted to leave me."

Angela Byrd was stunned. Tears welled in her eyes as she leaned over her husband. "Dennis, I can't believe you'd say that. I can't believe you'd even think of that."

She reached across the hospital bed and hugged her helpless husband. Together they cried as she held him. He knew he would never again have to fear losing his lifetime companion.

With the commitment of his wife sustaining him, Byrd renewed his commitment to rehabilitation.

Incredibly, today, Dennis Byrd walks again, and is the husband and father he always wanted to be.

"It's not the boy in the fight . . . it's the fight in the boy."
Happy Chandler, Former Major League Baseball Commissioner

Chad Hennings

Chad Hennings has delivered on his commitments—his commitment to his country, to his family, and to his team.

A steady player for the Dallas Cowboys throughout the 1990s, the defensive tackle is not an all-pro, nor does he receive great acclaim. But for those who know him, there is much about Chad Hennings to appreciate.

Following a sensational college career at the Air Force Academy, where he won the Outland Trophy as the nation's top interior lineman and was an all-American in 1987, Hennings had an opportunity to forego his military commitment and, through a special waiver, go directly to the NFL. But for Hennings, this was never an option.

"I knew that a professional football career was a possibility, but I knew I had to honor my military commitment," he says, "It was very important for me because that's the way I was raised. I look back on what would my parents think? What would my high school coaches, my junior high school coaches, my college coaches—everybody—what would they think of me? And most of all, how would I view myself?

"Commitment is very important to me. Loyalty is very important to me. It's something that, for myself, I never really had an option. I was going to serve the commitment no matter what monetary gain might have been [lost] from it. It didn't matter. The commitment came first."

Instead of the NFL, Hennings entered the elite Euro-NATO pilot program, where the air force trains top pilots. Following training, Hennings had a chance to test his flying skills in combat situations during the Gulf War. He was on the humanitarian relief effort to the Kurds and flew in great danger.

"All those people on the ground scurrying for supplies looked like ants crawling over picnic food," Hennings said. "The Kurds were devastated by dysentery and diarrhea. Little kids were dying. Families would drive up into the mountains to escape, abandon their cars at the snow line, and then walk farther into the mountain. So many didn't survive.

"Coming out of the academy, I was really gung ho. I wanted to die for my country. I wanted adventure, risk, to roll the dice and see if I'd win. To be honest, it takes a certain spirituality to give up your life for your country, for a friend, or for someone you don't know, which is the biggest sacrifice. I wasn't totally convinced I had that until I flew in the Persian Gulf. Then I knew I had what it takes."

Hennings flew forty-five missions in Operation Provide Comfort, totaling 195 flight hours during two three-month deployments between April 1991 and January 1992. He earned medals for humanitarianism, air achievement, and as a member of an outstanding unit, then he was promoted to captain.

After completing his service, Hennings joined the Cowboys, who had held his rights since drafting him in 1988. He immediately threw himself into his new role with the same attitude he exhibited during the perilous missions.

"Commitment is a way of life," says Hennings, "As the old adage goes, there are no shortcuts to success. You can't cut corners.

"You have to have that level of competition, that discipline to go the extra mile, to pay the price. Not just to go out on the field and perform, but do what it takes off the field. To do the weights, to do the running, to work in 105-degree temperatures and sweat until you think you can't take it anymore, but then go that extra mile.

"It's the same sort of commitment it takes to do what's right. Whenever you come to a crossroads, where that commitment comes in is to choose a path that is the correct path."

> **"My attitude has always been . . . if it's worth playing, it's worth paying the price to win."**
> **Bear Bryant, Former Alabama Football Coach**

Eric Liddell

The movie *Chariots of Fire* immortalized the amazing story of British runner Eric Liddell's controversial stand at the 1924 Olympics in Paris.

Refusing to run on Sunday out of commitment to his Christian faith, Liddell chose to miss the 100-meter finals, in which he was the favorite. Instead, he ended up winning a gold medal, as a late entry in the 400 meters, an event he had not trained for.

It was Liddell's integrity and commitment to God on the track that took center stage in the Academy Award-winning film. In real life, the same integrity and commitment burned well beyond the Olympics, until Liddell's untimely death in a Japanese occupied prisoner-of-war camp in China during World War II.

Before going to China, Liddell was in training, not only as a runner, but also as a missionary. He considered his athletic ability a means to glorify God and spread the Christian message. He devoted time away from training to preaching and teaching among the young men of Scotland. When he spoke, audiences listened attentively, schoolgirls were infatuated, and his opponents would forget their roles.

"The modesty and simplicity and directness of his words went straight to the heart," a Liddell contemporary once said. "He has got the great redeeming gift, the gift of humor. He made us quickly realize that running was not to be his career. Eric's faith enabled him to love people in a way even fellow missionaries in China could not. But this love was simply an extension of his own relationship to God, a relationship bolstered by early morning Bible study, prayer, and Scripture meditation."

A fellow prison camp internee recalled how prayer was a dominant part of Liddell's life. Praying was "a habit" with Liddell, she said, not only in the early morning, but also "all through the day." This discipline of prayer enabled Liddell to handle his emotions when facing the horrors suffered at the hands of hostile Japanese soldiers, after, in the midst of his missionary duties, he was imprisoned with British soldiers—as an enemy.

Liddell's faith gave him the ability to face the miseries of the prison camp while encouraging others around him. After the war, fellow prisoners had high praise for his ability to manage the stress of the times.

Liddell did not die at the hands of the Japanese solders. Rather, he suffered a stroke from the hard work he endured in serving others within severe physical conditions. He died in 1945 at a prison hospital, more than twenty years after he heard the cheers of the Parisian crowd in winning the gold.

Liddell may have been disappointed that his race ended so soon, but those who knew him agreed that he ran his race to win.

**"The race does not always go to the swift,
but to the ones who keep running."**
Anonymous Track Coach

Dot Richardson

On a summer Tuesday in Atlanta in 1996, Dot Richardson celebrated a momentous achievement with the rest of her victorious U.S. women's softball teammates. Team USA had just won the gold medal in the first ever Olympic women's softball competition.

Less than forty-eight hours later she went back to work. At 7 A.M. sharp, the power-hitting shortstop and forerunner of her sport returned to the powers of healing, reporting as scheduled for the morning shift at Los Angeles County-USC Medical Center, where she was completing her residency as an orthopedic surgeon.

She was met by quite a welcoming party, as dozens of her colleagues crowded the medical center's front steps. The USC marching band feted her with a fanfare. A dozen roses were pressed into her arms. Physicians and nurses waved pom-poms. Party balloons lifted into the sky.

"Ohmigosh!" Richardson told the crowd, showing the enthusiasm and smile that were fixtures of the softball competition. "When we won the gold medal, I said, 'It doesn't get any better than this.' But I tell you, today tops it. You guys are so incredible to be out here with me."

With three years remaining in her residency, Richardson had taken a yearlong leave from County-USC to pursue her Olympic dream.

At the time, County-USC was an earthquake damaged medical center in the middle of gang-infested turf in a poor east L. A. neighborhood. It was America's busiest public hospital, a place where knife wounds are nearly as common as sports injuries. It was a public, county-funded hospital that is the most critical link in caring for L. A.'s low-income residents. It also was a place where the emergency room, the nation's busiest, fills nightly with every sort of urban nightmare imaginable.

"Being a surgeon is the ultimate dream," said Dr. Dot. "I would trade in my gold medal to do what I do here. That's what it's all about."

Los Angeles County supervisor Gloria Molina called Richardson "a great role model, a champion in our community."

Richardson was again a stalwart of the team that represented the U.S. at the 2000 Sydney games, which after three agonizing defeats, rallied to again win gold.

To carry the load of both softball superstar and doctor is more than most could handle. But Richardson is a bundle of energy and the perfect spokesperson for the sport. Her commitment to seeing both careers succeed without expense to either is an example that makes her admired by all. But for Dot, she's just being herself.

"I think it just basically comes down to the love that you have for what you're doing and if you believe in what you are doing," says Richardson. "I have dreamed about both of my careers all my life. I've always wanted to help people and I've always wanted to be there for them, and in medicine I can help them in such a way that I couldn't in any other way. And as an athlete you're able to give back a joy that you're experiencing on the field to all those people that are watching and to your teammates. That's what keeps you going and that's what keeps your enthusiasm. When you're doing things for other people, it just makes you feel more alive than ever. I just enjoy what I'm doing.

"I'm living my dream every day. To be able to inspire people to enjoy life more and appreciate the talents God has given them . . . I'm living my dream."

"I have this sign on my desk that says,
'It takes eighteen years of hard work to be an overnight success.'"
Randy Pfund, Former Los Angeles Lakers Coach

Jason Taylor

Each year the NFL selects a Teacher of the Year, based on the choice of a player honoring one of his former teachers. Each year, Miami's Jason Taylor nominates the same two people—his mom and dad.

That's because when Taylor signed as a third-round draft pick of the Dolphins in 1996, he became the first home-schooled athlete to play in the NFL.

"Home schooling worked to my advantage," said Taylor, whose three siblings were also home-schooled. "It forced me to grow up faster, to be accountable for my own future.

"The only difference is home schoolers don't ride a yellow bus to school in the mornings. But anytime you do something different, something out of the ordinary, the world looks at you in a different light, like you're weird or strange.

"The truth is we're all the same. We all want to be successful. Some of us are just taking different routes."

Taylor completed his high school education entirely through the home school process. His mother and father worked hard to provide a quality education, while enrolling him in athletic programs at a local high school. Jason had the benefit of an all-around high school experience. He became a standout football and basketball player, and received a scholarship to play football at Akron (Ohio) University.

As a freshman at Akron, Taylor spent the first month wondering if he'd play sports at all in college.

Two days before the Zips' first football game, on Taylor's eighteenth birthday, the NCAA refused to honor Taylor's high school test scores, saying he hadn't met core course requirements. His football scholarship and athletic future was jeopardized.

Taylor continued going to class but couldn't practice. His family pursued legal action, getting help from the Home School Legal Defense Association. A month later, the NCAA reversed its decision and Taylor was back on the field, where he made a substantial impression on Dolphins' scouts and then head coach Jimmy Johnson.

His impact on the NFL as a rookie was immediate, and Taylor is now considered one of the best young defensive ends in the game.

Taylor's commitment to succeeding academically, and becoming a forerunner, helped pave the way for his standout career and for other home-schooled athletes in the future.

Jean Driscoll

When Jean Driscoll was born with spina bifida, doctors painted a bleak picture. They told her parents that as a result of the congenital birth defect—characterized by the incomplete closing of the spinal column— Jean would most likely never walk. She would have to be enrolled in special education classes, they said, and would be dependent on them for the rest of her life.

But Jean Driscoll has proven the doctors wrong.

More than thirty years after that fateful pronouncement, Driscoll is now one of the world's most decorated athletes.

When she won the wheelchair division of the Boston Marathon in 2000, it was her eighth title in the prestigious race. With her commitment to excellence and her indomitable spirit, Driscoll has become the most celebrated female wheelchair athlete in America. The competitive fires have burned in her ever since those difficult days as a child.

Because her condition occurred at the lower end of her spinal cord, Driscoll was able to walk with leg braces from the age of two until she was fourteen. She staggered awkwardly from side to side, dragging her feet and working hard to keep her balance. She insisted on being included in neighborhood games and races, and excelled at crawling through obstacle courses and playing "h-o-r-s-e" basketball, perfecting the art of shooting a one-handed shot with her right hand, while holding on to a fence for stability with her left.

In fourth grade, against the advice of her parents, Driscoll taught herself to ride a bike. One Saturday, she rode up and down the sidewalk in front of a friend's house for eight hours. At the end of the day, she rode home to show her parents.

"I can ride a bike!" Driscoll screamed as she rode by.

"You're going to break your neck!" her mother screamed back.

"I don't need my training wheels anymore!" she proudly responded.

Still there were numerous reminders that she was different from other children.

She remembers the days her sister and three brothers would take turns pulling her to grade school in a red wagon. She remembers how her mother made her wear rubber boots over her shoes when she went to the playground, to keep the blacktop from destroying her leather shoes. She remembers at fourteen, while riding her new ten-speed bike, she fell on her left hip and dislocated it. After five operations to strengthen the joint—and a year in a body cast living in either a hospital or her family's living room—when the cast was removed, the hip dislocated again.

"I was told I'd end up with a sit-down job," Driscoll says. "My only goal was to sit behind a desk, filing and typing. My sister could be the first female president, but I was supposed to become a secretary."

From that moment on, doctors said that because of her lack of lower body musculature, Jean would have to use a wheelchair and crutches to get around. When she returned to school, at fifteen, her peers began to make fun of her because of the wheelchair. She was devastated by the entire experience, fell into deep depression, and contemplated suicide.

"It was a blow you couldn't believe," she recalls. "I was very angry for several years. I couldn't make myself or others comfortable with the chair. I would ask God, 'Why don't you pick on somebody else?'

"I thought a wheelchair would be very limiting. I thought it was a barrier to life."

In fact, it was the wheelchair that removed barriers and enabled her to start living. All the while, Jean was trying desperately to prove she was just like anyone else. Now the world knows she is, in fact, most unique.

"I thought, *Now my life is over,*" Driscoll says. "But the thing I thought would limit me has enabled me more than I ever imagined. I've done what most people only dream about."

Now Driscoll's memories drive her to something greater.

She has become the best wheelchair racer in the world. She has set world records or world-best times in sprints and endurance events. Her strength and stamina are of the iron-man variety.

She has won at nearly every distance, including 800, 1,500, 5,000, and 10,000 meters, as well as the 4x100 meter relay. Among her triumphs at Boston is the world record of 1 hour, 34 minutes, 22 seconds, set in 1994. She medaled at the 1992 and 1996 Olympics, as well as the 1996 Paralympics. But the road to success as an athlete was formed through great despair.

"My disability was always an excuse. It was the reason I didn't get the boyfriends I wanted and the reason I didn't get baby-sitting jobs as early as my sisters."

While in school, Driscoll tried to find herself in academics, but even that went awry. She flunked out of the University of Wisconsin-Milwaukee after three semesters.

"I was suicidal," she says. "I didn't think I had anything to offer this world. It rips you apart inside when your only confidence comes from academics and you can't do that."

During her academic hiatus, Driscoll met the person who would be the catalyst for extraordinary changes in her life. During a year spent as a live-in nanny for a young family, Driscoll met then University of Illinois coach Brad Hedrick. Hedrick had spoken at a wheelchair sports clinic, then watched Driscoll and others play a game of wheelchair soccer. Something caught his eye.

"I saw lots of enthusiasm and talent that was unchanneled at the time," Hedrick says.

"He saw my speed and thought that could transfer over to the basketball court," Driscoll recalls.

Soon, Hedrick began recruiting Driscoll to come play basketball at Illinois, the nation's top program for wheelchair athletics. She jumped at the opportunity.

From 1987–91, she lettered four times and won three MVP awards for the Illini women's team, helping them to the national championship in 1990 and 1991. She was named amateur athlete of the year by the Women's Sports Foundation in 1991, and has been honored with Jean Driscoll Days in Champaign, Illinois, where she now lives, as well as in Milwaukee and by the state of Wisconsin. On top of all that, she graduated with distinction in speech communication in 1991 and received her master's degree in rehabilitation administration in 1993.

The family that had employed her as a nanny invited Jean to attend church with them. Her interest was sparked, and she eventually had a real encounter with God and became a Christian. A passage from the Bible became her personal creed: "Faith is being sure of what we hope for and certain of what we do not see" (Heb. 11:1). She began to see her disability much differently.

"Walking is overrated," she says. "Jesus Christ suffered and died on the cross for my sin. I now know, by faith, that he lives in me and gives me grace day by day."

Driscoll's success in racing was built upon the foundation of her faith and the confidence she gained from her impressive career at Illinois. She began to train for racing and quickly became a major force.

A Milwaukee businessman, Jim Derse, provided a racing wheelchair for Driscoll's first big-time national race, the *Phoenix Sun-Times* 10K. With little training behind her, Jean took third place. It kicked off a stretch in which she won races of varying distances all over the world. She came home from her first international event, in England, with nine gold medals.

It took Driscoll's coach, Marty Morse, two years, however, to convince Jean to enter a marathon before she finally debuted at the 1989 Chicago race.

"I hated the training," Driscoll says. "Instead of fifty-mile weeks, all of a sudden I was doing one-hundred-mile weeks. I thought I would get lost, abandoned, or attacked by a dog, or not even finish the distance."

Morse's gentle persuasion helped Jean stay on track. She finished 8 seconds under 2 hours in Chicago, qualifying her for the Boston Marathon in 1990.

"But I don't want to do any more marathons," she moaned to Morse following the Chicago race.

"You don't qualify for the Boston Marathon and not go," he told her.

She went. She also won the race in Boston in world-record time. It was the first of seven consecutive victories in the sport's most prestigious race, and the beginning of an amazing career.

"If you're willing to take risks, to dream big and work hard, you'll meet goals you never thought you could," says Driscoll. "So many people have a fear of failure. It paralyzes them."

What makes Driscoll so good? Her commitment to training is legendary. Around Champaign, her nickname is the "Jean Machine," for her two to three hours per day, six days a week, year-round regimen on the road and at the track. She logs as many as 130 miles a week.

"I plan my life around my training schedule," says Driscoll. "I love being in shape. I love being fit and strong."

None of her workouts compare, however, to Jean's hill repeats. She begins in the parking lot at Assembly Hall on the Illinois campus, doing fifty-meter sprints. After each sprint, she asks someone to hang onto the back of her chair, until she's so weighted down she practically spins her wheels—usually five people total on board. Then she sprints up the ramps to Assembly Hall, again adding a person to her chair on each climb—three is the usual here.

At five-feet tall, 110 pounds, she has the best strength-to-weight ratio of any woman in the sport. She has huge deltoids, bulging biceps, and taut triceps; bench presses 200 pounds; and can transfer that power each time she pushes the rims on the wheels of her chair. Her power enables as many as 130 revolutions per minute, while maintaining an average speed of 16.5 miles per hour. Because she is so light, she attacks hills with relative ease. Because she is so fearless, she thinks nothing of descending at close to fifty miles per hour. This has served her particularly well in Boston, where the marathon is well-suited for her strengths.

"Racing at Boston is a spiritual experience for me, more so every year," says Driscoll. "It's a big deal to win there. It's the race I want to win. I've placed a bigger priority on it than even the Olympics. I look forward to it every year. I feel stronger each year I race at Boston."

Aside from her physical prowess, what makes Driscoll a champion is her heart and her mental toughness. She developed a unique ability to concentrate as a child, spending long periods of time attempting to keep her balance and stand still.

"For most of my life, too many people placed limitations on me," Driscoll says. "Well, I'm making a living at a sit-down job, but it happens to be wheelchair racing.

"I went from feeling worthless to having Olympic medals and a fan base. It blows me away that people recognize me when I go to the grocery store."

With recognition has come responsibility. Driscoll is clear about her desire to be a role model to all people. She signs autographs with her personal motto, "Dream Big and Work Hard," a to-the-point message of her life that is the same one inscribed in large letters across her bright yellow racing chair. Driscoll has discovered that the words *you can't* have become a challenge to her to find a way.

"God has given me an incredible platform, and I'm really enjoying using it," she says. "For young people and adults, the biggest limitations are the ones you place on yourself. You have to experience failure before you can appreciate success.

"I am not a disabled person. That's not how people define me. I'm not a courageous person. I'm an elite athlete who's training for the same reasons as [any other world-class athlete]. I want to be the best in the world in my sport. I want to make a difference."

A champion puts the success of others above individual achievement.

CHAPTER 6
TEAMWORK

Being one of the better players on all of the teams I've played on, I had a tendency to want to try and do it all myself. Yet one reason I regret not being able to continue in my pro playing career is because I was beginning to really understand how much I need other people.

From the other starters, to the guys on the bench, to the training staff, to the coaching staff—everyone is important and must work together for a team to become a champion. A player must reach the point of maturity where he recognizes that it's about the common goal; he must do what he needs to do to enhance the opportunity to achieve that common goal.

When you're a young player in team sports, winning is important. But being recognized for your individual ability is probably right up there, maybe even superseding that. As you mature, however, you recognize that there's something bigger out there. It's about working together. It's about acknowledging what your strengths and weaknesses are, blending those with the team, and really enjoying the experience of working together toward something. The purity of the essence of teamwork—really embracing the other people that you're working with—is what makes the experience so fulfilling.

The one thing I miss most about playing the game is definitely the camaraderie—it's just so special. Going through the practices together. Going through training camp. Being screamed and hollered at by the coaches. Going through the conditioning. It's that shared experience that's so unique because it's at an intimate level. It's also very public at times, and it's emotional. Your passion is always at a high level; it just brings in so many dynamics that make it a special kind of environment.

You want to have that closeness and that sense of a common purpose. And when you do, it's really magical. You realize how important the other folks are to making you whole—and vice versa.

—C. K.

"If you're not on a great team, you don't get a chance to star."
John Wooden, Hall of Fame UCLA Basketball Coach

Scott Brosius

Once upon a time, Scott Brosius was a rather obscure but steady third baseman for the Oakland A's. Few outside of the A's organization knew of him.

In 1998, however, the entire baseball world found out who Scott Brosius is. And he has been showing them more ever since.

After four up-and-down seasons in Oakland, Brosius went to the New York Yankees in a 1998 preseason trade. That became a career year for the McMinnville, Oregon, native. He hit .300, with 19 homers and 98 RBIs from the ninth spot in the New York batting order, and became an American League all-star.

While the Yankees buzzed through the Atlanta Braves in four games to win the '98 World Series, Brosius hit two homers, drove in six runs, batted .471, and was named the Series MVP. He carried on in the 1999 season, with 17 home runs and 71 RBIs, and again played a key role in a repeat World Series championship.

After an all-star season, you'd think as a free agent Brosius would shop his services and consider an offer from a team closer to home. He didn't. Even before filing for free agency, he said he wanted to stay in New York, and signed a three-year contract to do just that.

New York was a rather unpleasant thought for Brosius prior to 1998. After a miserable '97 season, when he hit only .203 for Oakland, he was traded to the Yankees. When his agent called with the news, there was stunned silence.

"For a visitor, New York is the most uncomfortable place to play," Brosius says. "The thought of playing there for six solid months . . . it was a running joke with my agent whenever trade talks would come up. Anywhere but New York."

Brosius says the soul-searching focused on "really turning over my career to Christ. It's easy sometimes to turn over about 90 percent of your life, but there's always the part that you feel you have to control."

He calls the trade to the Yankees "a little slap" from the Lord, as if he were saying, "Scott, listen. You're going to a place that you know only I can help you go and enjoy." "Right from the start, it was so apparent that God was involved," Brosius says.

From day one in spring training, Brosius began to get a sense his new team was special. "Listening in the clubhouse, there was no talk at all about personal goals like, 'This is the year I'm going to hit 30 home runs.' Everything was team-oriented. Our goal was to get to the playoffs and try to win a championship. The talent on the team goes without saying, but we also have a group of guys who are really special in their character."

Brosius soon found out many of his new teammates were Christians. Their season-long discipline of daily Bible study before games began during spring training.

"So much of baseball is being comfortable where you are, and when you find some guys who share the same beliefs, who share the same thoughts that you do, when you have somebody to spend all that extra time with on the road, it makes the season go so much better," Brosius says.

Chad Curtis was the ringleader in both 1998 and 1999. Anywhere from six to a dozen players—usually including Andy Pettitte, Joe Girardi, and Darren Holmes—prayed and studied together at the ballpark before batting practice.

"I don't think we missed a day all year," Brosius says. He remembers the topic of their first discussion. A theologian would call it God's sovereignty. For these guys, the question was: What are we doing in New York? "And yet here we were together," Brosius says. "This was no accident."

A primary prayer, for both the fellowship group and the team, was for unity. Brosius believes the focus on team goals was God's answer.

"For twenty-five guys to come together like that is rare," he says. "A lot of teams have the talent, but very seldom do they have the focus that this team had. Every day there was no let up. It didn't matter how well we did the night before—today's game became the most important one. After a win, there'd be no music blaring, no partying in the clubhouse. Guys would shake hands, go about their business, and come back ready to play the next day.

"[Winning] wasn't our motivation," Brosius says. "We certainly appreciated how well the season went—this was something we may not experience again. But our motivation came from within, to go out and be our best every day."

Their 114 wins in 1998 set an American League record and created enormous expectations for the playoffs. Anything less than a World Series championship would bond the Yankees to the 1906 Cubs, who won 116 games in the National League but laid the foundation for a century of disappointment in Chicago when they folded in the Series.

With superior pitching, the Yankees had little difficulty with Texas and Cleveland in the Division Series and Championship Series. Brosius hit a home run in each series as the Yankees brought the World Series to the Bronx again. They repeated in 1999, sweeping the Braves four games to none, with Brosius again playing a key role in the series, hitting .375. In 2000, even without the likes of Curtis, Girardi, and Holmes, the Yanks took the series again, beating crosstown rivals the New York Mets. Again, Brosius came up big as a part of baseball's best team.

The Yankees had no season MVP, no batting champion, no home run champ—no individual awards. Yet they epitomized the team concept. And Scott Brosius was the epitome of how they became champions.

> **"We are just the seven mules.**
> **We do all the work so that these four fellows can gallop into fame."**
> **Adam Walsh, Former Notre Dame Lineman**
> **(on blocking for the famed "Four Horsemen")**

Annett Buckner Davis and Jenny Johnson Jordan

They make up the best team in U.S. women's beach volleyball. They are both African American. They are both God-fearing, Bible reading, genetically gifted superb athletes. And they are also best friends.

Annett Buckner Davis and Jenny Johnson Jordan both have great bloodlines. Johnson Jordan is the daughter of 1960 Olympic decathlon champion Rafer Johnson. Buckner Davis' father is former NBA player Cleveland Buckner. Johnson Jordan is married to former UCLA and NFL receiver Kevin Jordan. Buckner Davis' husband is Olympic-class swimmer Byron Davis.

They have played together since their indoor volleyball days at UCLA. They live two blocks apart in southern California. And, unlike most beach volleyball duos, they genuinely like each other.

"A lot of times, teams just don't stay together long enough," says Buckner Davis, who has been wooed by some of the sport's top players but is steadfastly committed to Johnson Jordan. "What's different is we made a commitment and stuck to it.

"Our life is balanced off the court. If you hate a person's guts off the court, that's not a very good feeling. You can't be at peace if you're like that. We know we have that peace.

"We have a lot of similarities too. I think if we didn't have those things in common, it would be harder for us to be together off the court. I'd be uncomfortable around her, maybe. It just makes it a lot easier this way."

Johnson Jordan agrees. "It's just the two of us, and we travel together, we room together, we do everything together," she says. "That would be hard if you didn't believe in one another."

The commitment has paid off. After leaving UCLA in the mid-'90s, they joined the now defunct four-person beach volleyball tour. They tried doubles for the first time in 1997, and in only their third tournament, became the first African Americans to play for a pro beach title.

Now, they reach for even greater success—and Olympic history—continuing to do it together.

"Going out there and working with the people on your team and all of a sudden it all comes together and all starts to click—that's the thrill I get nowadays.
That's what I look for . . . the whole combination. It's when those things come together and we rely on each other at the right time that makes a great team."
Jeff Gordon, NASCAR Champion Driver

Bob Christian

Atlanta Falcons fullback Bob Christian is a throwback to the day of the single wing when the quarterback was the blocking back. He's a fullback who blocks. That's his primary job. Sometimes that is all he does.

He came out of Northwestern a record-setting running back who carried the ball 25–30 times a game. When he gets to run the ball with the Falcons, it's stop-the-presses stuff. They do trust him with it on passes now and then.

"He can be dangerous when he gets his hands on the ball," Dan Reeves said. "He's as good a blocker as I've ever been around, but he can do more than block."

Football computes just about everything it does. No statistic is too obscure to be logged, but somehow blocks get overlooked. No record is kept of devastating blocks, killer blocks, pancake blocks. They keep records on half-tackles, but the blocker who clears the track goes unrecorded, except by the coach and the old blocker doing analysis from the broadcast booth.

"I get a lot of awards and stuff, but I should just hand them all to Bob," says Falcons running back Jamaal Anderson, who led the NFL in rushing in 1998. "There are things I don't even see when I'm on the field. When we're looking at the film on Monday, there will be this defensive lineman coming at me at full speed and Bob plucks him off."

Christian also is adept at picking up blitzing rushers, which has helped injury-prone quarterback Chris Chandler stay on the field.

"I've seen a lot of fullbacks," says Reeves, who has been around the NFL since 1965. "But none of them could block better than Bob Christian."

To be a blocking back, you have to play without fear.

"You've got to be fearless," Christian said. "It's not a natural thing to go running full speed into another guy who's trying to stuff the hole."

And the art of blocking is much more technical than the average fan realizes. You've got to keep your feet apart, your head up. You've got to stay lower than the guy you're blocking, making sure to roll the hips on contact while remembering to keep the feet moving.

"It's easy to say," Christian said. "But trying to think of all those things at once, sometimes it's real hard to keep things going.

"It's against human nature. You're bearing down on some guy as big as you are, both going full speed. If you flinch, you lose. I put my faith in God. I feel like he gives me the courage to do what I do, or I wouldn't still be here."

No pampered athlete here. He plays to serve, as he lives his life. In the spring of 1998, he and some other athletes made a Christian mission into South Africa and Zimbabwe—here *Christian* referring to his faith, not his name.

Blocking is no precise science. It has to be the nature of the beast, to stick his head in a lion's den and hope to get it back. Rare is the fan who has a full appreciation of it, unless it's in full view. It's a life of sacrifice, but here's a man who has the attitude for it. Christian the Christian.

"It's amazing how much can be accomplished if no one cares who gets the credit."
John Wooden, Hall of Fame UCLA Basketball Coach

Tom Hammonds

In 2000, as the U.S. "Dream Team" went after the gold at the Summer Olympic games in Sydney, Australia, one of the team's key performers was a late addition—power forward Antonio McDyess of the Denver Nuggets. While McDyess was rebounding over Spaniards, Russians, and Canadians, Tom Hammonds was sitting at home watching, with a big smile.

Tom Hammonds?

Yes, Tom Hammonds, the journeyman forward who has bounced from Washington to Denver to Minnesota and other stops in between. You see Hammonds and McDyess enjoy a unique friendship.

When then first-round draft pick McDyess made his NBA debut in Denver in 1995, his teammates watched a frightened, shy young man struggling to understand the NBA drama. McDyess comes from Quitman, Mississippi, where the head count totals 2,736 and could easily fit into one corner of the packed arenas McDyess plays in each night.

In a game where one man's failure is another man's opportunity, it would have been easy for Hammonds, at the time the backup power forward to the struggling rookie, to gloat secretly over McDyess' fumblings. Instead, Hammonds built a relationship.

"I offered him advice and friendship," says Hammonds. "I'm the elder statesman. I'm not really that much older [7 years], but I see my role as the one to hold the team together. I like to call myself 'the landlord' of the team."

Just as a landlord maintains buildings under his care, Hammonds considered rookie maintenance a priority.

"I don't get caught up in competition for a starting role, or the hot new talent that new seasons bring," says Hammonds. "My faith is in Christ, and I can only do the best I can with what he's given me."

Hammonds' faith and quiet confidence proved to be more than rhetoric, and McDyess gladly sat under Hammonds' gentle guidance. Hammonds became a mentor for the young star, helping him adjust not only on the court, but also to the NBA lifestyle. Because of Hammonds' influence, McDyess has remained grounded and has not fallen prey to the temptation that has beset so many of his peers.

With family and solid foundations tucked in their mental treasuries, McDyess and Hammonds developed a friendship that survived the competition and shallowness of professional sports. Most of what they offer each other comes in the form of encouragement, being there—at home or on the road—to offer support when a poor performance or loneliness could eat away at them.

"Antonio and I were like Amos and Andy," recalls Hammonds. "Wherever I went, he went."

Now the pupil has exceeded his mentor. And as the gold medal was placed around Antonio McDyess' neck in Sydney, surely for a moment his thoughts turned to the man who, like a big brother, showed him how to make it. And surely, somewhere, Tom Hammonds was smiling.

Bobby Labonte and Joe Gibbs

Joe Gibbs

When Joe Gibbs moved from the sidelines of the NFL to the garages of NASCAR, he brought his formula for winning with him. And now the man who built the Washington Redskins into football's most successful franchise in the 1980s is building a racing enterprise of equal stature. In 2000, Gibbs gained a title in a second major sport, successfully directing his No. 18 team to the Winston Cup season championship.

While the two sports have marked differences, the blueprint for success remains the same.

"Everything that happened to me in football is happening to me in racing because you've got people involved," says Gibbs. "And it's a people business. You don't win in football with Xs and Os and equipment. You win with people. It's the same thing in racing. You don't win with a car and mechanical things. You win with people.

"When you get fifty or sixty people together in any endeavor— business, sports, football, auto racing—you're going to have people problems; and you're going to have great success and thrills working with people. It's one of the hardest things in the world, but yet the only thing worthwhile in life, really, is people."

Gibbs' football résumé proves quickly he is a master of working with people to create a winning atmosphere. While in Washington, he created a dynasty, winning three Super Bowls, four NFC championships, and five division titles. Over twelve seasons he totaled 140 wins—tenth best in league history—and posted a winning percentage near .700. He led his teams to at least ten wins in eight seasons and earned eight playoff berths. Only six coaches ever reached one hundred wins faster, and his .790 winning percentage in the postseason has been surpassed only by two other coaches. Only four other coaches have taken their teams to at least four Super Bowls as Gibbs has; none have won three of the sport's biggest games with three different quarterbacks.

Former Redskin Eric Williams spoke for many of Gibbs' former players when he summed up the team's general opinion of their leader: "In a game with a lot of liars and cheaters and crooks, he [Gibbs] was different. He was a shining star. He was honest. He was brilliant at what he did. You couldn't ask for more of a coach, or a human being."

In 1996, Gibbs was inducted into the Pro Football Hall of Fame and selected by vote of a panel of NFL experts as the greatest coach in pro football history.

Now, as the owner of Joe Gibbs Racing, he is directing another championship team. After both of Gibbs' Winston Cup drivers—Bobby Labonte and Tony Stewart—finished in the top ten in the points standings in 1999, Labonte took the season championship in 2000, with Stewart finishing sixth and leading the circuit with six wins. In just eight years, starting from the ground up, Gibbs has once again built a potential dynasty.

Since beginning his second career in 1992, Gibbs has been riding in the fast lane. The learning curve for stock car racing was as accelerated for Gibbs as that of football. When Gibbs started coaching in the NFL, it took him two years to win the Super Bowl. After starting Joe Gibbs

Racing, it took Gibbs just two years to win the Super Bowl of NASCAR—the Daytona 500—an achievement Gibbs considered tantamount to any he had ever experienced on the football field.

"Winning the Daytona 500 in only our second year is like an NFL expansion team winning the Super Bowl in only its second season," said Gibbs at the time.

But success now comes from a different vantage point than it once did. No longer does Gibbs call the plays from the sidelines. Now he stands atop the team hauler, watching at a distance from his team's huddle in the pits. Instead of a quarterback, Gibbs now has a driver. His linemen are mechanics. His receivers and backs, engineers and machinists. Still, it is individual commitment to a group effort that makes the team work—whether on a field or a raceway.

"My role is different," says Gibbs. "In football, I was a coach. I hands-on made things happen, called the plays, designed the plays. Over here, that's not my job. I couldn't do that if I wanted to. Jimmy Makar is our crew chief. He's the coach over here. He makes the calls on the car. My role has changed. Now, by being an owner in auto racing, my job is to get the sponsors, pay the bills—which is a big deal—and to pick the people. I enjoy the change, really."

Enjoyment has brought expansion. Gibbs has added to his racing empire, with the debut of two additional teams in the Busch Series and two trucks in the Craftsman Truck Series in 2000.

Still, the methods for success and excellence remain the same. And Gibbs remains true to his strategy and his principles. At Joe Gibbs Racing it's not about Joe Gibbs; rather, it's about the team.

"We feel like we are a big family," says Gibbs. "I think that's how you win in business. How you win in sports is that people have to feel like they're valuable, they're a part of it. Certainly, we feel like everybody here at Joe Gibbs Racing is very important. Every single person—whether it's the front office and all the things we're doing here in the front office, or it's back with the race team, or people on the road representing us. We feel like it is family."

"We're fortunate to be hooked up with Joe because he's a great leader of the teamwork philosophy and the ability to communicate that," says Norm Miller, chairman of Interstate Batteries, the lead sponsor of Gibbs' No. 18 Winston Cup car. "When someone can impart to you the necessity that everyone's leaning on the other and the whole thing can't move any further than all the parts together in unison—the pit team, the guys back in the shop that are doing the engines, the fabricators—everyone together.

"The Bible itself teaches you how to respond to each other, to relate to one another, and to look out for other people's interests. It tells you don't just look out for your own interests, consider other people's interests at least equal to yours, and then we're told to put others first.

"So, we try to do that. People appreciate it. They feel comfortable and they trust you and you can trust them. So, the team can move on to higher levels without a lot of the petty things that go on in many relationships. We're just pleased as we can be that Joe drives that philosophy and that teaching from the Scriptures."

"He's a great guy to work for," says Labonte. "He brings the right aspect of living, the right aspect of families, the right aspect of winning to a team. I mean, he's got all the ingredients. It's not, 'Let's win and not do anything else.' It's not, 'Who cares about winning? Let's just have a good time.' He wants to have a good time, and he wants to win, and he wants family values to be right."

"There's a big responsibility when you've got sixty families that have come to work for you," says Gibbs. "I want their job to be the best—our benefits and all the things we offer, our bonus programs, the work environment, the things we offer for the entire family.

"It's hard to get fifty employees or fifty players to go in the same direction a lot of times," says Labonte. "Everybody's got different attitudes, different personalities. To make it all work, you've got to have somebody strong right there, and Joe does that. He makes a really strong race team, makes everybody feel like they're a part of it, and they all work toward the same thing."

"It all starts right there at the top with Joe, his beliefs and what he's brought to this team," says crew chief Jimmy Makar. "He cares about them as individuals. And so, when they come to work every day, they're coming to a place that's friendly; that they know they can come in and do their jobs and they're respected, they're well liked."

"We try and have a lot of things where we involve the wives," says Gibbs. "We have a once-a-month get-together where the wives try and come together and get an opportunity to do things together. And then we have different kinds of seminars, Bible studies, what have you, that the entire family can be a part of."

Part of Gibbs' plan to care for his team members and their families is the spiritual assistance that is offered. Gibbs' approach in that area is unique in that he employs a full-time corporate chaplain to help meet his team's needs. One-on-one and group counseling, Bible studies, devotionals, and prayer time are all a part of what Gibbs extends to his entire staff on a regular basis for their choosing.

"Joe Gibbs Racing is committed to people," says Bob Dyar, the team chaplain. "We want to see that people are ministered to and encouraged in many different areas. We meet together every Tuesday morning to pray for every single person on this team. That creates an atmosphere where we are pulling for people, encouraging people.

"It's not an environment where people are pointing fingers at each other. It's an environment where we want to help every person improve and aspire to all that they can be as a part of this team. That's pretty unique from my experience dealing with different companies and organizations—to have somebody [Joe] who cares that much."

"Any time you put teams together it's so critical that every person's important, all the small things," says Gibbs. "And it's really, normally, the teams and the businesses that do the small things the best are the ones that win."

Because of his winning ways, many were startled when Gibbs announced his decision to leave football in 1993, at a time most viewed as the pinnacle of his career. But here, again, the decision was all about the team. For Joe, it was an opportunity to build a winner from the ground up, to be hands-on in the sport of first love, and, most importantly, to get closer to his "home team."

"It's just time to move on. I want to spend more time with my family and pursue other endeavors," he said at the time.

Gibbs and his wife, Pat, live in Cornelius, North Carolina, just fifty miles southwest of his boyhood home in Mocksville and only about six miles from his race headquarters. In 1999, Gibbs completed building a new 134,000-square-foot, state-of-the-art racing facility in Huntersville, at which public tours are given and where the race team engine parts are manufactured.

Both of Gibbs' sons are involved in what has become a family business. J. D., a former football player at William & Mary, is president of Joe Gibbs Racing and also competes part time in the NASCAR Busch Series. Youngest son Coy, a former linebacker at Stanford, has worked with Gibbs' NHRA teams and, in 1999, won the NASCAR Slim Jim All-Pro Rookie of the Year award. In 2000, he ran a limited schedule in the MBNA Chevrolet, one of Gibbs' entries in the Craftsman Truck Series. Both sons desire one day to drive for their father on the Winston Cup circuit.

For Gibbs, this is indeed the best of both worlds. It's also a far cry from his days in Washington, when he went off to start the season, the boys went off to college, and Pat went to see the boys. The family being separated for so much of each year is the main reason Gibbs left football.

"I spend a lot more time with them," says Gibbs of his family. "And Pat, my wife, travels with me. I wouldn't have been able to do that in football. Football is not a life where the wife and family come with you. In fact, Pat never traveled to games with me, unless it was the Super Bowl.

"I think a dream for any parent would be that you could work with your kids. Certainly, this has been a real thrill because of that. Having J. D. and Coy working in the race shop with me, we see each other every day. We live within ten minutes of each other, so I'm always over there and they're over at our house.

"But more than anything, I think, getting to enjoy something—when you think about that, how hard is that? Something that everybody in the family would enjoy—working on racing, and then to build a business and a race team—it's, I think, very unusual. We're probably one of the luckiest families in the world to get an opportunity to do this."

"I couldn't think of working for another boss," says J. D. "I couldn't think of driving for anyone else besides him. It's great to have the father-son relationship away from business, but adding work to it brings kind of a new dimension."

"My family is the most important thing I'm going to leave on this earth," says Gibbs. "When all is said and done, it isn't the games that I've won, or the races we've won, or the money I've made; it's my wife Pat and the two boys."

Joe and Pat Gibbs were married in 1966. Thirty-five years later, they can look back on wonderful times as well as challenges. In 1980, Pat had surgery for an acoustic neuroma, an operation that left her partially numb on one side of her face. Today, Pat accompanies Joe to the races and keeps the most important part of the team functioning properly.

"If you look at it like, 'OK, we're a team. We both belong to the Lord; everything we have belongs to the Lord—including our children,'" says Joe, "it gives you the right perspective on your mate and your marriage. I believe that God made Pat especially for me and that he made me especially for Pat. When we married, we became a team."

While Joe Gibbs' passion for his family is unquestioned, his love for auto racing actually predates that of football. The sport first made his heart jump back in 1955, when his family moved from North Carolina to California. A stone's throw from the sun-splashed beaches, and in the shadow of James Dean, Joe began drag racing. He sold his racing equipment when he made a full-time commitment to football, but vowed to one day return to racing.

That day came in 1991. While still coaching the Redskins, Gibbs opened a modest race shop north of Charlotte with Jimmy Makar as crew chief and Dale Jarrett, Makar's brother-in-law, at the wheel. During the first three seasons, Joe Gibbs Racing, with its bright green No. 18 Interstate Batteries car, won two races. One of those just happened to be the Daytona 500. The win not only launched Gibbs' career as a stock car owner, but also launched the career of Dale Jarrett, who would leave the team following the 1994 season, then go on to win again at Daytona in 1996 and take the season points championship in 1999. It's clear to Jarrett his time with Gibbs was designed for more than on-the-track exploits.

"You look back over things and you always wonder what the plan is for your life," says Jarrett. "I had no idea why Joe Gibbs was coming into my life when he called me in 1992 about the possibility of him starting a team and the possibility of me being the driver for that team. I realize that there was much more involved than just becoming a race driver. It was changing my life totally and certainly for the good.

"It was a time that Kelly, my wife, and I rededicated our lives [to God]. Even though we were believers in God, we weren't living our lives exactly like that. We weren't honoring him like we should. It was that association with Joe Gibbs, who was a high-profile person—this is the way that he's living his life.

"We went to the Super Bowl in 1993 and went to the Redskins' team chapel service on the night before the game. That's where, without knowing it, Kelly and myself and Jimmy Makar and my sister Patty [Makar's wife], all stood up at the same time to rededicate our lives—with our eyes closed, not one of us knowing that the other was getting up. That was probably as big a thrill for me as anything that's ever happened. That surpasses any victories that I have here.

"That's when Joe Gibbs said, 'We've done something good here besides start a race team.' It was just a thrill. It changed our lives totally. So, Joe Gibbs is someone that we realize we owe a tremendous amount to in our lives, because he certainly made an impression on us for the rest of our lives."

After the 1994 season, Jarrett left to join the Robert Yates Racing team. Gibbs signed up-and-coming driver Bobby Labonte as his replacement for 1995. He added a second team in 1999, signing Stewart to drive the No. 20 Home Depot car. In 1999, Labonte finished as the runner up to Jarrett in the season points standing, with Stewart finishing fourth and being named the circuit's Rookie of the Year. Then in 2000, the championship season finally came. Still there is the unchanging perspective.

"If you're standing there trying to race these cars and saying, 'Man, I'm going to make this happen myself,'" says Gibbs, "I don't know how you could live. Because there are going to be so many things that are out of your hand out there. The only way we can have peace, I think, is to know that God loves me, knows what's in my life, he's sealed me, I belong to him, and in the end everything's going to work out the best for me."

Over the years things have worked out for Joe Gibbs. There have been shifting circumstances and changing drivers, but the principles and standards that govern Joe Gibbs Racing remain steadfast.

"Everybody out there is high stress because we're trying to do what? We're trying to be successful in life," says Gibbs. "And people ask me, 'What's being successful?' That's something everybody is wrestling with. And still our life winds up being [all about] relationships."

The principles that drive Gibbs are rooted in his deep faith, a faith that strengthens him, sustains him, motivates him, and gives him balance.

"You know, our lives are caught up in all these emotions and things that are going on," he says, "and unless we have the right priorities, unless we have God first in our life, I'll guarantee you it's a monumental struggle for everybody."

"Most people in racing have been of the belief that whatever it took to win races was OK," says Makar. "They call it fudging. They call it cheating. They call it lots of things. Joe is of the belief that you do things as hard and as well as you can do them, then leave the results to God."

"We make choices all the time," says Gibbs. "And at Joe Gibbs Racing, we say that if we were going to gain from something and it's wrong, we can't do it. And yet, if we would lose by doing something and it's right, we have to do it. We're driven by the fact that we want our principles here to be right in line with the Lord's."

"We want to win championships, but you know, twenty years from now, nobody's going to have any idea who won the NASCAR championship or the Super Bowl," says J. D. "But if you can realize what's most important in your relationship with the Lord and have that straight, then I think years from now, you're going to end up with treasures that are a lot more important than trophies."

It's been said the true measure of a man's success is not based on numbers, but rather in the legacy he leaves in the lives of those he touches. Perhaps it is in that arena that Joe Gibbs has made an even more valuable contribution than in either sport. His life has become an example to those around him, demonstrating what the essence of teamwork is all about, and showing that when excellence becomes a tradition, there is no end to greatness. The only thing that endures is character.

"To walk the talk—I think that's what my dad, if nothing else, he's always done that in my eyes, and I think in everyone else's eyes," says J. D. "He's a man after God's own heart. He's not perfect, and as usual the family is the first one to point that out to him. If it's not me or my brother, it's my mom bringing him back down to earth. But, he just really wants to do what's right in God's eyes. I think that encompasses so many different traits—loyalty and honesty and hard work—that I was able to witness growing up. It obviously made a big difference in my life."

"I would hope that people from the outside would look at this race team and say, 'Hey those guys are trying to do things the right way; there's something different there about their race team; that's the right way we should be doing things,'" says Gibbs. "To be a witness through the way we act and the way we race."

A champion understands that winning is not the only thing.

CHAPTER 7

PRIORITIES

One of the greatest challenges I, and probably countless others, face in the world of athletics as well as in the world of business is juggling the personal and the professional. It's a real challenge. This juggling "game" requires establishing priorities.

But priorities have to be born out of conviction, not circumstances, because convictions are less changeable than circumstances—or at least they should be.

One of the great challenges that anybody faces with priorities, especially those of us in the public eye, is that "good" and "best" are hard to discern. There are a lot of good things to do and to be involved with, and yet what's best may require refraining from getting involved in some of those things. The more public you are and the more opportunities you have to gain materially from your visibility and from the desires people have of you, the more difficult it is to say no—especially if you aren't clear on what your goals and priorities are.

I was faced with this dilemma when my contract with ESPN expired in 1997. It had been a matter of prayer for my wife Rosie

priority: taking precedence logically or in importance

109

and I to have me on the road less. I had been working for the Indiana Pacers and ESPN, which required an average of three to five nights away from home each week during the four to five months of the basketball season. It disrupted any semblance of stability for us as a family.

That's when the opportunity with CBS presented itself. It called for studio work on weekends and less travel during the week. I'm thankful for this answer to prayer. Not only am I on the road less—a priority—but God has elevated me to a more high-profile position, and at a higher income level.

But I wasn't looking for more money or a higher profile. It was simply a matter of priorities.

As you consider your priorities, you must ask yourself a few questions: What are you looking to accomplish? To whom is your loyalty and allegiance directed? In my case, as a follower of Christ, he receives my loyalty and allegiance. Therefore my priorities—if I'm going to walk the talk—must line up with the allegiance that I publicly state.

—C. K.

"My faith, my family, my city, and my friends are the valuable things in my life."
Art Rooney, Former Owner, Pittsburgh Steelers

Laurie Brower

In 1986, Laurie Brower, then a southern California junior golf champ and two-time Southwest Conference Player of the Year at Texas Tech, decided to try the LPGA's qualifying school. She felt ready to contend for a spot on the pro tour.

She was on her way to making the Tour when she tore the cartilage in her wrist while hitting a routine fairway shot. Her wrist became so sore she couldn't pick up a pencil. X-rays showed the bones in her wrist had fused together. Following surgery, one doctor told Laurie she would never play golf again.

Brower spent eighteen months rehabilitating the wrist before she was ready to give the Tour another shot. On the eve of making her comeback attempt, Laurie received an urgent telephone call from her father. He told Laurie her mother was dying of a brain tumor.

Brower had waited a year-and-a-half for the opportunity to prove she could play with the best golfers in the world. She had recovered from the wrist injury. It was her time to shine. Yet when her dad called, there was no hesitation as to what she would do.

"My dad asked me to quit work. I did," Brower says. "I never asked why. It was my mother."

For two and a half years in the late 1980s, Brower put golf aside and took care of her mom.

There were good and bad days. On the good days, her mom was normal, could hold a conversation, and remembered what life once was. Other days were far worse. "When she woke up from naps, she would scream with fear if nobody was there," Brower says. "So I tried to stay close by. I was there whenever anything bad happened."

Brower knew she was losing the best years of her golf career, but she didn't care. Her mom was more important. Her only practice came in the backyard of her parents' home, hitting balls into a net and putting on a small patch of Astroturf.

"I was very thankful for that time with my mom," Brower says. "Otherwise I wouldn't have been home with her and gotten to spend so much quality time. I wouldn't change any of it. None of it. I had to watch her deteriorate, but God took her in a very gentle way, and I was there for her."

Dorothy Brower died in 1989.

Shortly thereafter, Laurie got a call from a friend asking her to play in a minitour event in southern California. Brower initially said no. She still wasn't emotionally ready. After some persuading, however, she agreed to play.

Unfortunately, as she stepped up to the first tee, she realized it was the same course where her mom had last watched her play. She broke down. And took a nine. She was doubting her ability to finish when she "realized my mom wouldn't want to see me like this," she says.

Brower rallied to shoot a 75, finished fifth, and earned nine hundred dollars. "It was time to get the ball rolling," she decided. Less than a year later, in October 1991, she made the Tour, five years later than scheduled but much more fulfilled.

Tim Burke

Baseball had been a major part of Tim Burke's life since he first played Little League ball in his hometown of Omaha, Nebraska, at age seven. As a major-league pitcher, he played for the Expos, Mets, and Yankees. Over eight seasons in the majors, he became one of the preeminent relief pitchers in the game and made the all-star team.

In 1993, Tim was heading into camp with his new team, the Cincinnati Reds, for season number nine, when things suddenly changed. On February 27, 1993, Burke walked into the office of then Reds manager Tony Perez and general manager Jim Bowden and announced he was retiring from professional baseball. At the age of thirty-four he was simply walking away from a six-figure contract and the game he had loved for twenty-five years.

Burke's decision to leave baseball wasn't due to injury, money, or his loss of love for the game, but rather for his desire to spend time with his four children. Each was a special-needs child Tim and his wife, Christine, had adopted over the previous five years. Walking away meant leaving behind a $650,000 salary and perhaps additional millions before his career would have ended. The money didn't matter; his heart wasn't at the ballpark anymore. It was at home.

"Baseball will do just fine without me," Burke told reporters as he left the Reds camp. "It's not going to miss a beat. But I'm the only father my children have. I'm the only husband my wife has. And they need me a lot worse than baseball does."

Burke said good-bye at the height of his career. He collected 49 wins and 102 saves in his eight years, mostly for the Expos, and pitched 2 shutout innings in the 1989 all-star game. But success had not come without a price.

Tim and Christine had troubles early in their marriage from Tim's alcohol problem, their own difficult backgrounds, the heartbreak of infertility, and struggles over the decision to adopt. The baseball lifestyle only made things worse.

"She [Christine] was packed up and ready to go home and get a divorce two weeks after we were married," Tim says.

A disaster was avoided when the couple accepted a teammate's invitation to a Bible study. That evening, says Christine, "It all made sense. Our marriage wasn't working right, and the Bible had an outline for how a marriage does work." That summer they committed to Christianity, Tim stopped drinking, and their relationship improved. The couple then decided to make a family.

Each adoption brought both tears and joy. Stephanie was a premature infant from South Korea. Next, from Guatemala, came Ryan, who suffers from a thyroid disorder. Then Nicole, also from Korea, who was born without a right hand and with a serious heart defect, joined the family. Finally came Wayne, a Vietnamese orphan born with a club foot and hepatitis B. Even with a full house, the Burkes planned to adopt more children.

"Christine and I both have a lot of love to give away and feel that children are the ideal ones to receive it," Tim said.

In 1989, the Burke's planned to pick up Ryan from Guatemala during the all-star break. Four days before the trip, Tim learned he had been named to his first all-star team. "We talked about whether I should go with her [Christine] to Guatemala, and Christine insisted that I play."

After pitching two shutout innings, Burke caught a midnight flight from Los Angeles to Guatemala City, arriving at 6:00 A.M. to join his wife and new son.

It was Nicole's serious health problems that first opened the door to Tim's departure from baseball. Just one day prior to then ten-month-old Nicole's open-heart surgery, Tim was traded from the Expos to the New York Mets. He had to leave for New York while Nicole was in serious condition, leaving Christine to handle the situation alone. Nicole subsequently suffered brain damage from the surgery and experienced forty or more seizures a day for a time after the surgery.

"It's easy to be irresponsible. I was not responsible," says Tim. "Christine was the leader. She took care of the kids; she was their teacher and spiritual leader; she had to take care of the finances; she had to move us—thirty-eight times in ten years."

Since Tim's retirement from baseball, the Burkes have no regrets. The reward has come in fours, emphasized every time Stephanie and Ryan tell people, "My daddy retired from baseball because he loves us so much."

"Never let yesterday take up too much of today."
Tex Schramm, Former General Manager, Dallas Cowboys

Jeff King

Jeff King was the first overall pick in the 1986 amateur baseball draft, a highly coveted slugger from the University of Arkansas. He made his way through the Pittsburgh Pirates organization, constantly living with the bane of expectations.

He made it to the big leagues to stay in 1989, and by 1993 he had become one of the game's top run-producing third basemen. After the 1994 season, Jeff was eligible for free agency and appeared ready to move to a contending team for more money. After all, playing for the cost-conscious small-market Pirates wasn't where he would be compensated best.

Then something unusual happened. Jeff decided he wanted to be loyal to the team that had been loyal to him. He wanted to stay in Pittsburgh. So he put his priorities ahead of a paycheck, and negotiated a one-year deal that called for an 11 percent pay *cut!*

Jeff became a dichotomy in the world of sports—a successful player who turned down more money and took a reduced salary to stay with the team who had nurtured his career.

"I really didn't want to leave," King says. "I liked Pittsburgh, and my family's home was there. Maybe I could find a better situation as a free agent, but why risk it when I was perfectly happy where I was?"

Bernhard Langer

"My priorities have changed a lot since the day I accepted Christ in 1985," says Bernhard Langer. "Number one is God, number two is family, and number three is my job. It is hard to maintain this order, and sometimes I slip, but I believe and know when you have your priorities right, everything is much easier in life."

That sense of priority has helped Langer and his wife, Vikki, handle the challenges that come with life on the pro golf tour—challenges such as the one Langer faced at the 1991 Ryder Cup, perhaps the most pivotal moment of his career to that point. He was staring at the putt of his life. If it went in, the Europeans would continue a six-year dominance of the Ryder Cup. If he missed, the United States would win.

Hale Irwin, his match play foe, would later say, "There is no way I would ever, ever, ever wish what happened on that last hole on anyone. I really don't think anyone in the world could have made that putt. The pressure was unreal."

Langer's putt just missed going in. Europe had been beaten. For the first time since 1985, the Cup would stay in the United States.

The final score was U.S. 14^1/$_2$, Europe 13^1/$_2$.

Delirium prevailed for the Americans. Paul Azinger rode the back of a golf cart while clutching a small American flag. Lanny Wadkins cried. And Langer played the goat.

"The first moments were hard, very hard—I can't tell you how hard," Langer admitted later. "But after sitting back and putting everything into perspective, I knew I had done my best—and it was all I could do under the circumstances."

Less than a week later, Langer's perspective was rewarded at the German Masters.

"This was my own tournament, as important to me as the U.S. Masters would be to Jack Nicklaus," he said. "I wanted to win that tournament so badly, but all anyone over here wanted to talk about was the missed putt. I told the press that I would talk about the putt on Wednesday, but from then on it would be a closed issue. The Bible says to forget those things that are in the past and to look forward, which is what I was trying to do."

Again it came down to a putt. This time Langer holed a fifteen-footer for birdie in a sudden-death playoff over Roger Davis to win.

Later that fall he took the Million-Dollar Challenge in South Africa and set a record at the time for most money ever won by an individual playing golf during one year.

In 1993 he won the U.S. Masters for the second time. For Langer, it was his sweetest victory because it came on Easter Sunday. It gave the German a platform to point out his love for God to a golf world that was hanging on his words.

Langer is still hungry for more victories and more majors. "I hope my best is not behind me," he said. "Nobody knows the future. I take things day by day. It says in the Bible that every day has enough trouble on its own so don't worry about tomorrow. I go by that."

> **"The true athlete should have character, not be a character."**
> **John Wooden, Hall of Fame UCLA Basketball Coach**

Johnny Oates

During his four seasons managing the Baltimore Orioles, Johnny Oates won 291 games and lost 270. His last three clubs went 237–189, the seventh-best mark in the major leagues over that span. Nonetheless, in 1994, Orioles owner Peter Angelos fired him.

The Texas Rangers were all too happy to immediately bring Oates aboard to rejoin his friend, Texas GM Doug Melvin, and build the Rangers into a contender. Little did Oates know he was about to be hit by a family crisis that had been looming on the horizon for years.

"I haven't always balanced baseball and life," says Oates. "Unfortunately, my family had to suffer for me to learn that baseball can be very, very important to us, but it can't be the only thing in our lives. We in professional sports get so spoiled sometimes with the red carpet treatment we get everywhere we go. We become immune to the needs of our wives, our families.

"Our kids suffered a lot. My wife suffered a lot. I finally came to realize that I can still enjoy baseball, but it's not the only thing in my life."

On the afternoon of April 15, 1995, Oates hopped into his car, tore out of Port Charlotte, the Rangers' spring training home, and headed north toward Savannah, Georgia. That was as far as his wife, Gloria, had made it from Colonial Heights, Virginia, on her way to Florida for a visit with her husband. The daily pressures of carrying the family alone had overwhelmed Gloria. She was hospitalized for what Oates has said was "emotional and physical exhaustion."

Both Melvin and Tom Schieffer, the Rangers' president, told Oates to stay with his wife as long as he needed. Instead of getting in the car and returning to Florida, Oates drove his family home to Virginia. Gloria Oates checked into a Richmond hospital. Johnny told the Rangers he wouldn't be coming back for awhile. Gloria went for counseling. Johnny went for counseling. They talked. They listened. Decades of silence were broken.

It ended up as a sixteen-day leave of absence, but at the time no one was sure if Oates would ever be seen again wearing a Texas uniform. He has since told friends that in the depths of Gloria's illness, he offered to resign as the Rangers' manager. The season had begun without him. It would continue without him. He began planning life without baseball.

That willingness to walk away from his career, Oates has said, became a turning point in his wife's recovery. After Johnny told her of his decision to give it all up, Gloria's condition improved almost overnight. Soon, Oates felt his wife was well enough for him to return to work. "Not many people know what he went through and how tough it was," says Melvin.

For ten days, Gloria Oates watched her husband. Finally, she told him he should return to his team. "Go back," Oates says his wife told him. "Baseball is not your mistress anymore."

The couple talks daily now. When either one is not in Arlington, the phone calls range from one to three hours. "We have an agreement that we can call each other at 4:30 in the morning if we have to."

Many of the conversations often start and end with prayer, an acknowledgment of the source that gives them both strength. Ironically, since reordering his family life, Oates has enjoyed his finest managing seasons, leading the Rangers to three division crowns. He is now enjoying the fruits of a healthy balance of family and baseball, and says the situation with his wife and children has never been better.

Branch Rickey

In the world of baseball, Branch Rickey was a known genius, not just for his role in the integration of the game with Jackie Robinson but as an innovator. Rickey introduced baseball to the farm system, pitching machines, spring training complexes, and the batting helmet. Clearly he was a man ahead of his time.

He was the one who converted Stan Musial from a Class D pitcher to a Hall of Fame outfielder. He helped force expansion to the western part of the United States. He even was a cofounder of the Fellowship of Christian Athletes.

He could have gone into the ministry, authored books, or "if he'd gone into politics," said Howard Green, general manager of the Dodgers farm club during Rickey's lifetime, "he could have been president."

In the midst of all the innovation and activity, arose Rickey's desire to racially integrate baseball, and beyond that, American society. The concept first came to him as a coach at his alma mater, Ohio Wesleyan College. While the team was traveling to play other college teams, a black player named Charles Thomas was denied a hotel room in South Bend, Indiana. Only when Rickey intervened was he allowed a cot in Rickey's room. As Rickey told it, he later overheard Thomas crying and saw him pulling at his hands, as if he were wishing he could wipe off his pigmentation.

Rickey was motivated to make a difference and wanted to be on the cutting edge in this action, not just a follower. He had been looking for the right person to break the barrier for about three years, studying what would be necessary. He asked prospective Dodger players, "Would you ever have any objection to playing with a Negro?"

Some players did.

Rickey could have signed a lot of qualified players from the Negro Leagues, many with better baseball stature. But he had someone in mind, as he said in a 1945 letter to Dr. Dan Dodson, who headed New York's Committee on Unity, an organization interested in promoting the integration of major league baseball—someone who might not be the best player but was the best fit with Rickey's personality profile.

Rickey knew the right man for the role in history was Jackie Robinson. So he signed him to a contract and told Robinson of his intentions, then he prepared Jackie for what lay ahead.

Robinson himself knew the importance of Rickey's actions, writing him before he died, "It has been the finest experience I have had being associated with you, and I want to thank you very much for all you have meant, not only to me and my family but to the entire country and particularly the members of our race. I am glad for your sake that I had a small part to do with the success of your efforts, and I must admit, it was your constant guidance that enabled me to do so."

Though "the man who could have been president" never wound up in the White House, his legacy as the one man who made the integration of baseball and the nation his priority ranks him in history every bit as influential and presidential as those who have occupied the Oval Office.

> "Talent is God-given; be humble. Fame is man-given; be thankful.
> Conceit is self-given; be careful."
> John Wooden, Hall of Fame UCLA Basketball Coach

Chris Spielman

Chris Spielman knows what it is like to take a hit. As a star middle linebacker for three NFL teams, he was one of the league's hardest hitters in a football career that spanned 1988–99. But even this ferocious tackler was not prepared for the emotional hit he took in 1998.

It was then that Spielman learned his wife, Stefanie, a former model, had cancer.

Just one-year earlier, Chris had come face to face with football mortality, suffering a chilling neck injury that required surgery and threatened to end Chris' career at the age of thirty-two.

But the competitive fires still burned in Spielman, and the former Ohio State all-American was not ready to give up. He planned on a comeback with the Cleveland Browns in 1998. He prepared to show the NFL he was the same player who had been selected to the Pro Bowl four times as a Buffalo Bill and Detroit Lion from 1988–96. What he didn't plan on was having his wife fight cancer at the same time.

It was July 1998, after Stefanie suffered a miscarriage, that tests revealed a precancerous tumor in her right breast. While driving to the doctor for consultation, Chris became emotional and complained about the injustice of the situation. Stefanie provided perspective.

"How can you sit there and say those things with all the blessings we have in life?" she asked.

An ensuing mammogram and biopsy showed Stefanie needed a mastectomy. During the mastectomy, doctors found signs the cancer had spread to her lymph nodes, demanding further surgery and six months of chemotherapy.

Spielman made what was for him a quick and easy decision. He abandoned his comeback plans and stayed home to take care of his wife and their then four-year-old daughter and two-year-old son. He would walk through the rigors of recovery with Stefanie and become the primary caregiver for the children.

"I knew in my heart it was the right thing to do," Chris said. "We take our wedding vows very seriously."

None of this set well with Stefanie, who attempted to persuade her husband to go back to football.

"I knew how much he wanted to play," she said. "I knew how excited he was about returning to football. I didn't want to be the reason he didn't get to reach that goal."

Chris heard his wife's plea, but he heard his heart even louder. He gave up football. He had always talked about qualities like responsibility and concern for others. Now he had a chance to show those character qualities in action to his children. He thought about how Stefanie had been there unconditionally for him for ten years, and now it was his turn to be there for her.

Chris threw himself into a regimen every bit as challenging and demanding as training camp. It turns out the emotional preparation he put himself through for a football comeback put him in precisely the state of mind needed to help fight this opponent.

He made breakfast, bathed the children, dispensed their cold medicine, and took them to preschool. He helped them get dressed and took care of their daily needs. He built a Barbie dollhouse and repaired bicycle tires. In parenting, Chris was an all-star. He also took Stefanie to all of her chemotherapy appointments. When Stefanie lost her hair during chemotherapy, Chris showed his support by shaving his head.

"I don't know what I would have done without him being there," said Stefanie.

Early in 1999, the Spielmans received very good news. Stefanie's chemotherapy treatments were over, and she appeared to be cancer free and ready to resume a normal life. Doctors have officially classified her as being in remission.

The Spielmans established the Stefanie Spielman Fund for Breast Cancer Research and inspired the NFL to cosponsor the Susan G. Komen Breast Cancer Foundation's "Race for the Cure."

In 1999, Chris did attempt his comeback, with his hometown Browns. A violent collision in practice forced his eventual retirement on the eve of the regular season. However, Spielman was unflustered.

"Even in the worst-case scenario, my wife is alive," he said. "When you go through something like we've gone through, it's not a cliché—you really learn to appreciate every day."

Darrell Waltrip

The most successful driver on the NASCAR circuit during the 1980s, Darrell Waltrip won 57 races during that decade and captured series championships in 1981, 1982, and 1985. He was on top of the NASCAR world. Despite his overwhelming success, Waltrip's bulletproof attitude did little for his public image. But a crash at the Daytona 500 in 1983 changed all that.

"It was the beginning of a huge change in my life. I had success and was pretty much an 'I' person. I didn't really need anybody else's help. Pretty much could do it all on my own. I always liked what big Daddy Warbucks said, 'You don't have to be nice to people on the way up if you're never coming back down.' Well, I don't know how many people out there feel that way, but take it from someone that's been up there; you will come back down sooner or later. And the fall can be devastating if you don't have somebody there to catch you.

"I think that's where I found myself in '83. I had won the championship in '81. I'd won the championship in '82. And I was starting off my '83 season with the same expectations. I had become the center of attention, the focus of our sport at that time, and we were on a roll. We had it going. We won 12 races in both years, '81 and '82, 14 poles both years. I mean, I was just dominating the sport and just felt invincible. Really did. And then all of a sudden, that deal happened at Daytona, and it was a wake-up call. People say it knocked me conscious. I think as I look back, I think it really did.

"I think it got my attention because, up to that point, I'd never had an injury. That was the first time I'd ever been carried out in an ambulance and taken to a hospital. And that was a frightening experience because I realized, 'Hey, these things hit pretty hard sometimes. You could possibly get hurt doing this.'

"I got down on my knees, Stevie [his wife] and I did, and we just said, 'Lord, we have screwed up a lot of things; will you forgive us and come back in our lives, direct us and guide us and help us and save us? And we want to have a relationship with you.'

"And from that night on, when I think about where I was in 1983 and here I sit in 1998—I'm not anywhere near the same guy that I was then that I am now, and it's because of my relationship with our Savior.

"He put some humility back in my life, for one thing. He took my focus off of myself, which is where it had always been, and it softened my heart, and let me look at people differently. The fans, the people that I had dealt with, my associates in racing, all of a sudden, I had a different feeling toward them than I had prior to that. I had compassion for them, and it was really just a changing of my heart and how I felt and how I thought.

"I had been the most unpopular driver in the sport. People hated me. They called me Jaws. They booed me. They threw chicken bones and beer cans at me. They'd cuss me. . . . That was the way people perceived me. And from 1983 on, though, I made a conscious, 100 percent effort to turn that around, and in 1989, six years later, I was voted the most popular driver in the sport.

Cynthia Cooper

As the first star of women's professional basketball in America, Cynthia Cooper is an anomaly. She is gracious and unassuming off the court, but intense and driven when playing. At thirty-seven, she would seem to be an athlete past her prime, yet she finished her career in 2000 maintaining her role as the most dominant player in the WNBA.

Cooper was the league's first superstar and MVP during each of its first two seasons. She led the Houston Comets to championships in each of the league's first four years of existence 1997–2000. And when she retired following the 2000 title, she did so fulfilled in knowing she was the one person most responsible for giving the fledgling league a solid identity right from the get go.

But while Cooper was dazzling fans on the court night in and night out, her insides were churning as she walked through intense personal tragedy. Her smile and pleasant nature belie the burdens she has carried while lifting her sport to professional acceptance.

Those close to her know what Cooper has had to endure. They saw it when she affixed a pink ribbon to her uniform to signify her support for breast-cancer research. They saw it when she used to hurry into the Houston locker room after each road game to call her mother, Mary Cobbs, who eventually died from the disease in 1999. They saw it when Comets coach Van Chancellor moved practice back by a half an hour once in awhile so Cooper had time to take her mom for another battery of tests or a chemotherapy treatment session. They still see it when Cooper wistfully looks at photos or the jersey of former teammate, roommate, and close friend Kim Perrot, who also died of cancer in 1999.

After all, it was Perrot, herself, who used to stay up late at night with Cooper when the team was on the road, talking about faith, holding onto hope, and why bad things happen to good people.

Being on the court seemed to be a relief for Cooper. She was a pure scorer, who exuded an I-dare-you-to-stop-me attitude. The league's all-time scoring leader, she was equally as comfortable draining a jumper in a defender's face as she was whisking by them on the way to the hoop.

While she was vivacious on the court, Cooper tends to be stoic about herself and her off-the-court challenges. She will not easily volunteer information regarding the emotions she has struggled with or how she came to the aid of both her mother and Perrot. Few know, for example, that Cynthia escorted her mom through every stage of her cancer treatment in 1997. Or that she frequently stayed up until 3 A.M. to do the ironing and other household chores for her mother. Neither do many know that she has helped raise a niece and nephew and has adopted another nephew, Tyquon. All together, she now has five nieces and nephews who live with her.

For Cooper, playing through a hamstring pull or ankle sprain was minimal in comparison to what her mother endured or what Perrot went through.

Mary Cobbs learned she had breast cancer just weeks after she and her daughter received the joyful news that the WNBA had assigned Cooper to play in Houston, the family's adopted hometown. At least there, Cooper thought, she would be home enough to help care for her mother.

"It was unbelievable how it all worked out," Cooper says.

While the WNBA was marketed as the game that would be ruled by such media darlings as Lisa Leslie and Rebecca Lobo, it was Cooper who took the league by storm. The five-foot-ten-inch shooting guard displayed her all-around game, and for four years outplayed the others, quickly setting the league's single-game scoring record with 44 points when the league was only ten games old.

"She's the best all-around player I've ever faced," said New York Liberty guard Vickie Johnson. "She can go left if you stop her from going right, and she goes right if you stop her from going left. She can shoot the three; she can drive and score or pass off. . . . Nothing she does surprises me. She always seems to have something up her sleeve."

"The toughest thing about guarding her is that most of the time you know exactly what she's going to do, but you still can't stop her," says New York's Crystal Robinson. "She's incredible."

Cooper's success in the WNBA was a far cry from the tears she shed as a youngster. She spent her teenage years in a crime-ridden neighborhood in the Watts section of Los Angeles. Her mother made significant sacrifices to raise Cynthia and her seven siblings. Cooper's difficult childhood included being molested by a family acquaintance at age eight and the death of her brother.

Sports became a way out of the pain of a childhood partially lost. Even then, Cooper's basketball career didn't begin until she was sixteen, and then it was only accidental.

"I just happened to be in the gym at my junior high school one day and saw this older girl come down the court, put the ball behind her back from her left to her right hand, and then make a lay-up," Cooper said. "Up until then I had run track. But just like that I said, 'Oooh. Wow. I want to play like that someday.'"

By her senior year, Cooper was good enough to be recruited by colleges in the West. She chose the University of Southern California, where she played a supporting role on the 1983 and 1984 teams that won NCAA championships and featured Cheryl Miller and the McGee twins, Pam and Paula. She also played on two U.S. Olympic teams, earning a gold medal at the '88 games in Seoul, Korea, and a bronze at Barcelona in '92. But

through all that, Cooper says she never felt completely challenged to uti-
lize all of her talents.

"I never felt like I had given all I was capable of giving to one of my
teams," she says. "I was always the sort of player who was asked to pass
the ball to the marquee players and set picks, run the fast break. My role
might be to come into the game to be a defensive stopper, or a spark plug.
But all along, I told myself, 'This is not my game. This is not who I am as
a basketball player. And this is not all I can do.'"

The evolution of her game began during her eleven seasons as a pro in
Europe beginning in 1986. She became a "go-to" player with the teams
Alcamo and Parma in the Italian league. In the 1995–96 season, Cooper
averaged 35.5 points per game for Alcamo. She arrived in the WNBA as a
full-fledged, known scorer. To become such, her work regimen at times
included firing up 300–500 shots per day in practice. And it all paid off.

In the first WNBA season, Cooper led the league in scoring at 22.2 per
game and was also selected as the title game MVP after a 25-point effort.
She began to receive endorsement offers and to show up on talk shows
and in WNBA promotional spots. She was now the league's true marquee
player, much like those she had grown accustomed to playing caddie to in
previous years.

In the aftermath of that first, glorious season, Cooper said it was all the
sweeter for her in that she was able to share it with her mother.

"I've been tucked away in Europe for eleven years, and my mom hasn't
been able to share any of the special moments," she said at the time. "She's
my MVP."

In 1998, she repeated her performance in a nearly identical fashion,
scoring 22.7 points per game to lead the league, and again leading her
team to the title and a 27-3 regular season record.

But 1999 would provide the biggest challenge yet. Oh there were the
expectations to win a third consecutive title, but the burdens grew heavier
than that.

Cooper turned in her third-straight outstanding performance on the
court and in the finals, and again led the league in scoring at 22.1 points
per game, while also leading in assists at 5.7 per game. But in the midst of
her continuing excellence, she faced her most difficult defeats.

On February 12, 1999, Cooper's mother lost her battle with breast cancer. Ten days later, Perrot was diagnosed with lung cancer that had spread

125

to her brain. In six months, Cooper's close friend was dead at the age of thirty-two. Following the 1999 finals win, Cooper stood atop the media table near center court and held aloft Perrot's jersey, as if to tell the world she and her teammates had won it all for their fallen friend. It was a victory she seemed to will herself and her team to.

"There isn't but one Cynthia Cooper," said Chancellor. "She's not going to let you lose. She's got the greatest will to win of any player I've ever seen, man or woman. I've heard a lot about Larry [Bird], Magic [Johnson], and Michael [Jordan] having the greatest will to win, but I'm going to put Cynthia Cooper up there against anybody.

"She is the most focused basketball player I've ever seen. She practices, she plays, and she lets nothing bother her. She plays at a top level night in and night out. How she does it physically is a mystery to me."

"I don't know if there is another person on the planet who could have handled it the way she handled it," says Cooper's 2000 U.S. Olympic team coach, Nell Fortner. "Triumphed with the memory of her mother and Kim Perrot in the forefront and leading Houston to the finals at the top of her game. She's got an inner strength that I don't know if anybody can match."

Cooper finished her wondrous basketball tour with a fourth-straight WNBA title and fourth-straight finals MVP award in 2000. Then she simply walked away from the game the same way she first entered—with grace, class, and composure, and as a model of how to prioritize one's life.

Chester Pipkin, pastor of ReJoice in Jesus Ministry, Cooper's home church in Los Angeles, says Cooper's strength comes from her Christian faith.

"There are a lot of people who read Scripture and go to church," he says. "But there is a difference between rhetoric faith and real faith. She has real faith."

Cooper says her faith allows her to be strong enough to do what needs to be done on the court in times of trial.

"God has allowed me to be mentally tough," she says. "I can only withstand all the different things that have happened because of my spirituality and my belief in letting go of your problems and letting God handle them."

A champion knows that winning
is not necessarily measured
by the final score.

CHAPTER 8

SUCCESS

To me, success is modeling for my kids a vibrant living relationship with God. Doing that impacts every area of my life: the handling of my resources, the way I treat people, and the way I carry myself in every venue. That, to me, is what being successful is.

Part of success for me is in the area of stewardship. Are my needs being met? That doesn't necessarily mean that I have everything I want, but that my needs and my family's needs are met and we're still in a position to give—both materially and of ourselves—to the betterment of other people.

Professionally, success is obviously to excel in whatever work I do and to do it with excellence. But success to me really is based on the relationship I have with God, and how I live that out. It is finding contentment and peace in that relationship and modeling that for my kids. That is what drives me to be successful.

It's been said that money can buy you a house, but it can't buy you a home; it can buy you a bed, but it can't buy you sleep; it can buy you a lot of things, but it can't buy you true love or peace. I believe that. That's why success is more than what I have materially.

I think another aspect of success is finding your particular purpose according to what your gifts and abilities and passions are, then utilizing those gifts and abilities for God's glory and as a means to sustain yourself financially. Those, I think, are hallmarks of success.

Success is fulfillment in who you are. For me who I am is defined by my relationship with God. Everything else flows out of that. Success is fulfilling your destiny.

—C. K.

"Success is peace of mind, which is a direct result of self-satisfaction in knowing you did your best to become the best you are capable of becoming."
John Wooden, Hall of Fame UCLA Basketball Coach

Jackie Joyner Kersee

Some people who saw the way she grew up in East St. Louis would never have linked the name Jackie Joyner Kersee with the word *success*. Today, however, they see a woman called "the world's greatest female athlete" who has gracefully overcome hurdles on the track—and in life—to become the epitome of the American Dream.

Kersee was born on March 3, 1962, to poverty-stricken teenage parents Alfred Joyner Sr. and Mary Joyner in the depressed inner city of East St. Louis. Often the family slept in the kitchen because the stove was the only source of heat in the house. Kersee remembers wearing the same clothes two days in a row and keeping her shoes until they fell apart. But she thinks her childhood helped make her tough.

Kersee easily could have taken a totally different direction in life. But because of strong role models and a childhood commitment to faith, she beat the ghetto odds to become not only a hometown hero but a role model for the entire world.

"Although my parents had eloped and married young—my mother was fourteen when she had my brother, Al—they had a tremendous faith and love," Kersee says.

Kersee's road began at the age of nine, when she enrolled in a community track program and discovered running. She wasn't the fastest or best runner, but she tried harder than most of the other kids. Suddenly, at age thirteen, things began to click on the track, and it appeared she had a future. She sold penny candies to kids at school so she'd have enough money to travel with her track club.

"When I was nine, I did my first race—a 400-meter—and finished last," she says. "But that taught me I didn't have to win. I could learn just as much or more from not winning, such as how to do it better next time."

Racial incidents stung Kersee in her youth but didn't deter her. Rather, they inspired her and ignited a remarkable competitive drive to exceed the expectations of others and herself.

She remembers vividly an Amateur Athletic Union (AAU) track meet held in Poplar Bluff, Missouri, in 1976. She was fourteen and competing with the East St. Louis Railers. She landed a winning long jump in her last turn during the qualifying round, a jump that should have been long enough to put her in the final round—but a white official failed to record it.

"As a result, I was out of the competition," she explains. "At the time, I thought it was a deliberate oversight. The disappointment was all the more bruising because I had to finish in one of the top three spots to advance to the AAU regional competition, and to have a chance at ultimately competing in the AAU national meet. When the official told me I'd failed to qualify, tears welled up in my eyes and my body stiffened."

It was her coach who stepped in to give Kersee a sense of perspective, saying, "Rather than looking for someone to blame or to be mad with, let's learn from this."

From that point on, she worked harder on her jumps, and at the end of each long-jump competition, she would walk by the judges to make sure they'd recorded her results. She learned from her mistake, and it never happened again. Now she double-checks everything.

"I learned to handle controversy and adversity calmly," she wrote in her book *A Kind of Grace, The Autobiography of the World's Greatest Female Athlete* (New York: Water Books, 1997).

It was a lesson learned from her mother.

In a posthumous letter she wrote to her mom, Jackie expressed: "When I was just a little girl, you planted the seed that even though I was black and a woman and from a family for which nothing came easy, I could achieve great things in this world. The key to success, you said, was to set goals, keep them in focus, and not to be deterred by hardship or distracted by temptations. . . . Whenever I feel lost or perplexed about something, I try to think of what you'd want me to do. I hope that every time you look down on me from heaven, that no matter how I look on the outside, you always see beauty within me. If you do, Momma, then I'm a success."

"It brought home what Mom had always told me—that the next day or even the next second isn't promised to us," Kersee says. "She'd shared with me how important it is to keep in mind my goals and my eternal future with God. She was one determined lady, beating the odds as a teen mom living in the inner city. She truly was an example of someone who achieved what God asked her to do, no matter how hard the situation. Mom also encouraged me to grab hold of my dreams, small and big.

"From her I learned that whatever you do is a test of character, a test of heart."

Kersee's heart and talent shined brightest on the biggest of stages. At the Summer Olympic Games in 1984, 1988, 1992, and 1996, she gained a reputation as the world's greatest female athlete through her record-setting performances in the heptathlon and long jump. In each circumstance, she won and, a few times lost, with class.

Class emanates from Kersee in all she does, including reaching out to kids. She feels it's her duty as an Olympic champion to give something back to the community, and especially to kids.

She has given countless motivational talks at schools, hospitals, and churches; donated money to help reopen the Mary Brown Community Center in East St. Louis, where she first learned to run; funded a scholarship to a National Merit Scholar from her old high school; and sent teams of children from her old neighborhood to the AAU Junior Olympic Championships—not to mention the Jackie Joyner-Kersee Youth Center she's currently building in East St. Louis. She keeps a house and office in her hometown and visits regularly. It matters to her that she maintains a presence there, to become the symbol she never had.

"I've gained a lot of material things from athletics, but that's not what matters long term," says Kersee. "It's my soul, my character, that mean more to me than anything in the world. I hope everyone I interact with sees that.

"I want to give people the courage and determination to realize they can change their life. But I also tell them, 'Don't follow in my footsteps. Make your own.'"

> "Ninety-eight percent of success is in the head and the heart."
> **Cathy Ferguson, Former Olympic Swimmer**

Pete Maravich

Success came early to Pete Maravich.

He was a child prodigy of sorts. A living legend. A man way ahead of his time, who, with a few fancy passes and breathtaking shots, single-handedly brought the game of basketball into the modern era.

"Pistol Pete" was the original "showtime." He brought style, flair, and showmanship to a game that had been drab and without color. Fans came in droves to watch the young basketball magician perform his tricks—both on college and NBA hardwood.

A three-time college all-American, Maravich remains the NCAA all-time scoring leader, totaling 3,667 points for LSU from 1967 to 1970—prior to freshman eligibility status—while playing for his father, coach Press Maravich.

Pete averaged 44.2 points per game over his three seasons at LSU, another NCAA record, including a 69-point game against Alabama in the 1969–70 season—a feat that still amazes LSU athletic director Joe Dean, who was a television commentator at the time.

"He took this school by storm; he took this area by storm," Dean said. "They didn't care if they [LSU] won; they came for the show."

Maravich's other NCAA records include most 50-point games (28), field goals made (1,387), and free throws made (893). He averaged 43.8 points per game as a sophomore, 44.2 as a junior, and 44.5 as a senior—all before the advent of the shot clock or the three-point shot in college basketball. Those who have studied tapes of his career insist that had the three-pointer been around in Maravich's day, his scoring average would have been closer to 58 points per game.

"The Pistol" was a hero to a new generation of basketball fans. He made basketball fun and broke the staid and traditional characterizations of the game in doing so.

When Maravich was in grade school, Press was the head coach at Clemson. He would take his son into the team's locker room before and after games. There the game became ingrained in Pete. He watched the players dress, heard their talk, and was privy to both the good and bad times.

When Maravich was about nine, Press began challenging him to games of "h-o-r-s-e" at their backyard hoop. To keep his son's interest up, Press devised drills for him that sometimes came to the coach in his sleep. "When that happened, I'd just write the idea down, show it to Pete the next day, and we'd give it a name," Press once said.

When Pete was twelve, he told a sportswriter he was going to play pro ball, win a championship, and make a million dollars. "The guy fell off his seat laughing," Pete said. But while others were playing baseball and football and backseat tag, Maravich was at the gym, throwing two thousand passes a day and shooting "until I couldn't lift my arm."

When he wasn't playing with boys his own age, he was on the court at Clemson, challenging varsity players to games of "horse" and "around the world" for movie money.

As a five-foot-two, ninety-pound eighth-grader, Maravich made the varsity team and became a starter at Daniel High School in South Carolina, ignoring the skeptics. From there it was onward and upward—to the storied career at LSU, and then the NBA.

In 1970, as a senior at LSU, Pistol Pete earned Player of the Year honors from every voting organization, then became the No. 1 draft choice of the Atlanta Hawks, who made him the first professional athlete to sign a million-dollar contract. He had fan clubs, was given keys to cities, and had his own private jet. At twenty-two years old, he had it made . . . or so it seemed.

Maravich played well in the NBA for the Hawks, the New Orleans and Utah Jazz, and the Boston Celtics. He averaged 26.1 points per game in the pros and was the NBA scoring leader in 1977, but never won a championship—in either the college or pro ranks—leaving his most important dream unfulfilled. Frustrated, he retired in 1980, while still in his prime.

In 1987, seven years after his retirement, Maravich became the youngest inductee ever into the Basketball Hall of Fame—shortly before Press died of cancer.

Following his retirement Maravich opened "Pistol Pete's Homework Basketball All-Star Camps" in Florida, designed to emphasize the fundamentals of basketball and Christian ethics. He also produced four instructional videos.

Maravich had become a Christian in 1982 and traveled the nation sharing his personal story. It was faith that gave him a new perspective on success. He kept just a few trophies in the attic of his home only because his wife wanted his sons to know what he accomplished.

"Basketball doesn't really hold that many fond memories for me, except in my youth," he would say. "I experienced everything there is to experience. I've been wealthy. I've had fame and popularity. I've broken over a hundred records. I've [been] all over the world to do my 'showtime' exhibition. I've met kings.

"There is more than this life. God gives you something firm to hold onto that isn't drugs or alcohol or sexual lust. . . . [Without God] you will die a very lonely and sad person because nothing in this life will satisfy you."

Following five years of devoting his days to influencing people, Maravich died at the age of forty, on January 5, 1988, during a break in a half-court pick-up basketball game in California. An autopsy showed "Pistol Pete" had been born with only one fully developed coronary artery—an extremely rare heart defect that went undetected from birth.

Miraculously, Maravich's one artery was enlarged and fed blood to both sides of his heart. This allowed him to play basketball for all those years, when the condition would normally have killed a younger man enduring such a strenuous lifestyle.

His life was shorter than his millions of fans around the world had hoped for. Yet it was long enough for Maravich to change the game of basketball and to understand the true meaning of success.

"If people really want to know true peace, true joy, true happiness— money can buy you everything but happiness, OK? And pay your fare to every place but heaven. That's what I've found out," Maravich said. "And I've also found out that if you seek pleasure and happiness, you'll never, never find it. But if you have the wisdom to seek obedience in Jesus Christ, happiness will find you."

"It's what you learn after you know it all that counts."
Earl Weaver, Former Baltimore Orioles Manager

Bruce Matthews

Bruce Matthews can't be in five places at once, but sometimes it seems like he is.

The perennial all-pro offensive lineman for the Tennessee Titans has consistently been one of the top linemen in the NFL throughout his remarkable eighteen-year career. Through the 2000 season, the USC grad had played 280 games—fifth most in league history and the most ever for an offensive lineman.

But it is the way he's recorded that feat that has been so amazing— playing all five positions along the offensive line. During a three-week span in 1984, his second season, he started at center one week, right guard the next, and right tackle the one after.

While this may seem just a swapping of interchangeable parts, it is not quite so. In football, techniques, responsibilities, reads, and blocking assignments are all uniquely different for each position. At center, Matthews is the line's quarterback. On the right side he moves one way on run blocks and pass protection. On the left side it is a complete flip-flop. It's a little like going from driving a car in the U.S. to one in the U.K. Still, Matthews, a sure Hall of Famer when his days of football musical chairs are over, seems not to be inconvenienced at all.

"I never felt it was a big deal to switch positions," says Matthews. "The coach thinks it's best for the team—that's good enough for me."

Despite this peripatetic thread that has run through his career, Matthews has been selected to thirteen consecutive Pro Bowls—at three different positions. His motivation to continue playing at such a high level, snap after snap, game after game, season after season? Fear. The fear of getting beat. He can execute his assignments to perfection on 68 of 70 snaps in a game, but it's the two plays on which he misfires that stick with him.

"That's the thing that drives me," he says. "It's not so much throwing a great block that springs a guy for a touchdown. It's more—don't get beat for a sack, don't be the guy who causes the running back to get blown up, don't be the guy who makes the mental error that causes Steve McNair to get blind-sided."

Matthews values his role as the Titan's elder statesman and enjoys the opportunity to set an example.

"I try to be an example to them," he says. "The season's long and there are a lot of situations where you can get real negative with it. Just trying to portray a positive image, that I'm doing work for the Lord rather than for me, is what I hope they see."

"The thrill isn't in the winning; it's the doing."
Chuck Noll, Former Pittsburgh Steelers Coach

John Naber

John Naber saw the proverbial handwriting on the wall. He was a teenage swimming champion with an eye set on the Olympics. He knew that to become great he would have to focus his entire life toward that goal. Yet in pursuit of his dream, he found himself very unfulfilled.

"It had gotten to the point where I was the American record holder in the 200-yard backstroke and the national champion in the 100-yard backstroke," reflected Naber, "and things seemed to be going my way. Colleges were recruiting me heavily. I was student body president. I had a 3.6 grade point average, and I had a lot of good things going for me. But I didn't quite feel content; I didn't feel any calmness."

Finding hope through finding faith, Naber pressed on.

Following high school, while a student at USC, he qualified for the 1976 U.S. Olympic team. He represented the USA in five swimming events at the games in Montreal: the 100-meter and 200-meter backstrokes, the 200-meter freestyle, the 4x100-meter medley relay, and the 4x200-meter medley relay.

Naber rocked the world in Montreal by winning gold in each of his events, except the 200-meter freestyle where he took silver. He set individual world records in each backstroke event and was part of world-record team performances in both relays. It still ranks as one of the greatest performances in a single Olympics.

Naber's 100-meter backstroke swim so amazed his chief competitor, Roland Matthes—who finished third in the event—that the East German star later said he had wanted to halt the race at the halfway mark and applaud Naber.

As Naber himself reflects back on his accomplishments, he is still overwhelmed by what the achievements mean.

"Basically it was the fulfillment of all the hours I had spent," he says. "It occurred to me that this was just like taking the last step to the top of Mount Everest—there was nowhere else to go. It was something like coming to the end of a really good book."

That sense of finality led Naber to retire from competitive swimming right after he stepped off the last medal podium in Montreal. He felt it was time to begin the rest of his life.

For Naber, the price of success was great. He kept with him the lesson he learned as an eleven-year old, when he read the label on a root beer bottle that said, "No Deposit, No Return." That day, he says, he understood what would be required to become a champion. He swam ten miles a day, six days a week, eleven months a year during the course of his competitive career. That amounts to traveling the equivalent of twice around the planet on the earth's equator.

What did it take for Naber to win four Olympic gold medals?

"No single ingredient," he says. "Physical ability, a supportive environment, good coaching, and discipline are all important criteria for success. But probably the biggest thing you need is a specific, concrete, measurable objective.

"I often try to describe the thrill of receiving an Olympic gold medal, but I can't do the moment justice without recalling the months and sometimes years of effort that went into its achievement," Naber writes in his book, *Awaken the Olympian Within*. "To paraphrase Tom Hanks' baseball manager's character from the movie *A League of Their Own*—'The hard is what makes it great.'"

> **"It's all about being a role model and trying to shed light on how to be a winner. It doesn't make a difference how much you have in your bank, but how you carry yourself, how many lives you touch, the impact that you have on people."**
> **Mark Jackson, Toronto Raptors Point Guard**

Gene Stallings

Gene Stallings' existence is an example of how some of life's darkest times can be a catalyst for better things.

In 1972, Stallings had lost his job at Texas A&M where he'd coached the Aggies to a Southwest Conference championship and a Cotton Bowl victory over Alabama and his mentor, Coach Paul "Bear" Bryant. Getting the A&M job had been a dream realized for Stallings, in returning to coach at the school where he had been an all-SWC player. Then the Aggies abruptly showed him the door, saying they were going in a different direction.

Stallings was without a job until Tom Landry called and offered him the defensive backfield coaching position for the Dallas Cowboys. Stallings accepted but was apprehensive because he'd never coached on the professional level. He was a fast learner, however, and became an outstanding coach with the Cowboys and later as head coach of the St. Louis and then Arizona Cardinals.

When Alabama came calling for a head coach in 1990, they were looking for a Bryantesque figure to return them to their glory years. Stepping into the considerable shadow of his mentor, Stallings delivered, leading the Crimson Tide to an undefeated 13-0 season and the national championship in 1992. His teams also went 11-1 in 1991 and 1994, and 9-3-1 in 1993, and won a major bowl game each season. Stallings had become one of the most recognized coaches in college football.

While the coach was finally noticed for his accomplishments, the world was also beginning to see what kind of person he was.

Stallings is a throwback to the old-fashioned "family values" that often seem lacking in society. He and his wife, Ruth Ann, raised their children with discipline, faith, and love. To them, this is what success is all about.

This is personified in their son, John Mark. Because of Down's syndrome, doctors told Stallings that John Mark wouldn't live past the age of four. Nearly forty years later, he's still here.

John Mark was born on June 11, 1962. The next morning doctors told the Stallings their son was a "mongoloid" and had a congenital heart defect that is present in about 60 percent of those affected by Down's syndrome. Because of the heart condition, doctors told Stallings that John Mark could die at any minute.

Terrified of losing his son, Stallings would frequently awaken in the middle of the night and lay his head on his son's chest, listening for a heartbeat.

"I cried a bushel of tears," says Stallings. "I couldn't believe it. There's a certain embarrassment that goes along with it. How do you tell your mother, your daddy, your friends? It's sort of like there's a big X on you. You wonder if God is punishing you. That's not the case at all, but that's what you think."

It didn't take long in those first months for Stallings to realize how wrong he was. One night, as Stallings arrived home, his four daughters had a surprise waiting. On the porch was three-year-old Johnny, clutching General, the family's German shepherd. Suddenly Johnny let go of the dog, walked to the other side of the porch, clapped his hands, and giggled. It is one of Stallings' fondest memories.

Stallings and Johnny were constant companions during his coaching days. Johnny attended nearly all practices and games and would often nap in his father's office. With every day, it was Stallings who learned.

"As a result of Johnny, I'm a lot more generous, more compassionate," Stallings says. "I'm for the underdog. The player who was less talented, less gifted. He wasn't big enough, fast enough, strong enough, or good enough, but I enjoyed having him on the team. On the other hand, if I had a player who had talent and didn't lay it on the line, I didn't have much tolerance for him after watching Johnny struggle.

"My life wouldn't be nearly as rich without Johnny. Absolutely, no question about it. He's just fun to be around. If we had to do it over again, I wouldn't change a thing."

Stallings left Alabama in 1996 after six bowl appearances in seven seasons. He left primarily because of John Mark. Each loss was getting tougher for his son to handle.

"I felt like that was putting pressure on his heart," Stallings said. "He needed some air and space. Do you know why he wanted Alabama to win so much? Because he said it made Pop [Stallings] happy."

Amidst the wins, Stallings remained a constant example throughout his life in coaching. Those who know John Mark say he is the most loving person they have ever been around. Those who know Gene and Ruth Ann, say John Mark is a reflection of his mom and dad.

Stallings has a clear understanding of his coaching legacy. Yet he is still ever mindful of what he considers to be infinitely more important than his win-loss record.

"I would like to be known as a coach who was fair," Stallings says, "who knew what he was doing and had compassion for the players, and who appreciated the honesty and the integrity of the game. And I like to see the players succeed. I like to see an average player turn into a good player.

"My real joy [however], is seeing how my children turned out."

Jeff Gordon

How fast is too fast? How good is too good?

While Jeff Gordon has never asked himself the first question, he has definitely been left to ponder the latter.

Gordon is NASCAR's answer to Tiger Woods, Michael Jordan, Wayne Gretzky, and Mark McGwire. He is so good that he has actually been too good for many NASCAR fans.

Gordon burst onto stock car racing's biggest stage in 1993 and turned the racing world on its ear: Rookie of the Year in '93; Winston Cup season champ in '95; a repeat in '96; and again in '98, when he had a near perfect year for this circuit. He won thirteen races that year, tying Richard Petty's record for victories in a single season, finished in the top five in twenty-six of thirty-three starts, and banked a record $9.3 million in earnings.

And then the booing started.

In 1999, racing's boy wonder, who had almost single-handedly turned stock car racing into the fastest growing spectator sport in America, was actually hearing catcalls from the grandstands.

"I think everybody likes a winner," Gordon says. "But nobody likes somebody that wins too much. I understand that. I really do.

"When the boos started coming, I'd sit back and say, 'I don't blame 'em.' You win thirteen races in a season or ten races in a season [as he did in '97] and it's unheard of . . . and I was just as baffled with it myself as other people were."

"Nobody can find anything wrong with him, so they boo him," says three-time Winston Cup champion Darrell Waltrip.

"That's America, man," says driver Kyle Petty, son of Richard. "They pull for you when you're the underdog, and once you get to the top, they pull for you to get knocked off."

While Tiger and Michael have yet to face such a dilemma, it is old hat for the greatest teams in sports. The Boston Celtics, New York Yankees, Dallas Cowboys, and now Gordon's Rainbow Warriors. Dynasties all. The fact is, it's the familiarity of winning that breeds contempt.

But then Gordon has been somewhat of a contradiction ever since he first zipped past the track's hierarchy without so much as an "excuse me." He's a California kid running among the South's good ol' boys. He doesn't fish and hunt in his spare time; instead, he goes to New York or L. A. He didn't grow up working on cars in the garage of a racing family or learning the trade from his father or uncle like most of the circuit's stars. Rather, he was the star of the family early on, winning races as a five-year-old, and backed by a well-to-do white-collar stepfather. He hadn't paid his dues on the Busch Grand National circuit for years and worked his way from the back of the pack to an eventual contender. Instead, he hit the ground with wheels blazing as a confident twenty-two-year-old who won right away and won often. Apparently too often.

Perhaps that is one of the things that rubs some of this sport's following the wrong way. The man who brought NASCAR from the backwoods to Hollywood in a span of four short years is not one of "their own."

Gordon has gotten used to the resentment.

"Sometimes it's frustrating for me because people don't want to give me enough credit, or they don't have any idea where I've come from.

"I know what I've done and what I've gone through."

What Gordon is now is the new breed of racing star, who has opened the way for multibillion-dollar television deals, mega-sponsorships with mainline brands, and new state-of-the-art 200,000-seat race tracks complete with luxury suites in places like southern California, Las Vegas, Chicago, and Kansas City. Clearly Gordon has brought the worlds of Beverly Hills and Dixie together. NASCAR is trendy, and Gordon is the reason.

"He gave the sport's new white-collar fans a reason to take up the sport," says former Coca-Cola executive Hal Price, a consultant for JG Motorsports, Gordon's company. "This is a new breed of driver they can follow."

A survey commissioned by one of his sponsors to measure Gordon's Q rating—or popularity with consumers-proved as such. The survey found that Gordon is not only popular with the sponsor's target group of eighteen- to thirty-four-year-old males, but also with twelve- to seventeen-year-olds. His scores were also "extremely high" with eighteen- to thirty-four-year-old females, and not just in the NASCAR hotbed of the southeast. He is now single-handedly responsible for introducing more women and children to NASCAR than any other driver in history. His fan base not only breaks the NASCAR stereotypes by being comprised of 50 percent females, but also in that 50 percent are technologically savvy fans and those who are apt to prefer golf to deer hunting. He is indeed the face of this sport for the twenty-first century.

But don't be fooled by what you see. This young man with teen idol looks may be respectful of his elders off the track, but he has ruthlessly rendered their records obsolete on it.

"He's the prototype race driver," says Waltrip. "Everyone's afraid of him. NASCAR is scared of him. Why? Because they can't make enough rules to keep him from winning races. Drivers are because they can't keep him from breaking records."

And there is no reason to believe Gordon won't keep getting better, win more races, and become more popular. His early success becomes more impressive with a glance at his career numbers, which are staggering. At the end of the 2000 season, he had registered more than fifty Winston Cup race victories—fifth all-time—and more than $35 million in earnings—second most in history. His three season titles are surpassed only by Richard Petty and Dale Earnhardt, who have seven.

But to view Gordon strictly by the numbers is to evaluate a house on the real estate market simply by its curb appeal. You get a general sense of things but can only guess as to what's inside.

Such was the case with crew chief Robbie Loomis, who took over for longtime Gordon mentor and friend Ray Evernham for the 2000 season. Loomis, who was around Gordon for years while working for competitor Petty Enterprises, was surprised at what he found when he got to know Gordon.

"From the outside looking in, I thought Jeff was too good to be true, just too squeaky clean," Loomis says. "Now, to get to know him . . . it's a pleasure to see somebody who carries himself the way he does and know that's really the Jeff Gordon you see."

"Jeff's great with people, and he doesn't complain about being a star or the position he is in," said Charles Hudson, a public relations official for the DuPont side of Gordon's marketing team. "He knows that what he does helps the sport of racing, and it helps his sponsors. But he is genuine. The way you see him in the media or with his sponsors is the same way that you see him when he's just sitting around off-camera drinking a soda."

"Everybody says it's much easier at the top," says Gordon. "Sometimes that's true, but a lot of people try to tear you down when you're at the top. I can tell you when you get knocked down a notch, it's very tough. And I think you just earn a little more respect, especially in this garage area and from the fans, when you're not winning and you slide some wins in there."

As the victories piled up from 1995 to 1999 and the boos proliferated, Gordon seemed immune—smiling and waving through every catcall. His demeanor did not go unnoticed in the garage area.

"I always wondered why they were booing him, because it wasn't like Jeff had ever done anything to anyone," says Dale Jarrett. "He was just doing his job. He was in a very enviable position—to dominate like that."

"People think racing is what I am, and that's not true. Racing is what I do," says Gordon. "I'm not going to let a twentieth-place finish or a thirtieth-place finish make me miserable. If you do that, you can be miserable for a very long time."

Even with the changes in crowd response, Gordon remains NASCAR's Jordan or Woods—the top name on the marquee, the guy who sells tickets, the guy who commands everyone's attention.

"I think every sport, just like Hollywood, has their box-office stars, their superstars," says NASCAR chief Mike Helton. "Jeff Gordon probably came quicker and was more brilliant in his run to the top than anyone this garage has seen, maybe ever.

"There are drivers, there are good drivers, there are heroes, and there are superstars. With a superstar, you're either behind him or against him, but either way you're watching."

Still, for Gordon, the main focus in on the track, where he feels there is always room for improvement. He has worked hard to become a better driver, and those around him have noticed.

Jimmy Johnson, who oversees the three-team Hendrick Motorsports operation, says Gordon is not the same driver he was when team owner Rick Hendrick first hired him in 1992. Rather, he is calmer and more calculating.

"We put seventeen front ends and rear ends on Jeff's car in the first year," Johnson says. "He didn't know but one way to go, and that was try to lead every lap."

"Every year I try to improve on my driving," Gordon says. "It doesn't mean how to make myself drive fast. It's how can I be a smarter driver?

"As a driver, you are constantly thinking, 'Is there a different approach to this corner? How can I change the way I'm driving to make my car go faster?'"

By the time he was old enough to get his driver's license, Gordon was going fast enough to have won more than one hundred open-wheel races, often driving two or three nights a week. He was so good by the time he was in high school—racing sprint cars every weekend all over the country—that his stepfather, John Bickford, moved the family from Vallejo, California, to Pottsboro, Indiana—about twenty miles from the Indianapolis Motor Speedway—so Gordon could be closer to races.

"I didn't consider racing to be a career," Gordon says. "Maybe other people, like my dad [Bickford], were thinking, 'Where can we take this?' Me, I was just having a good time."

He won the U.S. Auto Club's midget championship at nineteen and the USAC Silver Crown title for oversized sprint cars the next year. But no one in Indy car racing seemed interested in someone so youthful looking. So Gordon turned to stock cars.

"When I started driving the stock cars," says Gordon, "I realized they were more similar to sprint cars than Indy cars were. When you're on a dirt track driving sprint cars, it's a long, long way to 230 mph. These cars go fast and run close to each other. I just loved it."

Once on the stock car circuit, Gordon's heart burned with a desire to become the best ever. "But it [success] happened without me ever realizing it," he says.

After winning a record eleven pole positions and three races for Bill Davis in 1992, Gordon left the Busch series to join the Hendrick team on the Winston Cup series.

"I knew from the first time I saw him race, Jeff was going to be a champion," says Hendrick. "What I never dreamed was it would happen so fast."

Fittingly, Gordon's Winston Cup debut came at the 1992 season-ending race at Atlanta Motor Speedway. It was the same race that became the farewell event for Petty, long "The King" of racing. Clearly and symbolically, the torch had been passed, and Gordon was on his way to taking the NASCAR throne.

Among his significant wins was the inaugural Brickyard 400 at Indianapolis Motor Speedway in 1994, just six miles from where Gordon had so much success racing as a teen. He won at the Brickyard again in 1998, pocketing the largest single-race purse in the history of auto racing— $1,637,625. In 1997, at just twenty-five years, six months, and twelve days, he became the youngest driver ever to win the Daytona 500. He repeated there in 1999.

Gordon's most important companion throughout his rise has been wife Brooke, whom the driver met in Victory Lane at the Daytona 500 while she was serving as the circuit's Miss Winston in 1993. They were married in 1994 and have rarely been apart since.

"I knew the second I met her, no way was I going to let her get away; she's the best thing that's ever happened to me, and getting married was the best thing I've ever done," said Gordon. "She's brought me closer to God. She's almost been an angel."

Brooke is a major factor in Jeff's race day preparation. They share Bible study at the track with other drivers and wives on Saturday evenings. On Sunday mornings, they attend the driver's chapel at the track garage. Then, Brooke walks with Jeff to pit row for driver's introductions, prays for him, and kisses him before he hops into the car. Then she gives him a Bible verse as a reminder that God will be with him throughout his four-hour trek around the track.

"The night before every race, Jeff and I look through the Bible and try to find a Scripture that says something to him and says something to me—it's meaningful," says Brooke. "I'll put it on a little index card, and he tapes it to his steering wheel, and he looks at it during cautions and yellow flags. He tells me that it helps him get that inner peace . . . and it helps give him patience."

While he seeks more patience, Gordon continues on the fast track. He is still one of the youngest drivers in the series but has a remarkable sense of flexibility. Some days he stands on the gas, and others he will not tip his hand until the closing laps. He cares nothing about developing a signature style, preferring to pursue a variety of ways to win.

As he does so, he also continues to be blown away by his own success.

"I pull into victory lane and say, 'I can't believe this,' and people laugh," says Gordon. "They're thinking, 'Yeah, right, you can't believe this. You do it every other weekend.' And I want to say, 'No, you don't understand. I really can't believe this.'"

"He's got the potential of doing what athletes like [Arnold] Palmer and [Muhammed] Ali, Joe Namath and Babe Ruth and [Joe] DiMaggio did," says Charlotte Motor Speedway president Humpy Wheeler, "and that is to transcend the sport they're in."

"I'm very fortunate, very blessed, that my life turned out the way it has," Gordon says. "I'm very happy with my life, and if other people can't understand why I'm happy or resent the fact that I am, that's something I can't control."

Meanwhile, he remains committed to winning and improving until driving is no longer enjoyable.

"I hope that never happens," Gordon says. "I mean, I know there's going to be a day when that happens, but I hope I'm forty-something years old when it does. I'd like to think I've got at least another ten good years in me."

Jeff, so does NASCAR . . . and the sport's massive following.

> A champion lives by a
> higher standard and stands firm
> when others around him fall.

CHAPTER 9

CONVICTION

conviction: the state of being convinced; a strong belief.

Courage is the word that jumps out right away when I think of conviction.

To stand for what you believe in the face of adversity, ridicule, or not being accepted takes courage. It takes inner courage—real strength—to stand firm in what you believe and not be easily swayed, not be easily influenced by peer pressure, and not be distracted or taken off course.

When you're truly committed to an ideal or principle based on living by your convictions, you're not easily swayed.

At times in sports, you can do something right, yet your action goes completely unnoticed or somebody else gets the credit. At those times, what's important is just recognizing who you are, what your role is, and what your responsibilities are and accepting that doing what you're supposed to do is normal.

If what you do receives acclaim, fine. If it doesn't receive acclaim, you still know that you're on the right track because you're doing what you are supposed to do. And you do what you are supposed to do simply because it is the right thing to do.   **—C. K.**

"Be more concerned with your character than with your reputation because your character is what you really are, while your reputation is merely what others think you are."
John Wooden, Hall of Fame UCLA Basketball Coach

Justin Armour

Justin Armour seems to have it all. He is six foot four inches and 215 pounds, a Stanford grad with GQ looks and an old-school attitude. He is the kind of young man every mother wants her daughter to bring home. And are there ever lots of daughters who come calling.

Yet the NFL wide receiver is still strong enough to realize there is a plan for his life. And in the playground atmosphere that often accompanies life as a professional athlete, Armour receives recognition for being a virgin in a sport where sex outside of marriage is accepted and even expected.

"Temptations are easily available to those who look for them," says Armour. "But if you don't make yourself available to those women who would take advantage of you, they rarely approach you. I encourage young people to make the decision to be abstinent before they go out into the battlefields of life. If you don't decide beforehand, you'll lose the fight.

"There's a whole lot more to being abstinent than not having sex; it's a lifestyle," he says. "I've got . . . Christian friends who hold me accountable for my actions. I can be completely transparent in front of them."

Recognizing he can't win the war against his flesh alone, Armour has chosen to rely on a small group of men for assistance. He takes strength from having accountability. One particular friend Armour often leans on is his best friend, Steve Strenstrom, his quarterback at Stanford, who now also plays in the NFL.

"You need someone who is going to get into your life and hold you accountable for walking with Christ," says Armour. "Steve has been that for me. He knows everything about my life, good and bad, and there's nothing he won't hold me accountable for."

As an athlete, Armour first gained national attention as a high school senior. *Sports Illustrated* ran a feature article on the then all-American quarterback and basketball star from tiny Manitou Springs (Colorado) High School. It was there, as one of the most highly decorated and recruited athletes in the nation, that Armour had his first taste of personal adversity. His parents divorced, and Armour was left to become the man of the house while still a teen. Rather than running, he turned to his faith in God.

After graduating as class president, valedictorian, and a consensus all-American in football, he moved on to Stanford, where he graduated with a degree in public policy and set a school record with 2,482 receiving yards in his career.

A fourth-round draft pick by the Buffalo Bills in 1995, Armour bounced around the NFL for the next five years trying to find a home. From Buffalo to Philadelphia to San Francisco, he stuck with the Denver Broncos in 1998, playing a role on the Super Bowl XXXIII championship team.

His breakthrough season came in 1999 as he caught 37 passes for 538 yards and 4 touchdowns for the Baltimore Ravens. Armour became a free agent in 2000.

While Armour's perseverance would be tested on the field, his convictions were tested off of the field. He recalls a particular incident that put him in a potentially compromising situation long before he played in his first pro game.

It happened during preseason camp in 1995 when Armour—then a naive rookie—came across a scene he now describes as "incredible."

He had joined some Bills teammates for a night on the town. After dinner, they wound up at a club down by a lake.

Soon Armour's teammates began disappearing. One by one, they left the club and headed down to the dock, where they boarded boats—armed with young women.

"It was probably the most eye-opening experience I've ever had," Armour says. "I saw men leave on boats with two or three girls, just disappearing into the night.

"I had heard about things like this," he says, "but I had no idea what it was really like. I was so naive."

Later that night, some of those same women started approaching Armour. He reacted the only way he knew how.

"I got out of there as fast as I could," he says.

As a football player, Armour was used to running away from pursuit but mostly from linebackers. Now he'd have to run from temptation too. It was quite a welcome to life as a professional athlete.

"That's just the way it is," says Justin. "If I wanted to be promiscuous, night in and night out, I could be."

Armour has heard all the rhetoric about safe sex, but he prefers to *save* sex for marriage.

"God promises that sex is something he will bless in the context of marriage," he says. "I'm willing to wait.

"I've seen people who've had a lot of sexual relationships, and they're scarred. Every time you have premarital sex, you give a little piece of yourself away. By the time you're married, how many pieces have you given out? And how many do you have left to give?

"But the biggest blessing of choosing abstinence is this: You fall in love and get married for all the right reasons. You fall in love with someone because of how they motivate you, how they encourage you, how they hold up your life. And if you fall in love for those reasons, it'll be that much better.

"There's so much more to choosing abstinence than just saying no. You're not just saying no to sex; you're saying yes to . . . a life of real meaning, of real joy. That's the most liberating thing there is."

"Learn as if you were to live forever; live as if you were to die tomorrow."
John Wooden, Hall of Fame UCLA Basketball Coach

Terry Blocker

When Terry Blocker was asked to become a replacement player for the Atlanta Braves during the baseball strike of 1995, the onetime big-league outfielder never knew the special purpose he would realize.

Blocker, who spent the better part of nine years in baseball as a minor-league player and portions of three years in the big leagues with the Braves, had been retired since 1993. He came to camp looking for something more than just a chance to play again. He was hoping to have an impact on a handful of would-be players.

After one spring training practice at the Braves' complex in West Palm Beach, Florida, Blocker approached a teammate, thirty-year-old pitcher Dave Shotkoski. Blocker asked Shotkoski if he had time to talk. Blocker wanted to discuss matters of faith with the pitching hopeful. Shotkoski, a husband and the father of an eighth-month-old daughter, said he was interested in talking, but he had to take care of some family financial obligations. He told Blocker he would be happy to talk with him the following day.

For Dave Shotkoski, that next day never came.

Just hours after speaking with Blocker, Shotkoski was murdered in a robbery attempt in West Palm Beach. News of the murder floored Blocker. He knew he had to do something.

"When I was told about the death by some other teammates, I cried," recalls Blocker, who is also a husband and father. "I prayed to see if there was anything I could do."

He decided to help find the killer.

Although he knew how dangerous it could be, Blocker proceeded against the counsel of friends, disregarding the danger to his own well-being.

The search took Blocker to some of the meanest streets in West Palm Beach, where he eventually approached a young drug dealer, seeking information. The drug dealer was not in a mood to comply. He threatened Blocker's life. But Blocker remained undeterred.

The next day, the murderer was overheard bragging about the killing to several people—one of them the man Blocker had spoken with. He promptly called Blocker, who informed the Braves. Eventually an arrest was made, and Dave Shotkoski's killer was apprehended.

> **"The truth of the matter is, all professional athletes are role models. The choice you have to make is whether you're gonna be a good one or a bad one."**
> **Steve Largent, Seattle Seahawks Hall-of-Fame Receiver**

Mark Dewey

The year was 1995. The date, July 28. The San Francisco Giants were holding a pregame ceremony at Candlestick Park called "Until There's a Cure" Day, as a show of solidarity with AIDS volunteers.

Then Giants relief pitcher Mark Dewey refused to join in the ceremony. He wore his red AIDS ribbon sideways, making the looped ribbon resemble a Christian icthus, or fish symbol.

In the aftermath, Dewey wrote an open letter to area newspapers in the wake of the negative reaction he received for his actions and comments.

"Much speculation has been made about my character, but very little is based on the intent of my heart," Dewey's letter said. "Everything I have done and said has been to express love and compassion for all people with AIDS, their friends and families, and those who have lost loved ones to the disease without compromising the teaching of the Scripture. I have no hatred or ill will toward homosexuals. I have concern for all who have AIDS, and I'm not opposed to the search for a cure or action taken by people to raise money for research.

"I do, however, hate sin, and the Bible clearly teaches that sexual immorality (fornication, adultery, homosexuality, etc.) is sin. I could not be involved with the ceremonies because sexual immorality was condoned and in some cases encouraged. I altered the [AIDS] ribbon for the same reason. I wore the ribbon like a fish to show my love and compassion for lives as well as souls. All I did and said was out of love for God and people. The bottom line is this: The deadly disease we are battling is sin (it kills body and spirit). ALL HAVE SINNED. There is a cure—the shed blood of Jesus Christ."

Giants officials responded by saying Dewey was entitled to his opinion and that the club did not condone his actions or comments.

> **"It's not whether you win or lose; it's how you play the game."**
> **Grantland Rice, Former Sportswriter**

Ben Hamilton

As a college football offensive lineman, he is grateful for any recognition . . . except this one.

University of Minnesota center Ben Hamilton turned down a spot on *Playboy* magazine's 2000 preseason all-America team because he feels the publication conflicts with his beliefs.

"It really was hard because it is an honor, and playing on the offensive line you don't get too many honors, and they don't come along too often," said Hamilton.

Hamilton knew the all-America team had little to do with the magazine's reputation because Minnesota coach Glen Mason assured him it was legitimate. Hamilton spoke with some players who had been selected to get their opinions as well.

"People would tell me things like that [legitimacy], but . . . I didn't want to portray the wrong idea of the kind of person I am," Hamilton said.

Hamilton, the son of former Minnesota Vikings offensive lineman Wes Hamilton, had already been named to several preseason all-America teams prior to the notice from *Playboy*. Still, his decision actually drew the attention of some front-office members of NFL teams.

"From a character standpoint, you know you don't have to worry about Ben Hamilton," said Vikings player personnel coordinator Scott Studwell.

"A champion is not always going to be somebody who wins every game or wins every battle. I think a champion is one who makes the right decisions."
Sean Elliott, San Antonio Spurs Guard

Reggie White

Reggie White, a licensed minister and the father of two, has always been a man on a mission.

Whether it is in chasing down quarterbacks—which he has done better than anyone in the history of the NFL—or trying to stomp out social ills, White is a man led by strong convictions, who it seems will not be deterred from his goal.

In what was likely his most prominent stage—at Super Bowl XXXI in New Orleans as a member of the Green Bay Packers—White addressed the media each day during the week prior to the game with an agenda in mind.

He had said he always wanted to play in a Super Bowl, in part, because he felt it would give him a chance to spread his message to a worldwide audience. For hours over four days that week in 1997, he presented his message to three thousand somewhat skeptical journalists.

He was not exactly preaching to the choir. When White began to talk about his faith, a number of reporters rolled their eyes, shut off their tape recorders, or simply walked away.

Finally, at the end of the week, White was asked about a *New York Times* report that indicated league officials were concerned White might use a victory celebration on Super Bowl Sunday to lead a prayer on international television.

"Why would the league be concerned?" White responded. "You guys, the league, people around the country are crying out for us to be positive role models, but they don't want us to do the things that Dennis Rodman does.

"They're crying out for us to be role models, to be heroes, and when we choose to do it that way and we have a positive effect on the community, then they try and tell us when to pray, when not to pray, and sometimes how to pray.

"It's unbelievable to me that the league—our league—would be concerned about Reggie White, or anybody else on a platform, using it. It amazes me that that's a concern."

White has always been the main proponent of the circle of prayer, during which NFL players from both teams gather at midfield after a game to pray—an action that has polarized many football followers, and made White somewhat of a lightning rod.

"Some of the media are very interested because they are seeking for truth and peace in their own lives," says White. "Some of them are sarcastic. They don't feel we should force it on the public, but we're not forcing it on the public. It's something we do for ourselves."

As many have discovered, White is much more than just a defensive end. He is every bit the activist. Yet it is hard to fit him into a particular box. White is conservative, yes. But he has a heart for the poor and the inner cities. He is quick to speak out on the plight of minorities in America and rails against the evils of racial inequality.

So it was one night a few years ago when flames engulfed the Inner City Community Church in Knoxville, Tennessee, burning it to the ground. No one was more saddened by the act against this church than its associate pastor, Reverend Reggie White.

White's second home has long been his church in Knoxville, where, when he was in town, he regularly preached thunderous sermons.

All that ended in January 1996 when that beloved church was torched—one of more than seventy Southern black churches to be set on fire that year. Investigators found that a combination of kerosene, gunpowder, and eighteen Molotov cocktails had been used to burn the building to the ground. Lest there remain any doubt about intentions, the messages Die Nigger and Die Nigger Lover were left behind.

Yet the act of hatred was followed by an outpouring of love from White's mostly white fans in Green Bay, who immediately raised

$300,000 for the future of ICCC. One of White's favorite donations consisted of ninety-two pennies pasted on a piece of cardboard by a child.

White has been actively spreading the good news at each stop in his NFL career.

"The only way you can have an effect on people is to get down in the trenches. Go where they are . . . [show] them you're no more important than they are," he said.

White's years of ministering in that way made him increasingly aware that while inner city residents urgently need to hear the gospel, they also need practical solutions that could better their lives. His answer was to start a Community Investment Bank in Knoxville, kicking in a million dollars as seed money. The bank's goal is to provide loans ranging from $500 to $15,000—primarily to refurbish rundown housing—to people who couldn't otherwise qualify to borrow from a full-service bank. Community Investment Bank also offers finance seminars, provides credit lines for small-business owners, and encourages the start-up of low-overhead home-based businesses. White's dream is to establish similar nondepository banks in other inner cities all over America.

White and his wife Sarah have also created a home for unwed mothers, a football camp for underprivileged ghetto youth, and a number of other ventures to help the needy. He is always thinking of ways to reach out to people.

White knows that as a leading sports figure he is himself a role model for thousands of children, and he takes that responsibility seriously. He makes it well known that he doesn't smoke, swear, gamble, or drink, and he always makes time to talk to young autograph seekers. "I do my best to lead by example," he says.

And while he is closing out his storied career with the Carolina Panthers, White is still known for tossing three-hundred-pound opposing players into the air as though they were kids' action figures, then politely asking, "Are you all right with Jesus?" as he helps pull them to their feet.

> **"I never wanted to fall short even for the fan's sake.**
> **When I was going to cross those white lines, I was going to give them their money's worth.**
> **I was gonna give them everything I had every day."**
> **Gary Carter, Former Baseball All-Star Catcher**

Danny Wuerffel

NFL quarterback Danny Wuerffel is no playboy; he proved that back in 1996, just prior to his Heisman Trophy-winning senior season at Florida.

That was when Wuerffel, the son of an Air Force minister, declined an invitation to be named a member of *Playboy* magazine's all-America college preseason football team and their National Scholar Athlete of the Year. His decision cost him an all-expense-paid trip to a posh Phoenix resort, site of a photo shoot with the other twenty-three college players selected to the team.

"It didn't take any thought at all," said Wuerffel. "I'm sure there's a good bit of the population out there that would think I'm silly for doing this. But there's also a good bit of the population that would understand that's not the type of person I would want to portray myself as."

Wuerffel explained at the time why he could not accept the award—he speaks frequently at churches and schools, and he believes his appearance in such a magazine would undermine his work as a role model and "confuse" those who look up to him.

In college, the young role model led Florida to three straight SEC championships, passing for more than 10,000 yards and 114 touchdowns—second all-time—and compiling a 163.6 passing efficiency rating, an NCAA career mark. Then it was on to the NFL, where he has continued to excel as a model of character.

Yet for Wuerffel, the quality character that oozes out of him is merely a byproduct of the conviction he lives by, both on and off the field.

"What really drives me is that I'm just trying to do the best I can," Wuerffel says. "My commitment is to represent God in all I do."

A. C. Green

A. C. Green is anything but your typical athlete. He is quiet and humble, almost self-effacing. He is consistent. A man of amazing self-control, with an iron will and subtle inner strength. He is a man who works and lives according to his convictions.

Green is basketball's answer to the Energizer Bunny. The NBA's version of Cal Ripken. He is the sport's iron man. Following the 1999–2000 NBA season, in which he helped lead the Los Angeles Lakers to the NBA championship, Green had played nearly 1,100 games consecutively without taking a night off. That's fourteen seasons without calling in sick, playing hooky, resting a weary and injured body, or simply saying, "I need a break." To put it in perspective, Green has not missed a game since Ronald Reagan was president.

In this age of prima donna sports stars, where players have flat-out refused to enter a game at a coach's request, Green has played fourteen years straight—through pulled muscles, sprained joints, and even missing teeth. Not that much fanfare has been made over Green's achievement.

While Ripken's streak-breaking night was broadcast on national television and included celebratory ceremonies, Green's feat has been practically unnoticed by the majority of the sports world. Alas, this seems fitting to Green, whose philosophy on his streak is simple. He is merely doing what he is supposed to do.

"If I can walk, and I can breathe, I can play," Green likes to say.

And play he has. In 1998, Green broke the existing NBA record for consecutive games played when he logged No. 907 for the Dallas Mavericks. Then he just kept right on going . . . and going . . . and going.

"That's just what I'm supposed to do," Green says. "My standard that I've put on myself, and that really I feel God puts on me, [is] to do the best that I can, as well as to consistently do it. It starts with doing it and then doing it the best you can. And it's just something that I do, and something I'm supposed to do."

Green has put up with the incessant questioning about his streak. He is polite in his responses, yet continually understates what he has achieved. He is convinced that his achievement is not so different from that of his father, A. C. Sr., who detailed Fords at a dealership in Portland, Oregon, or his mother, Leola, who worked as a machinist at the Jantzen sportswear factory. Like them, Green is blue collar to the core. You do your job, and you are held accountable for what you do.

"Both parents working, just trying to make ends meet and provide for us kids . . . that set a pattern," says Green. "It set an impression in my mind that, if I wanted the by-products of hard work, I was going to have to sacrifice. I was going to have to make the sacrifice to enjoy the benefits of that. And I'm not afraid of sacrifice today. I'll go out and work hard because I know it's worth it in the end."

But it is not all quite as simple as Green makes it seem.

If he were a six-foot-two-inch point guard, or a six-foot-four-inch shooting guard, then maybe. But Green is a six-foot-nine-inch somewhat undersized power forward, whose role is to pound constantly on much bigger men, often giving away as much as four to five inches and forty to fifty pounds. It is constant shoving and elbowing, pushing and banging. Make no mistake about it, he is definitely getting physical.

"You're constantly making contact with each other's body, and it's body to body," he says. "You expect to get hit upside the head. You expect to get elbowed, not maliciously, but at the same time, you just expect physical contact. . . . You've got to learn how to dish that out because, if you don't, you're going to find yourself looking up all the time like, 'Somebody help me up off the ground because I just got beat down one more time.' It's constant contact. It's very aggressive. It's very physical. But it's the mentality that you have to have."

Says Green's former coach and general manager with the Dallas Mavericks, Don Nelson, "You play power forward in our league, you can't run away from anybody. You've got to get in there and duke it out every night. It's hard to even talk about it [the streak], because it's just such an incredible feat that I don't know how to describe it. We've seen him play when he probably shouldn't have . . . but he still gets out there and straps them up."

Green has battled through deep thigh bruises, almost constant back pain, torn ligaments in his left thumb, a neck so sore he could only turn it in one direction, jammed fingers, and lost teeth. Yes, that would be teeth, as in the hard, bony structures on the jaw used for the seizing and chewing of food. In this case they were found lying on an NBA floor, apparently not much good for anything, almost costing Green his streak.

It was February 25, 1996. Green was playing for the Phoenix Suns, who were playing the New York Knicks, then the NBA's "bad boys." Knicks' forward J. R. Reed threw a nasty elbow that knocked out one of Green's bottom front teeth and loosened another, which Green later yanked out in the locker room.

"Just take his reaction when that happened," says Green's former Suns teammate Kevin Johnson. "A. C. just looked at the guy, picked up his tooth, and walked out. Nobody in his right mind would react in such a calm manner."

Nobody seemingly in their right mind would have had themselves fitted with a hockey style protective mask and played the very next night either. But then again, that's what makes Green such a special athlete, and what strikes peers like Johnson with awe.

"It's incredible," says Johnson. "You appreciate what Cal Ripken has done in baseball, and A. C. has done the same thing in basketball. He's not out there just playing four minutes and chalking up another game. You love playing on the same team with A. C. Green. You hate playing against him because he's a warrior."

Green claims his streak actually goes back to his "peewee" league days, and that's why it has become second nature to him. He is content to leave the hyperbole to his peers. It certainly won't come from the media.

Green has actually been underappreciated for his work wherever he's been. In Los Angeles in the mid and late 1980s, he was a fixture on the league's best team, starting for back-to-back champions in 1987 and 1988 in the showtime era with Magic Johnson, Kareem Abdul-Jabbar, and James Worthy. He did the dirty work—grabbed rebounds, defended opponents' top scorers, made key passes, set bone-jarring picks, and did all the intangible things that helped the Lakers win. He was all grit and no glamour.

He was unrecognized, yet invaluable. He never scored more than 15 points per game, nor averaged more than 10 rebounds. He was named to the league's all-defensive team in 1989 and voted to the all-star team in 1990. Other than those, accolades have been few and far between. But as comedian and basketball fan Woody Allen once said, 80 percent of success is showing up. And that's just what Green has done since November 18, 1986, when then Lakers coach Pat Riley last put him on the bench for an entire game. Every night for nearly fifteen years he has played hard, played well, and played selflessly for some thirty minutes per night. He has shown up.

"The thing is, this is such a normal job. I mean, the preparation, your attitude," says Green. "You wake up in the morning, and, trust me, you do not feel like going to work. No, I don't want to go to practice. There's nothing inside my body that tells me I need to be at practice. And I have a right. I can call in sick. You know, I've played enough practices, enough games, that I've accrued enough, you know, vacation time that I can take two days if I wanted to take two days, and I think my coaches would even understand. But that's not me, and that's not how I play the game, and that's not how I prepare for the game. So, there's been many a day, trust me, that I just think, 'No, I'd rather not,' but there is just something within me that drives me on and motivates me just to get there to that game, to that practice, and not only to it but through it."

While few have taken notice of Green's consistency on the court, many in the media have grabbed hold of Green's other streak.

Now just a couple of eighty-two-game seasons away from his fortieth birthday, Green remains a virgin. And proud of it.

Here, again, he is unique among professional athletes, particularly in the NBA, where in recent years national publications have reported on the number of prominent players who have fathered multiple illegitimate children with a varying number of women. Being abstinent in a veritable lion's den of temptation, Green stands out like a modern-day Samson.

"It's very, very simple to be mediocre today and do nothing, and you can just be normal," says Green. "No opinion, no ideas, no convictions, just living to be living. So many people settle and fall into that. But then to have a conviction about anything and to stand for that, especially one on abstinence or your sexual preference, which normally people say is so personal, people ask, 'Why are you putting it out in the public.'

"I was on *Oprah* [in 1998] right before the season started. The whole show was geared around professional athletes having children out of wedlock, and why aren't they taking care of their responsibilities, or are they being set up by women? And I'm on this show being a virgin, first of all, so obviously, I'm not having sex, but I know I have a message and I have a point for being on this show. So they had different ladies and different guys on the show, and Oprah went on in her introduction of why are these guys being set up or are these guys just having sex just to be having it? She says, 'A. C., what do you think about it?' And I'm like, 'Well, first of all, I don't know why they're doing it in the first place.'

"That's really where I'm coming from. Why are we so irresponsible in our thinking? Why are we believing this one message that you can just have sex, forget responsibility, forget accountability, forget any repercussions, just doing it because it feels good. No, it's a lot deeper than that. There's a lot more to it than that. And I'm still dumbfounded. I think I'm normal."

Normal is hardly what Green's lifestyle might seem like to his peers. On most days he is up early in the morning, usually around 5:00 or 5:15. He is up to spend time with God, praying and studying the Bible. It is this time, Green says, that keeps him strong and enables him to walk out both of his streaks.

"I am curious about sex," he says. "But not curious enough to go to the violation point. I figure God created it, so it must be good. But he has created it to take place at a certain point of time—within the confines of marriage. If I'm going to live according to the rules God laid out, then there are rules A through Z. There can't be situation ethics.

"I'm not superhuman. . . . You know what I'm saying? I'm so human. I am 100 percent man without a question. But there's just an extraordinary gift that God's given me. . . . It's very simple to me. And so I'm very happy. I really am. I mean, that's just the way it should be done."

The challenges Green has been presented with throughout his career have tested his character. With Laker girls and groupies ogling him on a nightly basis during his rookie season, Green's teammates challenged him, declaring that with a big paycheck and plenty of willing company in Tinsletown, Green's chastity wouldn't last.

"That first year about four guys were saying, 'We've had guys come on this team before talking that Christian stuff. We're going to give you six weeks,'" Green recalls.

In two years, Green convinced the Lakers that his convictions would not be shaken. And while he hasn't exactly changed the NBA, the NBA hasn't changed him either. Some teammates over those years have come to him privately when needing guidance. Some have asked him to help them find the same peace they see in him. Through the years, Green has become perhaps the most respected role model in the NBA.

"A lot of people talk about a lot of things," former teammate Magic Johnson says, "but A. C. lives everything he preaches—not for notoriety but because he feels it's the right thing to do."

"If there was ever a player that was the consummate professional basketball athlete and role model for kids, it would be A. C. Green," says former Lakers coach Pat Riley. "While a lot of current professional athletes may not think they have a responsibility to the youth of this country or to something bigger than themselves, A. C. doesn't feel that way."

For Green, that responsibility also means taking advantage of his reputation and platform to influence young people. To do so, he created the A. C. Green Youth Foundation, which has initiated a number of programs to reach out to inner city youth—basketball camps, mentor programs, and educational curricula. His biggest project is an abstinence program called "I've Got the Power," which was released to junior high and high schools in 1999.

"It's a six-week study course talking about abstinence, really helping kids understand that you have the power within you if you learn how to set boundaries," says Green. "You have to define lines. You decide on what's right, what's wrong, that your no means no. And it's powerful. And why? Because they're powerful, and they just need to know that. It's not something they've always got to be told, but they've got to start believing that and absorb that, and that's really what the 'I've Got the Power' curriculum is all about. . . . I want to give them the tools and skills to know how they can [practice abstinence] also."

As a result, Green is seeing many young people responding and becoming empowered to make better choices.

"With our Web page at the Foundation, we get so much E-mail. We get so many letters. We get so many faxes from young people, saying, 'You know what? I've been waiting to hear this message.' Now we're not the only ones saying it. There are other organizations and other people out there saying the same thing. Hopefully, there are other parents saying the same thing, and we can just be more of a confirmation. But we're receiving a lot of letters that are just really applauding the message and just saying, 'Keep doing it because it's affecting me.'

"I remember a boy wrote me, a fourteen-year-old boy, and said, 'I feel like having sex with my girlfriend. We both go to church, and I know it's really not right, but I just have these feelings sometime. And I think of you and I'm just like, How, how can he stand it? I mean, how's he been able to do this? And it just encourages me to stay strong, and I'm able to not do it. And I just want you to know you've been an encouragement.' That is so cool. I mean, you don't know how you affect people. You really don't. You're really doing it because you know it's right, and whatever comes of that, hopefully you're happy with. That was just so encouraging to me."

Green seemingly has everything under control, including his own desires. He is committed to wait until marriage to partake of the good thing God has created. He looks forward to one day marrying and becoming a father, but is in no hurry to get there. And, he says, in this streak, there are no war stories, no near misses.

"God is so sufficient that he satisfies every void that we were once created with," Green says. "He's able to satisfy those needs that we have. We still have wants, but he'll give you the needs for you to have a successful life."

When asked about how long he can keep succeeding in his remarkable show of endurance, Green is ever humble and to the point.

"I'm not surprised, and I don't know where this streak will end up. I think I'll retire before it ends," he says.

While the debate will endure as to which streak Green refers with his remark, one thing remains certain. As long as he plays the game, Green will be the focus of any discussion around durability. While he understands that, he prefers that the focus be on the character that drives him, rather than the streak itself.

"That defines me as a person. That defines how I play. That defines how I prepare for the game. That defines how I live off the court. And that's defines how business affairs are conducted about me and around me. That's life."

> **A champion is one who lays down his own desires for the benefit of others.**

CHAPTER 10
SACRIFICE

Our culture is such a culture of comfort and convenience. To me sacrifice means giving up comfort and convenience for the sake of blessing and benefiting somebody else.

Unfortunately, sacrifice is something that many of us either avoid or fail to embrace as we should. Yet to be a friend—a true friend—you will be inconvenienced at times. You must be willing to be inconvenienced. I think that's what sacrifice is—being willing to be inconvenienced in order to enhance someone else's life.

Part of sacrifice is to give a piece of yourself. I think about that with my own kids. For me to know them individually and to impart to them values that I deem important, I must give them part of who I am. That takes time, energy, and effort. It's not something to simply aspire to do—I must get in there and make conscious choices to make it happen.

The Bible tells us that it is more blessed to give than to receive. This applies to more than material resources. We must also be willing to offer from our personal experiences—even our lives in some situations.

When you sacrifice to benefit someone else, more times than not the fulfillment and joy you feel as a result are far greater than anything you would have imagined beforehand.

—**C. K.**

"The real make of a man is how he treats people who can never do anything for him."
Darrell Royal, Former Texas Football Coach

John Amaechi

No one was more surprised than Orlando Magic center John Amaechi when the Basketball Hall of Fame came calling for his uniform.

Sure, he's the first British citizen to play in the NBA. And he became a true contributor on the floor during the 1999–2000 season. But let's face it, no one would mistake him for Magic vice president Julius Erving, a true Hall of Famer.

"I happened to make the first basket of the millennium, even if it isn't really 'til next year," Amaechi said at the time. "The shot was an extremely ugly left-handed hook that rolled around the rim four times before falling in."

So right there, in the Hall of Fame in Springfield, Illinois, hanging among the jerseys bearing the names Jordan, Bird, West, Abdul-Jabbar, and Chamberlain, is one with the name Amaechi.

You can almost picture children strolling through the building with their fathers, asking, "Dad, I see Michael's jersey and Kareem's and Magic's . . . but who is *that?*"

Ironically, it is kids who Amaechi values more than the game he plays. His plan is to play in the NBA as long as he can, then take his earnings back to England to finish his doctorate in clinical child psychology and then open his own practice.

For Amaechi, the lifestyle of a basketball player is not such a great thrill. He finds enjoyment in more intellectual areas.

"I know I'm different from the norm," he says. "I'm actually quite proud of that. I don't feel any pressure to conform and be more like a real basketball player. In fact, in all honesty, I play up the differences. I'm probably worse now—more British, more quirky, more different—because I find I quite enjoy it."

Amaechi's mother, Wendy, died at age fifty while he was overseas studying at Penn State. The loss is the deepest tragedy of Amaechi's life. Wendy was a general practitioner who made house calls. As a child, John often rode with her and watched her work. Her life, he says, is what inspired him to want to be a healer himself.

Next to his late mother, literature has most impacted Amaechi's life. In particular, the one book that influenced him most is *The Lion, the Witch, and the Wardrobe* by C. S. Lewis.

He was assigned the book in grammar school and then read the other six books in Lewis' *The Chronicles of Narnia* series on his own. Even in this age of Harry Potter, these books remain extremely popular. At their center is Aslan, the great lion who shows others the way to life.

"I always related to the lion," Amaechi says. "It sounds really pompous, I know. You're supposed to relate to the children. The lion sacrifices himself and comes back to life—it was all very noble. I like that. There's little nobility in many people's lives at this point. There's not much nobility in basketball. That's for sure. Intrinsically it's not a noble profession. Teaching is. Medicine is. A doctor, a physician."

How about a child psychologist?

"Yes," he says, "yes, a child psychologist. That is a noble profession."

He is a lion of a man, running up and down the courts of the NBA, but he also has a lion's heart. Just as Lewis' noble Aslan led the way, the NBA's noble lion, Amaechi, is showing NBA peers a better way.

He'll continue that in his next career as a healer of troubled children.

> **"You have to be totally focused and determined
> to sacrifice whatever it takes to get there.
> You have to pray and you have to work."**
> **Junior Seau, San Diego Chargers All-Pro Linebacker**

Coy Bacon

He was once one of the most feared defensive ends in the NFL. A Pro Bowler and member of the L. A. Rams' "Fearsome Foursome," in the 1970s, Coy Bacon worked alongside Merlin Olsen and Deacon Jones in one of the best defensive lines in football history. But when his career ended, his life nearly did as well.

After years of trials, Bacon was given a new lease on life in 1987, and he is now giving that life back to his community.

"I thank God every day for the jobs I have," says Bacon, a staff member at the Ohio Center for Youth in Pedro, a facility for eleven- to seventeen-year-olds who are experiencing problems at home.

In addition, he manages a minority outreach as a part-time counselor with the Family Guidance Center in his hometown of Ironton. He desires to teach these young people about the same solution he found—God— but as he notes, "You can't talk to 'em about the Lord until you get 'em off drugs and alcohol."

Still an imposing figure, the six-foot-four-inch, 280-pound former defensive end tries to steer young people away from the path that nearly led to his premature death.

The five-time all-Pro speaks to youth groups in the region, relating the havoc drugs caused in his life and how God spared him. He counsels them to avoid associating with users "because pretty soon you start doing what they're doing."

Near the end of his career in the early '80s, Bacon slipped deep into drug use, eventually squandering his entire pro football savings. The habit culminated in his arrest for cocaine possession in 1986.

To prevent him from "squealing" on the stand, a gunman stopped by his suburban Washington, D.C., apartment a week before the trial and put a .38-caliber bullet in his stomach.

"God saved my life as soon as the bullet hit me," he recalls. "I felt his presence. I grew up in church, but I was never committed to God. All the way through [my time in] the hospital, I prayed and repented of my sin. That's why I'm alive today."

Returning to his hometown, Bacon recuperated for six months before going out to warn young people about the dangers of drug abuse.

Now, the one-time sack master, once nearly sacked himself, is helping pick young people up, giving them a second chance as he has been given.

"If I make a key shot, I'm excited and I'm thrilled, but if I can put the ball in the right hands and that guy knocks down the shot, not only am I thrilled, but that guy is thrilled and my teammates are thrilled because of the unselfish act and it becomes contagious. That's what it's all about."
Mark Jackson, Toronto Raptors Point Guard

Carl Erskine

Carl Erskine knows about personal trial. He was a teammate of Jackie Robinson's on the 1948 Brooklyn Dodgers' team the year after Robinson broke baseball's color line. He saw Robinson endure unthinkable abuse and, from him, learned how a man perseveres under adversity—something Erskine would understand firsthand a short time later.

Erskine had become one of the National League's top pitchers during his twelve-year career in the major leagues. He won 122 games while losing only 78. His .610 winning percentage is still one of the tops in Dodgers franchise history. He pitched in five World Series and was a twenty-game winner in 1953.

But Erskine's career nearly ended before it began. He tore a muscle in his right shoulder during his very first major-league start in '48. From then on, he battled arm miseries on and off throughout his career. On a good day, however, Erskine could give the game's best hitters fits with his magnificent overhand curve. His most impressive performance came in 1956 against the Dodgers' vaunted rivals, the New York Giants. He recalls that day in vivid detail.

"I was having tremendous arm trouble and was in a very low mental state. I was scheduled to pitch that day, but I was debating whether to tell Walter Alston I couldn't," Erskine says. "Then he came to my locker and gave me a new baseball—the warm-up ball. By taking it, I indicated, 'I'm ready.' For some reason, I couldn't say, 'Skip, I can't pitch today.'

"I went out on the bench and, man, was I low. I watched the people coming into the park and I thought, 'People are paying money to see me pitch, and I'm not even sure I can warm up.'

"I'd had cortisone treatment on my arm in Chicago on a quiet basis. I went to a trainer on the Cubs because I was embarrassed to keep going back to our trainer. In those days, if they didn't see blood and bone hanging out, they'd say it was all in your head. That added to my psychological low—that I was having so much arm trouble, I was afraid to go to my own trainer.

"But, right then at that low point, I remember praying to God: 'You must have some reason for bringing me to this point. I have very little to offer. I may not even be able to warm up. Help me do the best with what I've got.'

"I got through the warm-up and pitched the first inning—remarkable! I pitched the second inning . . . pitched the fifth inning. There was no score until the seventh inning, when we got three runs. Each inning I finished, I couldn't believe it. And remember, I was no kid. I was a veteran pitcher, and nothing should have surprised me.

"While walking to the dugout [after the eighth inning], it occurred to me; *The Giants don't have a hit yet!* Then, it was just as though God said to me, 'What did you expect? It's what you asked for.'

"When I went out for the ninth, I got the first man out right away. Next, Whitey Lockman hit a sharp grounder right at me. I went down to field the ball and didn't get it. It looked like it was through for a base hit. But when I raised up, I saw I'd pinned the ball between my mitt and the ground. It was laying there like an Easter egg! So I threw him out. Then, Alvin Dark grounded out, and I had a no-hitter.

"The game was the spiritual high of my life. The fact that it was a no-hitter was not the significant part. The significant thing for me was that I got to a point where I truly surrendered my total will.

"It's a story I've been reluctant to tell because it sounds too perfect, too made up. It came out a no-hitter. But if you'd realize what really happened—not only to my arm, but also to my soul—you'd know why it was the spiritual high of my life. And to think I came so close to telling Alston, 'Give me another day's rest.'"

Erskine's willingness to selflessly sacrifice for the team brought tremendous personal dividends. It was a lesson he would not soon forget.

Shortly after retiring in 1959, Carl and his wife Betty were completing their home team. After three children, a fourth was born in 1960. To the Erskines' shock and surprise, son Jimmy was born with Down's syndrome.

Shortly after Jimmy's birth, Carl met with a local doctor whose son had multiple disabilities. The former pitcher listened as the doctor explained the lack of local services available for their boys. Shortly after that first meeting the two were working with other parents to form an organization that would help meet the special needs of children like their sons.

Through hard work, the Erskines helped found the Hopewell Center, which provides specialized help for Down's syndrome children. And with a lifetime of love, Jimmy Erskine is doing just fine.

> "My family instilled in me growing up that you have to give back. Your value as a person is directly correlated to how much you give back and help out people that are less fortunate. And that's natural for me, you know, I get credit for it. You don't do it for credit. You do it because that's one of the permanent things."
>
> **Kevin Johnson, Phoenix Suns Guard**

Tom Landry

"A lot of times through those years, when I was on the sidelines, when we had difficulties and problems . . . you know, I felt God's presence with me," Tom Landry once said. "And that made all the difference in the world in how I reacted and how I handled people."

Clearly, Tom Landry knew the final score.

When the legendary coach of "America's Team" died of leukemia on February 12, 2000, he left a legacy that will be difficult to match. "America's Coach" knew the purpose for his seventy-five years was more than winning football games. Win he did, totaling 270 wins—third-most in NFL history—over his twenty-nine seasons, with a record twenty consecutive winning seasons. He led his Dallas Cowboys teams to five conference championships, thirteen division titles, and eighteen playoff births. His teams won two Super Bowls.

He was an innovator, responsible for developing the 4-3 defense, the "flex" defense, the multiple offense, shifts and motion, and restoring the spread or "shotgun" formation. But more than that, Tom Landry was devoted to developing winning people—beyond the game of football. All who knew him said Landry was a living example of character.

His innovative mind, steely game face, meticulous preparation, and plaid fedora were all hallmarks of the man who walked the sidelines. But more importantly, he touched hearts and changed lives with his humble moral fiber, flawless integrity, transcendent character, and Christian faith. The impact he had on the lives of so many others is Landry's true legacy.

"Coach Landry wasn't one to preach to you every day," says Dan Reeves. "He led his life. He walked the walk. He also had the vision of knowing that football wasn't the ultimate success, and that's the reason he became a Christian. The things that Coach Landry talked about and showed in his life personally have helped me to become a better person. Hopefully I can

171

have the influence on half as many people as Coach Landry influenced in his life."

"He was like my second father," said Cowboys Hall of Fame defensive tackle Bob Lilly. "He imparted principles and integrity and character in us that we probably lost when we went to college. When I went to that first meeting and he told me about his priorities—God, family, and football—I thought he was kidding."

"When I got into coaching, he was the guy I looked up to, he was somebody I kind of patterned my career after," says Hall of Fame coach Joe Gibbs. "He was a rare guy."

"He made you want to follow him by example," says former Dallas defensive lineman Randy White. "I didn't understand what he was talking about back then. But while he was teaching us Xs and Os, he was teaching us about life. We all understand that now."

"The real testament about Tom is that—you watch—he'll teach us more now that he's gone than when he was here," says Hall-of-Famer Mel Renfro. "We were learning from him and we didn't even know it at the time. Now we know."

"I remember when my dad died the night before we played a regular-season game up there in Denver," recalls White. "I didn't tell anybody except [linebacker] Bob Breunig. I didn't want to tell anybody. When I got introduced before that game, Coach Landry shook my hand and looked me in the eye. I kind of had some tears in my eyes. He said, 'Randy, you take as much time as you need with your family.' He always would tell you God should be first, family should be second, and football should come next."

Drew Pearson remembers a story that perhaps most of all typifies Landry. After the 1983 season, Pearson helped organize a team of Cowboys who traveled the area playing charity basketball games. One night, the bus carrying players from a game arrived around 1:30 A.M. Drew had been accompanied by his brother, Carey, who was then twenty-eight and helping out as the team's ballboy.

On the way home Pearson's sports car weaved and hit a truck that was parked on the side of the road. The impact killed Carey instantly. Drew suffered multiple injuries, including a bleeding liver. He woke up two days later and saw, standing at his bedside, his mother, Roger Staubach, Harvey Martin, and Tom Landry.

"Every time I'd wake up, every day that I was in the hospital, Coach Landry would be there," Pearson said.

That was just like Landry—to be there. So it was more than ten years earlier when Dallas traded Ron East and Pettis Norman to San Diego for Lance Alworth in the spring of 1971. Landry's policy was that no player should hear news of such a move from the media or other sources, so the announcement was delayed while Landry drove to the bank where Norman worked during the off-season to tell the player himself.

His former secretary, Margo Kelly, used to talk about how Landry would write numerous letters to people who were ill or in need—not form letters, but expressions of hope and perseverance that she said were heartfelt.

"If the NFL had a Mount Rushmore, the profile would be of Tom Landry," NFL commissioner Paul Tagliabue said. "He's one of the greatest gifts ever to the NFL."

"He was also a father to me," said Bob Hayes, whom Landry testified for during a drug trafficking trial.

"He was our rock, our hope, our inspiration, our coach," Staubach said. "The world was a better place with him in it."

Former quarterback Danny White added, "We're all better people for having known him. You can see a little of him in a lot of us."

Landry's words still ring true in the hearts of many men who once played for him: "Your priorities must change. It's not enough just to go to church and sit in the pew," he said. "Your priorities have to change. And mine changed. God became first in my life, and my family became much more important to me. And of course, football became third."

> **"There are three kinds of baseball players: those who make it happen, those who watch it happen, and those who wonder what happened."**
> **Tommy Lasorda, Former Los Angeles Dodgers Manager**

John Wetteland

John Wetteland was about to leave for the ballpark one day in 1997 when his doorbell rang. He opened it to find a young boy, maybe twelve years old, nervously shifting from foot to foot.

"Is Mr. Wetteland here?" the boy asked.

"That's me," the then Texas Rangers reliever replied.

Stammering, the boy asked if Wetteland could come outside and play catch.

A lot of big leaguers would have brushed off the boy's request. Not Wetteland, who is still a boy at heart himself.

One problem. All his baseball equipment was at the ballpark at Arlington.

"My wife and I searched the home for a glove and couldn't find one," Wetteland says. "I felt so bad, I told him, 'Look, I can't play now because I don't have a glove, but when I come back from the next road trip, I'll bring one home and we can play.'"

Wetteland did, and, sure enough, the boy came back.

"We went out on the front lawn and played catch for about thirty minutes," Wetteland says. "He wanted me to help him with his pitching mechanics. I was sweating bullets, but I loved it. It was fun—pure, unadulterated baseball."

Betsy King

You wouldn't know it from observing her, but Betsy King is the most successful women's professional golfer on the planet.

In 1995, she became the first female golfer to reach $5 million in career earnings. Also that year, she won her thirtieth tournament and was thus immediately inducted into the LPGA Hall of Fame.

In 1992, she became the only golfer ever—male or female—to shoot all four rounds of a major championship in the 60s. Through 2000, she had won a half-dozen major tournaments and more than $6.5 million in winnings—tops on the all-time money list. In 1984, 1989, and 1993 she was voted the Tour's top player. She is by many accounts the finest player ever in her sport.

Yet to label Betsy King *composed* is an understatement. She is known among her peers as quiet, humble, and unemotional. The dichotomy then is this woman of the stoic exterior, who has a searing intensity to be the best roaring inside her.

"I'm pretty conservative by nature," says King. "I don't get very emotional. I'm not loud and excitable, and I have a tendency to keep things to myself, unless you know me real well."

Thus, it was a complete surprise to the entire golf world when King, upon winning the 1992 LPGA Championship, ran down the fairway at 18 giving high-fives to the gallery.

"When she ran down that fairway, I almost fell over," said then LPGA commissioner Charlie Mechem at the time. "I always tell our players, 'If you feel genuine emotion, show it.' But Betsy?"

King is as self-controlled an athlete as you'll find in any sport. Most of this has to do with her upbringing. She was raised in the rolling farmland of eastern Pennsylvania, in the small town of Limekiln. It was there her love of sports and competitiveness were forged, while taking on her brother and his friends on the family basketball and tennis courts.

"Betsy was always good at everything and seemed to understand any game with a ball," says her father, Dr. Weir King. "She only got to play golf about six to eight weeks a year because of the weather, but by the time she was fifteen, I thought she might be a professional athlete, and I was hoping it would be in golf, despite the limited amount of time she put into it."

King put more attention to her golf game during her college days at Furman University, while also playing on the school's field hockey and basketball teams. But golf would not have come first had it not been for a knee injury in field hockey that ended her run at the more physical sports. She ended up becoming an all-American in golf and led Furman to the 1976 NCAA championship.

Turning pro in 1977, King would wait seven years to experience success at that level. But when her first win finally came at the 1984 Kemper Open, it was as if she had opened a veritable dam of victories. She followed with nineteen more over the next five years and was on her way to the Hall of Fame.

King credits two specific events for vaulting her into the spot as women's golf's preeminent player: "I switched teachers . . . and I became a Christian. I think I improved in all areas—emotionally, mentally, and in technique."

Her association with Chicago teaching pro Ed Oldfield began in 1980 when he became King's coach and completely reworked her game over the ensuing three years.

At the request of friend and LPGA Tour player Donna White, Oldfield observed King hitting balls off the practice tee before a tournament in Portland, Oregon, that year. Oldfield saw about twenty things in King's swing he thought needed changing.

"She had serious problems," says Oldfield. "Her divots were going way right, and the ball was going way left. I watched her play, and on one par-5 she couldn't carry a fairway wood 100 yards over water. She had to lay up with a wedge."

After hearing of Oldfield's critique, King arranged to spend the off-season in Phoenix—site of Oldfield's winter office. Her father accompanied her to provide support. The day of her first lesson, Betsy and her dad went out early in the morning to hit balls in private at a deserted playground.

"She was hitting balls, and I was chasing them—and a cop came and chased us," says Weir. "I think that was the low point in her career. But that afternoon Ed told me that she was going to be one of the five best players in the world."

She exceeded even the plans of her coach.

"She was very quiet, pretty much a loner, when she first got out here," says Oldfield. "But no one has ever worked harder than Betsy. She was dedicated, made lots of changes, began winning tournaments, and simply built on her success. She has no weaknesses."

Just prior to hooking up with Oldfield, King discovered her own internal weakness. She found herself looking for a source of inner strength and peace that was missing during those first lean years on the Tour. It was White, again, who played a key role. She was to speak at a Christian golfers conference in 1980. King wanted to hear White speak, so she accepted an invitation to attend the conference. During one of the morning sessions, in response to a speaker's invitation, King prayed to become a Christian. While she still had to work on the mechanics of the game, King felt for the first time that her inner game had been taken care of.

"The truth is, I don't know where I'd be if I hadn't become a Christian," says King. "But I don't think it would be where I am today.

"I was work-oriented, but I had a lot of my self-worth tied up in how well I played golf. I definitely feel more at peace."

That peace gave her a new fire for the game, and an understanding that her fervent faith and a dedication to her game could coexist.

"I had the notion that if you were fully committed to Christ, it would mean being in the full-time ministry. When I realized you could be both totally committed to Christ and totally committed to your occupation, it had a releasing power on me. I felt he had given me a talent, and I could give my 100 percent effort to developing it.

"I saw that God wants his people in different walks of life. He can use them wherever they are—if they serve him with all of their hearts.

"When I'm out there playing, I'm certainly going to be probably more intense than just about anybody else."

And, on most occasions, better.

"Betsy tries harder than anyone I've ever seen," says Tour rival Cathy Gerring. "She's a wonderful player, and she's done great things for women's golf."

"She's one of the most focused people I've ever known, very tough and aggressive to play against," says friend and opponent Meg Mallon. "She's quiet, sure, but there's also a side to Betsy that not many people see."

Back to the emotional side of King, which she says is greatly misunderstood.

"I'm a very emotional person, but maybe not in front of a crowd," says King. "I really try to control my emotions on the golf course and try not to get too upset for two reasons: First, as a witness to my faith in God; and second, because it hurts my golf game. . . . Others say I'm not emotional, but I really am—just not in front of a thousand people.

"I'm a combination of my mom and dad, I guess. My father was a physician, very intellectual and analytical. Being a doctor, he was controlled, unemotional, which I think you have to portray to your patients. I picked up some of that.

"My mother was quite the opposite. She was very talkative and emotional. Most people would never guess it, but I'm very emotional inside too."

Her emotions come to the forefront when the topic turns from golf to people, particularly those who are in need. This is the area that most affects Betsy King. It is what ignites her passion.

Such was the case in 1993, when just two days after birdying the final hole of the last tournament of the season—to lock up her third LPGA Player of the Year title—King was surrounded by Romanian street children.

In mid-November of '93, King and four fellow LPGA players traveled to Romania with a group called Alternative Ministries for a week of work with Extended Hand of Romania, an orphan-relief group in Bucharest. The trip followed a whirlwind week for King. After winning the Toray Japan Queens Cup in Kobi, Japan, she took a red-eye flight to Phoenix, Arizona, then spent a day at home in Scottsdale unpacking and packing, then hopped on a plane for Bucharest.

"I went from celebrating an incredible win and season to extreme sadness," says King. "I was so happy, and then it all became very, very clear. I said to myself, 'How important is golf, anyway?'

"We were standing in the snow, freezing, dealing with young children who live under a train station. It gave me a perspective that has changed my life."

King and her golfing partners experienced the desolate living conditions in Romania. During their trip, they stayed with a family who had no indoor plumbing. King and Alison Nicholas were so moved by the family's plight, that they gave them the money to cover the cost of installing plumbing indoors.

"We experienced firsthand what it was like to live without the basic necessities that we take for granted," King says. "Their home was barely heated, but in spite of their poverty, they gave us everything they had. We ate all the time, it seemed. Their faith was so strong that it made mine even stronger."

King and her friends had come to help, so with a renewed perspective, they went about their mission. They visited several orphanages scattered throughout three cities, delivering food, clothing, and medicine, and extending love and hugs.

"We spent a couple of days just going down to the train station and meeting kids who were living on the streets," recalls King. "We took them some food."

One night King and a local church youth group went to the train station to sing songs. Some were familiar choruses like "Amazing Grace." King was touched as she watched many of the street teens find comfort and hope through the songs and the expression of love.

The experience left an indelible impression on the entire group. In 1994, they returned to Romania to again bring needed basics to more orphaned children.

King remembers a particular moment from her Romanian adventure that seemed to crystallize the entire experience. Her group located a five-year-old boy named Daniel who was being adopted by a family in the Seattle area. The golfers picked up Daniel from an orphanage and dressed him in a new outfit provided by his adoptive parents. Daniel stayed with King and the others throughout their trip, becoming so attached that he cried when they said their "good-byes" in Bucharest prior to the boy's flight to the U.S.

"He is one of the lucky ones," King said. "It was wonderful to be able to help make things better for him. The whole country is so poor. It's sad to think about the children we left behind."

King's commitment to those who have been left behind extends beyond Romania. She has spent time in Korea, using golf as a tool for aid work. And each off-season for the past several years, she has helped out on domestic soil as well.

Since 1993, King and a handful of other golfers have been involved in projects with Habitat for Humanity. Each year in mid-October, following the end of the Tour's domestic season, the women put down their clubs for a week and pick up saws, hammers, nail guns, and tool belts, volunteering to build houses for poor families in various parts of the country. It means one to two weeks of hard labor, from 8 A.M. to 4:30 P.M. every day. It also means experiencing spartan accommodations during that time for the golfers, who all contribute personally to cover much of the cost of building materials.

King, who has spearheaded the project that has seen as many as thirty golfers involved at one time, says of the effort, "We believe you're called to serve others."

In 1993, King and friends built a home in Guadalupe, Arizona, just outside Phoenix. Upon completion, the women attended a dedication ceremony for the new home where they watched a family move in that had previously lived in a shack.

"The sister had a trailer and allowed her sister [and her family] to have this plywood shack next to it," says King. It actually burned down, so they moved into the new home earlier than they were supposed to, before it was finished, just because they didn't have anywhere to go.

"We thought it would be a really neat idea to not only raise the money for the house, but also to try and build it by ourselves.

"We made a difference, I think. Obviously, you don't change the world, but you try to change the world you're in."

Friend and Tour pro Robin Walton says the Habitat connection never would have come about without King's persistence.

"The thing that really strikes me about Betsy is once she gets a goal or an idea in mind, nobody pursues it as hard as she does," says Walton. "She wanted to see the Tour get involved in the Habitat for Humanity project. She really pushed for it. I don't think I could have made it happen the way she did. She really throws herself into something.

"That's her greatest attribute and her greatest talent. Her tenacity. She gets onto something and she really wants to see it all the way through."

King has seen to it that her giving efforts remain a constant in her life. The Betsy King Classic tournament, a regular stop on the LPGA Tour since 1996, serves to raise money to benefit children. She runs youth sports camps for the Fellowship of Christian Athletes (FCA) and has even volunteered as a high school basketball coach in her home area.

Her efforts have drawn attention. In 1993, she was selected by the Golf Writers Association of America to receive the Charles Bartlett Award for "unselfish contributions to the betterment of society." Her peers continue to acknowledge her commitment to reaching out to people.

"I've never known anyone, let alone a professional athlete, who lives their faith more than Betsy," says John Dolaghan, director of Golf Ministry for FCA. "I've never met someone with a servant attitude like hers who wants to learn more and grow. She's as authentic as they come."

Says Bill Lewis, a retired U.S. Navy captain, who formerly conducted chapels on the LPGA circuit, "I've never met a superstar athlete with so much humility."

"There is always a need, but you can't do everything," King says. "It's not, 'What am I gonna do for God,' but, 'God what do you want me to do? Where are you working and how can I help?'

"All I can do is live one day at a time and do things with all my heart."

> **A champion gets up one more time
> than he's been knocked down.**

CHAPTER 11

PERSEVERANCE

During my playing days with the Indiana Pacers, we weren't very good, so not many fans came out to watch us. As a matter of fact, with a 16,700-seat capacity, Market Square Arena would pull curtains over the top part of the arena because we wouldn't have enough bodies in there to fill it. We would have four or five thousand people there—unless we played the Lakers or Celtics. Then we'd have a sellout, with two-thirds of the crowd cheering for them.

So to gear up and get motivated while knowing that you would probably lose because your team just wasn't good enough—it was a lesson in perseverance. Even while you're aspiring to win, it's easy to become deflated in the process if you think you don't have the ammunition.

It all comes down to wanting to give your best. It's doing what's right even though people aren't watching because you know that's what you're called to do. That's where you will get satisfaction. Give the effort. Don't give up. Don't get down.

perseverance: to persist in spite of difficulties

It's OK to get frustrated. It's OK to get angry, but stay in control of yourself so that it doesn't negatively affect the kind of effort you give on the next play or the next game or the next practice.

I believe the biggest obstacles to perseverance are failure, uncomfortable resistance, discouragement, lack of vision, lack of focus, lack of confidence, and lack of belief.

Sometimes you need encouragement. You need a boost. You need something that shows you the light at the end of the tunnel. You need something that can keep your fire stirred.

I see this need in one of our children. Our middle child, Alex, is very talented, and yet he can be a drifter. But when we offer him encouragement within his space, then he lights up. His chin is up, his prance is different, his gaze is clearer, his focus is better, and it's all because of encouragement. He can be easily discouraged. If he bumps into somebody as big or as quick as he is, he can get discouraged and frustrated. But he's learning that with encouragement and through perseverance, he's got something to offer as well.

Perseverance is not something that comes and goes. It's an everyday thing. There are a lot of different things that come at us in life that can discourage us, knock us down, or tempt us to settle for our circumstances, but perseverance keeps us pushing forward.

—C. K.

"Time proves all things."
Branch Rickey, Former Brooklyn Dodgers Owner

John Stephen Akhwari

It was Mexico City. The 1968 Summer Olympic games. Late at night, in the main track and field stadium.

Out of the cold darkness, John Stephen Akhwari entered the stadium at the far end. He hobbled slowly, and unsteadily. Pain filled every step. Blood ran down his bandaged leg.

Over an hour earlier, the winner of the Olympic marathon had already been declared. All other runners had completed the 26.2 miles shortly thereafter. Only a few spectators remained in their seats. There was no cheering, no flag waving. Yet, the lone runner pressed on.

As he neared the Olympic Stadium, word circulated that there was one runner still on the course. Other Olympians and spectators quickly came back to the stadium to watch the scene unfold. As Akhwari came to the finish line, the crowd began to roar with appreciation.

After it was all over, a reporter asked Akhwari why he had not retired from the race, as he had no chance of winning.

Akhwari seemed confused by the question but finally answered. "My country did not send me to Mexico City to start the race. They sent me to finish."

> **"Success is never final. Failure is never fatal. It's courage that counts."**
> **Winston Churchill, Former British Prime Minister**

Avery Johnson

Over the first eight years of a nearly unnoticed NBA career, Avery Johnson became just the second player in league history to increase his scoring average in each of his first eight seasons. He also became one of the game's top assist men. And he led the San Antonio Spurs to a world championship in 1999. But for all of his accomplishments, the one thing Johnson seemed not to have achieved was respect.

It has been Tim Duncan, David Robinson, and Sean Elliott who have received most of the credit for the Spurs' success throughout the '90s. One would think NBA personnel folks have rarely seen the good in the Spurs point guard and catalyst. Since signing with Seattle as an undrafted free agent in 1988, he has played with Denver, San Antonio, Houston, San Antonio again, and Golden State, before coming back to the Spurs to stay and guide the team that had released him twice previously to their 1999 title.

But don't think Johnson isn't appreciated. In San Antonio, Johnson is beloved by fans. Best known for his quick cross-over dribble and for his nice-guy qualities, he is the little left-hander with size 10 shoes. He is a little big man with the Bayou drawl, who often leads teammates in pregame prayer and has a motivational locker-room speech rivaling most Baptist preachers.

More than all that, Johnson is thankful he is still in the league. He understood early on how he was viewed and what he needed to do to stick around.

"When I first came in the NBA, I couldn't make a lay-up," he says. "I was strictly a passer. So I had to work on finishing in the lane. I had to work on getting an eighteen-foot jump shot to be effective in the NBA. . . . You have to get out there and practice. As you practice more, you get more confidence. Life is about confidence. Life is about building up confidence in yourself."

"Avery has thrived on that," former coach Del Harris said. "He has just sneaked in and become a very good point guard, a very key player. I think by now people have to realize that you do have to guard Avery Johnson, and you do have to treat him with the same kind of respect other point guards get."

For Johnson, the pursuit of the R-word has been torturously slow but also enlightening.

Throughout his odyssey, two Johnson strong suits were constant—the speed to blow past even the NBA's more highly regarded point guards and a willingness to listen, work, and improve. Fortunately for Johnson, at least one key person noticed—Spurs coach and general manager Gregg Popovich, who signed the point guard to back-to-back long-term contracts (Johnson had gone those first eight years with nothing more than a one-year deal).

"It's a story of perseverance—just hanging in there," says Johnson. "Every day you wake up is not going to be a great day, but it's still a good day because you are still alive. Basketball has not been everything that Avery Johnson is about, so the times that it was taken away, . . . I believed in myself. Even when basketball was taken away I still felt good about Avery Johnson. So, you just persevere.

"I just try to keep it all in perspective. I'm in a temporary job as it is. Hopefully if I live thirty years after this I gotta find something else to do."

Spurs fans hope that day does not come soon.

> "You wonder how they do it and you look to see the knack,
> you watch the foot in action, or the shoulder, or the back,
> but when you spot the answer where the higher glamours lurk,
> you'll find in moving higher up the laurel spire,
> that the most of it is practice and the rest of it is work."
> **Grantland Rice, Former Sportswriter**

Tom Lehman

In 1989, Tom Lehman was practically broke. He had made no money to speak of as a golfer. He was down to his last three hundred dollars, which he and his wife, Melissa, decided to spend on entering a tournament in South Africa, to give this game one last shot.

That last shot became a shot in the arm, as Lehman won thirty thousand dollars at the tournament, setting off a new sense of confidence and a complete turnaround of his game. Among the upper echelon of players throughout the 1990s, Lehman was named player of the year in 1996, when he won more than $1.7 million. His career earnings now exceed $7 million. So it seems that that three hundred dollars was a good investment.

"I wouldn't trade those years for anything," says Lehman. "I look back and there's nothing but good memories. It was difficult. You really had to want to play golf and get good in order to go through it. You have got to do whatever it takes. So I look back at that and say, 'We did it.' Melissa and I together, we did whatever we had to do to get the job done.

"I just wanted to get as good as I could possibly get. I didn't care if I never got rich or famous. I wanted to play because I wanted to be good. And I always believed that I had the ability to be a really good player."

The lessons Lehman learned during the days he nearly quit have been put to good use since he established himself as a consistent contender on the PGA Tour.

Four times, Tom Lehman has played in the final group of the U.S. Open. Four times, he's watched someone else win. For Lehman, the Open is more like open wounds. For four consecutive Junes—1995, 1996, 1997, and 1998—Lehman either held or shared the lead after three rounds. On each occasion, he ended up making a consolation speech to the media.

It was 1996 that provided the most interesting Open drama. For the final round, Lehman was paired with his friend Steve Jones. They were deadlocked after 71 holes, two pals on a stroll that would reward only one. Jones shot 69 and looked to the heavens. Lehman shot 71 and looked to next year—again.

But it is what happened en route to the final score that typifies Lehman's outlook on his 0-for-Opens. It was Lehman who kept Jones calm as he played in this first major championship since the 1991 British Open.

He gave words of encouragement to Jones as they played together. He broke the ice as they walked down the first fairway.

"Twice during that final round, Tom quoted from the Book of Joshua to settle me down," Jones recalls. "He said, 'You know the Lord wants us to be courageous and strong, for that is the will of God.' I really got to thinking then. I said. 'Yeah, that is right.'"

"If I saw Steve Jones just walking down the street at home, I would walk over, we'd talk, and I would say something nice to him," says Lehman. "If I could encourage him in some way, I probably would. So if we are playing the last round of the U.S. Open, it shouldn't be any different.

"He was nervous; I was nervous, but he hadn't been in that situation for a long time. . . . So I gave him that verse from Joshua that says: 'Be bold and strong! Banish fear and doubt. For remember, the Lord your God is with you wherever you go.' [1:9 TLB]. It was just so he would know that no matter what happened throughout that entire day, that God loved him, God was with him just like he is with everybody else."

This fickle game has met its match in Lehman's faith. The same faith that carried him through the lean years has given him perspective on his Open travails.

"For a while, my entire life revolved around golf," Lehman says. "When I got my priorities straight, that changed. It used to be golf first. Now it's God first, family second, golf third."

But no one can question Lehman's tenacity, endurance, and determination. Jim Flick, his teacher since 1990, says, "There isn't anyone who learns from disappointments as much as Tom Lehman." To which Lehman replies, "I've had a lot more dealings with disappointment than the other extreme."

The disappointments include a heartbreaking loss at the 1994 Masters.

"That was always my greatest fear," Lehman said. "To die and have it written on my tombstone: Here Lies Tom Lehman; He Couldn't Win the Big One."

But a month after Jones' triumph in 1996—at Royal Lytham and St. Annes for the British Open—Lehman's day arrived. He won the major he least expected to win. Sometimes, even golf can be fair.

When average golf fans root for Tom Lehman, they're pulling for a part of themselves, realizing how much hard work it required for him to make it on the PGA Tour. It doesn't hurt that Lehman's integrity and values hit home with fans. When they look at Lehman, decked out in his familiar Dockers and with a receding hairline, they see an image of what they would look like as a pro.

"A lot more people are going to go through the school of hard knocks than people who jump right in and are instant successes. Both ways are just fine. But I think more people can relate to going through some tough times before the good times," he says.

"That is where you have to keep the balance in your life. You are a golfer; that's what you do. Obviously you want to be good, but there are things beyond golf that are far more important, and that is who you are on the inside."

"Quitters never win, and winners never quit."
Bob Zuppke, Former Illinois Football Coach

Jackie Robinson

On April 15, 1947, Jackie Robinson crossed the white line—the white chalk line that outlined the baseball diamond, and the line of color separation that kept America's game in bondage to bigotry.

But Robinson didn't just break baseball's color barrier by becoming the first black major leaguer of the century. He also set into motion the most sweeping social changes in the nation's history. For the first time, America had a black hero at the very center of the country's consciousness. More than his talent, it was Robinson's resolve that made that possible.

Brooklyn Dodgers president Branch Rickey was the visionary who signed Robinson with the intent of seeing him as the torchbearer for integration in baseball. Rickey prepared his young player for the barrage he would have to endure in '47, knowing the first black player would have to survive all manner of provocation—emotional and physical. In Robinson, he saw a man with the fortitude to withstand even the harshest of opposition.

Robinson swallowed hard and endured the most vicious treatment any athlete has ever faced. He was the target of racial epithets and flying cleats, of hate letters and death threats, of pitchers throwing at his head and legs, and catchers spitting on his shoes. In the midst of this chaos, there was a circus-like quality to Dodgers games, with Robinson on display. Large crowds, including many blacks, cheered his pop-ups and ground-outs. The daily papers singled him out as the "black meteor," the "sepia speedster," the "stellar Negro," the "muscular Negro," the "lithe Negro," and "dusky Robbie."

"More eyes were on Jackie than on any rookie who ever played," recalls Rex Barney, a Brooklyn reliever that year.

As the first days unfolded, the pressure increased. Police investigated letters that had threatened Robinson's life. "He turned them over to me," announced Rickey. "Two of the notes were so vicious that I felt they should be investigated."

The pressure also involved Robinson's lodging when the Dodgers arrived in Philly. The players usually stayed at the Benjamin Franklin Hotel, but when they arrived there, the hotel manager turned them away, telling the team's traveling secretary, Harold Parrott, "Don't bring your team back here while you have any Nigras with you!" The Dodgers ended up staying at the Warrick. Parrott later wrote that Robinson looked pained over the incident, "knowing we were pariahs because of him."

In the midst of such turmoil, Robinson soldiered on. "I'm just going along, playing the best ball I know and doing my best to make good," he said. "Boy, it's rugged."

Robinson eventually won over most observers. He was named National League Rookie of the Year in '47 and went on to be voted the league's Most Valuable Player two years later. During his ten seasons, the Dodgers won six pennants and a world championship. He was the team's catalyst, a second baseman who found numerous ways to beat the opponent. He was daring and exuded a competitive fire. He won a batting title, drove in 100 runs in a season, stole home 19 times, and hardly ever struck out.

Robinson's middle infield partner, shortstop Harold "Pee Wee" Reese, remembering his friend's display of courage, said, "I don't know any other ballplayer who could have done what he did. To be able to hit with everybody yelling at him. He had to block all that out. To do what he did has got to be the most tremendous thing I've ever seen in all of sports."

"I'm not concerned with you liking or disliking me," Robinson said. "All I ask is that you respect me as a human being."

Respect came from the entire nation, as did admiration. Robinson had not only carried the future of the game on his back, but also the future of an entire people. The sense of burden was not lost on him, yet he never showed it publicly. In so doing, he gave to baseball and his country more than he had ever dreamed possible.

"You're never a loser until you quit trying."
Pete Post, Illinois Special Olympics

Lake Speed

The true test of a man's character comes when he is beset with road-blocks and there seems no possible way he can reach his goal, yet he keeps striving.

The world of NASCAR provides a constant challenge for the driver—both mentally and physically—to break from the pack and make a name for himself. One such driver made a name by consistently overcoming obstacles. And an unusual name it is.

When Lake Speed joined the stock car circuit, he had already won six national championships in carting. Without top equipment, or sometimes even a sponsor, Speed was successful on the Winston Cup circuit because of his perseverance, tenacity, and persistence. He kept pressing on toward his goal even when the wins didn't come.

Lake Speed won only one race in his NASCAR career, yet he never wavered on what's important to him, nor forgot what a long journey it's been.

"You go through a lot of things in life where you have your own per-ception about what the future's going to be," said Speed. "Believe me, after my first win at Darlington in 1985, things did not work out the way I had them envisioned. I said, 'OK, fine, now we've got this behind us. Now we can go on and win a lot more, and everything will be fine,' but it didn't work out that way at all. Our season took a dive after that.

"It was one of those times when things just didn't work out the way that you thought they should. At the end of the year, sponsors didn't come, and we went into almost a tailspin from there with our career for quite some time before it started coming back up and things started looking good again.

"I love to see guys come out of nowhere and win championships. It doesn't matter whether it's basketball, baseball, football, racing, or whatever it is. I think that the majority of the people are sitting out

191

there, and, in their heart of hearts, they've got to pull for the guy that doesn't have everything behind him, doesn't have that support. So, you have hope.

"I hope that, if nothing else, my career and the life that I've led gives other people hope. Maybe some people who don't think that the odds are in their favor, and maybe they aren't in their favor, but yet it makes no difference. Just because the odds are stacked against you, it just does not mean you can't be victorious and you can't be an overcomer, whether it's in a career or whether it's in life itself. They can still be overcomers, and they can still be triumphant if they'll just continue to persevere."

> **"Champions keep playing until they get it right."**
> **Billie Jean King, Former Tennis Champion**

Paul Wylie

He knew in his heart he could skate well. Not win a medal necessarily—that was never the goal—but skate well. So twenty-seven-year-old Paul Wylie stayed on in amateur figure skating long after his peers had retired or turned pro. Stayed on past the 1988 Olympics, in which he finished tenth. Stayed on past the 1990–91 world championships in which he finished tenth and eleventh, respectively. Stayed on to skate in the 1992 Albertville Games despite all too often being a disappointment waiting to happen. Stayed on when others said it was time to turn his attention to something else. Stayed on and proved them all wrong.

In Albertville in 1992, in the most surprising and uplifting performance of his life, Wylie showed nine judges, nine thousand wildly approving spectators, and a worldwide television audience what his coaches, friends, and family had known for years—that here was a singularly talented skater whose gift was all the rarer because it was steeled by extraordinary determination.

Wylie's quiet belief in himself was sometimes misinterpreted as an unwillingness to face reality. Make no mistake, though; that resolve earned him a silver medal—many observers actually thought he should have won the gold—which capped an Olympic experience that Wylie later referred to as "serendipity."

Wylie had long been admired in the skating community for his intelligence, friendliness, and artistry. People rooted for him even though he was known as a "practice skater." Yet, they never thought he could win.

But in Albertville, he skated his short program perfectly, with the grace and dazzling spins and footwork that his fans have admired for years. In the long program, he followed favorites Kurt Browning and Victor Petrenko. Browning stumbled and Petrenko was flat. Still, the judges gave Petrenko high marks, seemingly determined to make him the first male singles skater from the former Soviet Union to win a gold medal.

Wylie was better. He skated by far the most compelling program of the night. He mesmerized the audience with dynamic spins, dramatic lines, and flawless timing, and brought the audience to their feet.

"I did allow myself to think, for about a half hour, how it would feel to win the bronze," Wylie said afterward. "How it would change my life and vindicate my decision to stay in the sport after Calgary. Now I have a silver medal.

"I wanted to stick around so I could have a good Olympics. And that was my goal for the whole four years. It wasn't necessarily the placement or medal, although that would have been nice, but it was mostly just to skate well.

"The silver medal God enabled me to win is to this day a sort of unprecedented, unrepeated feat, and it wasn't my doing. I am the only person in skating history who medaled in the Olympics without also being a national champion."

Kurt Warner

He is a family man and a man of God, an out-of-nowhere sensation whose story was called by announcer Al Michels, "too schmaltzy even for Hollywood." But on the football field, Kurt Warner is the quintessential quarterback—a leader who wants the ball in his hands when everything is on the line, as he showed the world in Super Bowl XXXIV.

In a storybook season, Warner came from football oblivion into the public consciousness and the football record books in 1999, leading the St. Louis Rams to the NFL championship and, in the process, proving that some dreams really do come true. It was the most spectacular and significant rise of any one player during one NFL season in history.

Warner's story is about perseverance, overcoming significant obstacles, and being in the right place at the right time. It's also all about great things happening in the life of a genuinely good human being.

Kurt Warner's odyssey reached a moment of truth zenith during the 1999 preseason. The Rams had signed free-agent quarterback Trent Green away from the Washington Redskins to lead the team in what they felt could be a breakthrough season. But Green went down with a season-ending knee injury in the Rams' next-to-last exhibition game, and the team was suddenly placed into Warner's hands.

"We were in shock when Green went down," says Rams offensive line coach Jim Hanifan. "We had centered everything around him. He was the quarterback we wanted—and then this, to face the season with a backup."

No one on the Rams coaching staff knew what to expect—nor did the players, fans, or anyone else. Few people outside of the Rams' organization had even heard of Warner. Worse than a no-name, he was often confused with former Seattle Seahawks running back Curt Warner, who had retired in 1990.

But by the end of the 1999 season, everyone in the sports world had become very familiar with this man and his journey.

Kurt Warner's unlikely odyssey to NFL stardom began in his lone year as a starting quarterback at Division I-AA Northern Iowa, where he sat the bench for four years. When he finally got his shot in 1993, as a fifth-year senior, he led the Panthers to the NCAA Division I-AA semifinals and was named first-team All-Gateway Conference, throwing for 2,747 yards and 17 touchdowns.

That performance earned him a free-agent tryout with the Green Bay Packers in 1994, where he was cut after running just ten plays in six weeks. With Brett Favre, Mark Brunell, and Ty Detmer in camp, Warner didn't stand a chance of making it, nor was he ready. Once, Steve Marriucci, then the Packers quarterbacks' coach, told him to go into a minicamp scrimmage, but Warner felt so unprepared that he refused.

"There were obviously some good quarterbacks there," says Warner. "From a mental standpoint I felt that I had a ways to go after only playing one year in college, just to get oriented to the system and to be able to pick up the offense. I knew it was going to take me a while within a system . . . to really get comfortable with everything that I could do, and the speed and quickness of the game. But from a physical standpoint, I felt that I definitely could play."

Warner went home to Cedar Falls, Iowa. He moved in with the parents of then girlfriend Brenda Carney and took a job stocking shelves at a twenty-four-hour supermarket. He continued to prepare for his shot at the NFL, working out and studying football film at his alma mater each day before heading off to work at night. There wasn't much time for sleep.

At the Hy-Vee store, he happily took home $5.50 an hour, while telling coworkers he would someday be playing football again.

"I think inside they were probably thinking, 'There's probably no way; I mean this guy's working in a supermarket—how's he ever going to play in the NFL?'" says Kurt. "They listened to me and humored me at the time, but I'm sure deep down nobody really expected me to be able to get to the point where I'm at today. I can't blame them. It's a strange story. If I was looking at things from the outside, I would probably have thought the same things as they did."

Still, celebrity beyond the check-out counter did come. Out of the blue, the Iowa Barnstormers of the Arena Football League called. At first, Kurt wasn't thrilled about the prospect of playing eight-man football, but he figured it was better than not playing at all. He struggled initially because he lacked the speed and agility needed for the quick scoring game. But he adapted and became an Arena ball star, passing for 10,164 yards and 183 touchdowns, and leading the Barnstormers to two Arena Bowls in three seasons.

He had a tryout scheduled with the Chicago Bears in 1997. But it was canceled after Kurt's elbow on his throwing arm swelled to the size of a baseball, thanks to a spider bite suffered on his Jamaican honeymoon.

While his quest for the bigger and better game seemed at a road block, Warner refused to be discouraged and clung to his dream of playing in the NFL, even when it seemed he didn't have a prayer.

"I've always believed in myself," says Warner. "I always believed that I had the talent to get to this level and to be successful. . . . I was just waiting for the opportunity. I was waiting for that door to open, to get a chance to prove to everybody that I could do it."

Despite his Arena League success, Kurt couldn't get another look from an NFL team. But then Al Luginbill, the coach of NFL Europe's Amsterdam Admirals came calling. Warner told Luginbill he'd rather keep playing for the Barnstormers for $65,000 a year than go abroad, unless an NFL team signed him and optioned him to Europe for training. A dozen teams told Luginbill no, until Charley Armey, the Rams' personnel director, decided to take a chance.

Warner then had what he considered a "horrible" tryout with St. Louis.

But during that look-see, he gained two key backers, namely Armey and assistant coach Mike White, who persuaded the team to sign him. The Rams then sent Kurt to Europe to play for Amsterdam in the spring of 1998.

It was a smart move. Warner led NFL Europe in passing yardage (2,101) and touchdowns (15), and gained a new level of confidence. His experiences off the field with the open culture in Amsterdam challenged the conservative quarterback and prepared him to be a leader.

"I think the Lord put me there for a reason—to test my faith and see where I was so that I would be ready for the situation that I'm in now," says Warner.

Warner returned to the States in the summer to compete for a spot on the Rams' roster. He barely held on to the third-string quarterback job for St. Louis that fall, nearly being released in favor of the well-traveled Wil Furrer. While the Rams were going 4-12 in 1998, Warner saw mop-up action in just one game, completing 4 of 11 passes for 39 yards. His future was still very much in doubt.

At the Rams 1999 training camp, Warner moved into the No. 2 quarterback spot, to back up Green. Rams head coach Dick Vermeil assumed Warner was good enough for the team to get by with should Green get injured. But he never expected a twenty-eight-year-old journeyman to play well enough to be the reason the Rams won.

Warner, with all of his minor-league experience, burst onto the NFL scene like a seasoned veteran. His success was clearly not of the flash-in-the-pan variety. Personnel people from around the league watched in amazement as Warner lit up the NFL's best defenses.

What they saw was a player of average size (6'2", 220 pounds) and speed but with impressive arm strength and great touch, and the ability to make all the throws—from laser-like deep outs across the field, to feathery-soft corner lobs, to on-the-money long strikes. Few quarterbacks in the game today can make the deep throw with any consistency. Warner does it with regularity, going over the top of the secondary and dropping the ball in to his receiver in the tightest of coverage.

They saw a man with maturity and leadership intangibles; equipped with pinpoint accuracy, poise under fire, toughness, and an uncanny adeptness for reading defenses very quickly—something that takes rookies three to four years to learn. Playing Arena ball, with its small field and wide-open style, Warner had become proficient at making quick throws, based on even quicker reads. His accuracy is uncanny. When his receivers come out of their breaks, the ball is usually right there.

They also saw a student of the game with a voracious appetite for watching film and an ability to learn. He's known for seeing something once on film or live and never forgetting it. He knows where every receiver should be on every play.

And they saw a quarterback with an unusual feel for the game. Warner has such a complete grasp of his offense and opposing defenses that he most often knows what he will do before the ball is snapped, making decisions on the way to the line of scrimmage. He rarely changes plays at the line, instead simply recognizing that a particular option is most likely to work and then going for it. Such poise is rare for any quarterback, much less one without NFL experience. But then, for Warner, pressure isn't a zone blitz—it's going to Amsterdam to prove himself.

In the end, 1999 was a year in which Warner generated the second-finest statistical season by a quarterback in NFL history. He completed 65 percent of his passes, and threw for 4,353 yards and 41 touchdowns (in league history, only Dan Marino has thrown for more TDs in a single season). His passing rating was the third highest all-time. He led the Rams from their 4-12 mark in '98 to a 13-3 record and a spot in the Super Bowl, and was named the NFL's Player of the Year.

At the Super Bowl, Warner continued his mastery, eclipsing Joe Montana's eleven-year-old passing record by throwing for 414 yards. He completed 24 of 45 passes and tossed two touchdowns, including the game winner with 1:54 remaining in the contest, and was named the game's Most Valuable Player.

"When you're a little kid, you dream about holding the trophy up after throwing the winning touchdown, or scoring the winning touchdown," said Warner. "This is what it's all about. It's what we play for all these years.

"To be the starting quarterback in the Super Bowl, to have won the MVP . . . you can't ever really think that's going to happen in your first year. But I've always had confidence. I've always felt I could play well."

"He is not a one-year flash-in-the-pan," said Vermeil following the '99 season. "I've never seen someone like him. And I've been around this game a long time."

Through it all, Warner remained unfazed, humble to the core, and ever insistent on putting the focus elsewhere.

"My faith is the most important thing," says Warner. "Everything that happens to me is just a platform for me to share my faith and to share what I believe. God's bigger than a football game, and he wants to touch people's lives. That's what my goal is, and he gives me the platform."

Warner's unflappable demeanor comes directly from the perspective he gains through his faith, and the situation at home. Because of that, perspective is one thing Warner has in abundance.

Kurt's ten-year-old adopted son, Zachary, suffered brain damage and blindness as an infant. In 1996, Zachary's mother, Brenda, whom Kurt was dating at the time, lost both of her parents when their home in Arkansas was leveled by a tornado. Kurt married Brenda in 1997 and legally adopted her two children—Zachary and Jesse—shortly thereafter. He has been a father to the two in every sense of the word, loving them like his own.

"I've just got an unbelievable family," says Warner. "My kids, they mean the world to me."

Zachary is a walking miracle. His condition was caused when his biological father accidentally dropped him in the bathtub. The baby's head slammed against the side of the tub, scrambling his brains and rupturing his retinas. Doctors initially told Brenda, who at the time of the accident was working as an intelligence officer in the Marines, that her son would most likely not survive, and if he did, he would probably never walk, talk, or even sit up again. But, like Kurt, Brenda refused to give up. For the next seventeen days she sat in a rocking chair next to Zachary's hospital crib, watching as her infant son suffered repeated seizures. She recited Bible verses and asked God to perform a miracle.

Ten years later, Brenda's prayers have been answered. Zachary is only partially blind, able to read words and see objects that are held close to his face, and he gets around fairly well. He is mainstreamed in many classes and is enrolled in special education classes to learn math, spelling, and how to tell time.

"I don't think of him as disabled," says Brenda. "He's got it in him. He just has to work a lot harder than other kids." Much like his adoptive father.

"My son is everything. He's the most special child I've ever met, with the things he's been through and that he does on a daily basis," says Kurt. "Everything is a struggle for him. You know, for me to go throw three interceptions on the football field, to get down on myself, to worry about that, to me is a joke because his life is so difficult, and it just gives me a humbling sense, and it gives me a sense of what's really important in life."

Now the Warner family celebrates the date of the accident, September 6, calling it Zachary's Day.

"What point is there to hate life?" says Brenda rhetorically. "What good does that bring to our children's lives? We need to help make them better people. You do that by loving them."

And love them Kurt and Brenda have done indeed—both Zachary and Jesse, along with a son they had together, one-year-old Kade. Another child is due in 2001.

"I can go home every day and not worry about what people think from an MVP standpoint," says Warner, "or what people think from the standpoint that I didn't play very well on the football field. I know that my family's going to be there loving me. And to them I'm just 'Dad.' And to me that's the most important thing."

"Kurt's the most grounded person you'll ever meet," says Rams cornerback Todd Lyght.

That grounding is important in light of Warner's instant celebrity. His face has shown up nearly everywhere since the Super Bowl. He's done the talk-show and banquet circuits, promoted products, and spoke at a Billy Graham crusade. He now receives about one thousand pieces of mail a week. And he even has a breakfast cereal, Warner's Crunch Time.

"Kurt Warner is Kurt Warner," Vermeil said following the Super Bowl triumph. "He is not a fairy tale. This is real life. He is an example of what we all like to believe in on and off the field. He is an example of persistence and believing in himself and a deep faith. He was willing to work and play a subordinate role until he got his opportunity. What else can you write? He is a book, he is a movie, the guy."

"The biggest thing I've learned is that the Lord's got a plan for me," says Warner. "We don't always know what that plan is going to be, or how we're going to get to where he wants us to be—but I've learned a lot along the way. I've learned about perseverance. I've learned about being humble; being able to enjoy everything . . . and to thank the Lord for everything that I've gotten.

"I wouldn't change anything from how it has turned out. I've become a better player and a better person throughout the experiences . . . . I wouldn't change anything. This is as good a script as I could have ever written."

> **A champion knows his talents
> and success are God-given, not
> self-developed or endowed by others.**

CHAPTER 12

FAITH

To me, faith is everything.

The relationship I have with God through Christ is based on faith. To come to God, you have to earnestly believe. To see God, you must be one that believes he exists and that he rewards those who seek him. So faith is the foundation of my existence as I know it today in relationship with God through Christ.

Faith is the anchor of my life. It's the foundation on which I base my thoughts. It's the foundation that influences and controls my attitude. It's the foundation that fosters the way I approach relationships and the way I approach my resources.

There's just no way I can compartmentalize my life because faith is the foundation of it. It's like a house. The foundation is part of the whole house. You don't see it in every room, but it's part of every room.

That's the way my faith is in my life. It's the foundation. Every aspect of my life is impacted by, and built around, that personal relationship I have with God through Christ. **—C. K.**

"People always talk about my great seasons, but they don't want to talk about my Christianity. A lot of times I wish people would ask me, 'Tell me about your faith in God.'"

Cris Carter, Minnesota Vikings Receiver

Ron Brown

The most important recruit Ron Brown ever signed never played a single game.

After months of wooing, Brown, the Nebraska University receivers coach signed Victor Stachmus, a top football recruit from the state of Oklahoma in 1988. Stachmus, a six-foot-five-inch, 250 pounder from McAlester High School, whom Brown lured away from the rival Oklahoma Sooners, was excited about playing for the Big Red.

But the happy news turned to distress later that year when Stachmus was diagnosed with acute lymphoblastic leukemia. Doctors did not give him much chance of living more than twelve months.

At the first opportunity, Brown flew to California to visit Stachmus in the hospital. He knew he needed to speak with the young man about faith in Christ.

The day when Brown arrived, Stachmus was so sick that he had been inactive and barely alert; he had slept most of the day. But when Brown walked into the room, Stachmus was awake and alert, as if the moment had been provided for. Stachmus looked up in pleasant surprise and greeted the man who had treated him like a son during the recruiting process.

"Coach Brown!" he said.

"Hey Victor," Brown responded quietly.

"Did you have a good trip?" Stachmus asked in a weak voice. "Are you comfortable?"

"Yes, I'm fine, Victor," the coach replied, amazed at the young man's selfless attitude.

Brown sat down next to Stachmus' bed and grabbed his limp right hand. The boy's face was pale, with a sick greenish tint. He appeared close to death. But Brown, caring now not about a football player's future, but rather for a young man's eternity, knew he still had time to ask Stachmus some important questions. The room was silent. Brown spoke.

"Victor, what are you thinking right now?" he asked.

"Coach, I'm scared," Stachmus responded.

"Vic, there's not much I can do for you," Brown said. "But would you like to pray?"

"Yeah, I sure would, Coach," said Stachmus.

Brown and Stachmus closed their eyes and talked to God. Brown prayed with fervor for his young friend. Stachmus, although weak, managed to join Brown in communicating with his Creator. When the two men finished, Brown noticed tears rolling down Stachmus' cheeks. He knew God had touched the sick young man's spirit.

Stachmus smiled.

"Thanks, Coach!" he said. "I feel great. I want you to know that I'm not afraid to die anymore. I'll never forget you." He paused for a breath and continued. "I want a Bible. I want a whole Bible like yours."

On January 23, 1989, just two weeks after he had prayed with Stachmus in the hospital, Brown received word from Stachmus' mother that the young man had died. With his new Bible at his side.

"To have your name inscribed up there is greater yet by far,
than all the halls of fame down here and every man-made star.
This crowd on earth, they soon forget the heroes of the past;
they cheer like mad until you fall and that's how long you last.
I tell you, friend, I would not trade my name however small,
if written there beyond the stars in that celestial hall.
For any famous name on earth or glory that they share,
I'd rather be an unknown here and have my name up there."
Unknown

Irving Fryar

Irving Fryar was born into a household of faith. His two sisters, Faith and Hope, sang in the choir; his mother a was a devout congregant of a church that was just a post pattern away from the door of their Mt. Holly, New Jersey, home. From the first day, Fryar crossed up his parents—something he would repeat many times later on—who were expecting a girl they would name Charity and round out the trio. Instead, they were blessed with Irving.

The name doesn't quite roll off the tongue the same way as those of his sisters. His childhood was filled with brawls defending his name. Be a boy named Irving in New Jersey and you better know how to defend yourself. It was a rough existence, but not as rough as it would become.

Fryar's father worked two jobs, and when he was home, he was usually drunk or mad, or both. Somehow Fryar fought his way into a football scholarship at Nebraska, where he became a high-profile receiver and kick returner and a bona-fide star.

Off the field Fryar became involved in drugs and was accused in one news report of intentionally dropping a pass in the Orange Bowl to throw the game (no charges were brought). Still, he became the No. 1 pick of the 1984 draft—the first receiver ever so selected—by the New England Patriots. By his own admission, he was a time bomb ready to explode.

The Patriots expected Fryar to lead them to NFL glory, but at the time he was incapable of leading himself anywhere but into trouble, much less leading a team. Despite his becoming an all-Pro in his second season in the league and helping the Pats to the Super Bowl in 1985, the team grew impatient with Fryar's immaturity, poor work ethic, and bad decisions.

He would disappear for days at a time on cocaine binges; he was pulled over for carrying a rifle loaded with hollow point bullets; he was caught packing a pistol in his cowboy boots during a bar brawl. He even toyed with the idea of suicide. After a while nobody trusted Fryar, and he trusted no one. It seemed nothing could reach Irving Fryar.

"At that point in my life, I didn't like myself. I didn't like other people. No one really had anything good to say about me, and I had nothing good to think about myself," said Fryar. "Even though I was a professional athlete in the NFL, first-round draft pick, had money, had whatever I wanted . . . I was one of the worst people in my mind that I could ever think of."

Just when it didn't seem like anything could save Irving Fryar from his own self-destruction, a "miracle," as Fryar calls it, happened. It came in the form of a baby girl the Fryars knew was sent by God.

Adrianne Fryar was born on April 22, 1990, with two holes in her heart, two arteries unconnected, and a valve missing. For once Irving had someone besides himself on which to focus. He started changing for his daughter—trying to keep clean from drugs and alcohol. At the same time, it also looked like Adrianne might make it. Fryar thought there was a connection.

One evening in October 1990, Fryar decided to give himself a break and go to a club with teammate Hart Lee Dykes. A little after 1:00 A.M., Dykes ended up in a fight with five bar patrons outside the club.

When the police arrived, they arrested Fryar for carrying a pistol without a permit. He spent the night in jail (the charges were later dropped). The police took his clothes, left him with a rap on the head, and locked him in a cell. Nobody came to get him that night. Fryar was left alone, bleeding and naked. His life had hit rock bottom.

"Now here I am, a person who supposedly had been getting it together . . . and I sat in that jail cell that night, bleeding, with no clothes on, and it was cold," says Fryar. "And Jesus came into that jail cell. And he let me know that, 'I don't care what it is you've done; I don't care how bad you feel about yourself—here I am. You've got to give me everything.'

"And that night, I accepted Jesus and I rededicated myself because I had no where else to go. I was at the bottom of the barrel. The only place I had to look was up. And I looked up and Christ was there for me."

Fryar now had somewhere to go, and he went there constantly. He studied two years to get his license as a Pentecostal minister and began to preach. His play improved. And his daughter was making a complete recovery.

Things got even better when New England traded him to the Miami Dolphins, where he could now be on the receiving end of some serious passes from quarterback Dan Marino. To Fryar, it was the NFL equivalent of heaven—a chance to really show what he was made of.

With the Dolphins, Fryar returned to all-Pro form, catching more passes than in any previous season. Almost equally as surprising, he was cited by the Dolphins for his work ethic and for being an example to younger players by being voted the team's most inspirational player. When that word got out, players from around the league were asking if this was the same Irving Fryar. Indeed it was . . . but then again, it wasn't. He was a new man.

Fryar moved on to Philadelphia in 1995, where for the next three seasons he was the leader of an Eagles offense and became a Pro Bowler again. He set the franchise single-season reception mark in 1996 with 88 catches, and seemed to get better with age. Away from the field his reputation grew as a man who returned from the deepest darkness to a life of influencing others for God.

He was nominated by his peers for the NFL Man of the Year Award and was selected, again by his peers, as the recipient of the 1998 Bart Starr Award for character. It was a far cry from his early days, and a welcome change.

"I gave up pain," he says. "I gave up sleepless nights. I gave up friend-lessness. I gave up a lot of stuff that was just negative in my life, and that all turned to positive."

By 1998, Fryar had not only climbed all the way out of life's gutter, but he had also climbed into the top ten all-time pass catchers in NFL history. In 1999 and 2000, Fryar continued that ascent with the Washington Redskins, by the end of the 2000 season moving into the top-five receivers all-time with more than 800 catches. The once all-Pro mess-up was even being spoken of as a possible Hall of Fame candidate. And a changed man.

"My life is more fun, more gratifying, more satisfying, more whole and rounded than it's ever been," Fryar says. "I'm having more fun because I can wake up in the morning and I can look in the mirror and know that I'm doing the right things. That I'm on the right track. That I'm working to be a great father. I'm working to be a great husband. I'm playing football the best way I know . . . because I'm doing the things that I'm supposed to do."

> **"I learned very early in life you're always going to find people who are going to tell you what you can't do. My mother told me I could do anything I wanted to if the Lord was with me. I always believed that."**
> **Mike Singletary, Chicago Bears Hall-of-Fame Linebacker**

Barbara Nicklaus

For those interested in seeing an example of a professional athlete's wife who is a model of faith, many who know her would point to Barbara Nicklaus. For forty years, the wife of golfing legend Jack Nicklaus, or "Momma Bear" as she is affectionately known, has been the strength behind the Nicklaus family, which includes five grown children.

While Jack has won eighteen major championships, he figures Barbara "has meant at least fifteen" to him, partly because of her undying support, and also because she has in the words of her husband, been "99 percent responsible" for raising their kids.

Barbara says her faith in Christ and her prayer life have been the source of strength for her during a challenging lifestyle. As such, she has been a true picture of humility and self-sacrifice, something that has not gone unnoticed.

"She's really made her life second to mine," Jack told the *Palm Beach Post*. "She's never said, 'Jack we're going to do this.' She'll always say, 'We've got your schedule. We'll go do this. Then if we have time, we'll do the other.'"

For her lifetime of support and example, Barbara was given the inaugural PGA First Lady of Golf award in 1999.

> **"I wouldn't trade my position in Christ for a thousand NBA championship rings, for a thousand Hall of Fame rings, or for a hundred billion dollars."**
> **Pete Maravich, NBA Hall-of-Fame Guard**

Joe Girardi

After seven seasons behind the plate for the Chicago Cubs and Colorado Rockies, Joe Girardi left the National League following the 1995 season in a trade that sent him to baseball's biggest market and most volatile atmosphere in New York City. The Peoria, Illinois, native and former Northwestern University star knew he was about to put on Yankee pinstripes, but he had little idea about what else to expect. Still, he and his wife, Kim, were excited about the change.

"I was in a comfort zone in Colorado," says Girardi. "Getting traded was a faith-builder, and as the season progressed, I began to see what God was doing in our lives.

"When I was traded to New York, I knew it was going to be hard," Girardi says. "The fans and media loved the catcher from the year before, Mike Stanley. I was booed before I even put on a uniform. Once the season started, I felt even worse. I didn't know anyone, and I was playing poorly.

"Kim met me on a road trip and really handed me the truth. She reminded me that God had put me in New York for a reason, and I needed to seek him. The next day Don Zimmer, one of my coaches, gave me the same speech. I couldn't believe it. I started to feel more comfortable being myself, and I asked God to give me some kind of sign to show me why he had me in New York."

The signs came, but not necessarily on the field. More often they were things happening in Joe and Kim's personal lives.

"I started to develop some friendships that were key to my growth as a man and as a Christian," says Girardi. "John Wetteland challenged me to grow in my faith. Andy Pettite was also a close friend. I grew more [that season] than all my other seasons combined."

Girardi soon became a part of a powerful movement among a group of Yankees players who were committed Christians. They studied the Bible together and created times on the road to help keep each other accountable. The group became the core of the team's sense of unity, which led to a cohesiveness on the field.

By the time the Yankees entered the playoffs in October of '96, the attitude on the team had intensified to a focus on a championship.

"We were in our zone," says Girardi. "God's zone. We prayed for each other. I prayed every day that, whatever happened, God would give me the strength to handle it. We prayed for the team and everyone on it. It took away the pressure and let us focus on the reality of what was happening."

Storybook endings do happen. The underdog Yankees beat the favored Atlanta Braves four games to two in the World Series, with Girardi pounding a clutch triple in the decisive game 6—a hit that led to the Yankees' victory.

When it was all over, there was Girardi running from behind the plate into the arms of Wetteland, who had registered the final out. The moment signified more than a championship, more than a ring or a winner's share. It embodied what had taken place all year as a group of grown men were bonded together through a common faith and united goal.

That scene was repeated for Girardi in 1998 and again in 1999, and included many of the same cast of characters. On each occasion, Girardi played a key role.

Prior to the 2000 season, Joe and Kim decided their time in the Big Apple was finished. Girardi accepted an offer from the Chicago Cubs to return home to the area where he grew up as a child, leaving the place where he grew up as a ballplayer. He knew that home was to be his next stop. And while being a part of three World Championships in New York was the apex of his professional career, Girardi knew it was not the ultimate source for his life.

"People think winning the World Series had the impact," says Girardi. "It is so much more than that. We are overwhelmed with God's goodness. I'm reminded of that every day. The World Series now is just on tape; God's reality is a daily event."

> "We're only here on earth for a short period of time.
> When I die and go to heaven, that's eternity. . . . Eternity is a long time.
> And my relationship with Jesus Christ guarantees me that eternity."
> **Kyle Petty, NASCAR Driver**

Jerry Schemmel

It was a crystal clear July day in 1989 when Jerry Schemmel, then deputy commissioner of the Continental Basketball Association, and his close friend Jay Ramsdell, commissioner of the league, boarded United Airlines flight No. 232, bound for Chicago.

Schemmel and Ramsdell were given the last two standby seats on the aircraft ready to depart from Denver. They were headed to Columbus, Ohio, where the CBA's draft of college players was to be held. It would be a short trip, one in which the two men intended to work out specifics of the league's television production package and make sure the draft went smoothly.

When they arrived at the airport for their early flight, they found their scheduled flight was canceled. They were forced to make adjustments and find a different way to get to Columbus. After a six-hour wait for an open flight, they finally found themselves on board an east-bound plane.

United 232 was the first flight with available space. Schemmel and Ramsdell made it on board but were not seated together. "When I plopped down in seat 23G," Schemmel recalls, "the thought occurred to me that I'd never been happier to sit down in an airplane in my entire life."

Those thoughts would quickly change.

An hour into the flight, the rear engine of the DC-10 exploded, causing complete hydraulic failure. The crew flew the crippled plane for forty-five minutes to Sioux City, Iowa, preparing for an emergency landing. The pilots had very little control of the plane.

"I began to pray, thanking God that my wife Diane was not with me," Schemmel recalls. "Then I began to take inventory of my life. 'Take me God, if you have to,' I quietly prayed. 'I'm ready.'"

The plane's captain, Al Haynes, flew the crippled aircraft using engine thrust—an unprecedented procedure. With no steering or brakes, the crew made arrangements with ground personnel in Sioux City to attempt landing the plane on a runway surrounded by cornfields.

Haynes gave the passengers a final message. He would give the command "Brace, Brace, Brace" thirty seconds before touchdown. And he added, "Folks, I'm not gonna kid anybody. This is going to be rough."

As the command to brace came from Haynes, Schemmel sensed this would be much worse than a crash landing. He realized it was more a case of an airplane falling out of the sky.

At 4:00 P.M.—thirty-seven minutes after the explosion of engine two, the DC-10 hit the runway.

As Schemmel struggled against the laws of physics, the section of the plane he was in flipped over and slid to its final stop in a cornfield.

"I was still upside down when the plane came to rest," says Schemmel. "The next moment I was standing up, with no detailed memory of how I managed to unbuckle the seat belt and ease to the floor—which was actually [now] the roof of the cabin."

Schemmel was struck by the chill of seeing passengers wandering around a dark cabin while others were dead, still strapped to their seats. These images were the first glimpses of what would later torture Schemmel in repeated nightmares.

After taking a few steps away from the airplane, Schemmel heard a muffled cry from inside the wreckage. It was the cry of a baby. He quickly headed back into the burning wreckage to see if he could find the child.

"I kept moving until I seemed to be standing right over the cries," says Schemmel. "Feeling the floor in front of me with my hands, I realized the child was buried beneath the debris. I reached into a hole, which I would later guess to be an overhead storage compartment grabbed an arm, and lifted the child out. I pressed the child's head against my chest and stepped back out onto the cornfield."

After running from the wreckage to an area where a few survivors sat, Schemmel handed the baby to a young women. "Would you please take this baby?" he said. "I don't know who she is or where her family is. I just grabbed her from the plane."

In all, 112 of the 296 passengers aboard perished, including Ramsdell.

The year that followed was a difficult one for Schemmel. Although he returned to work a week after the accident and even filled in as temporary commissioner, he was distraught. He couldn't seem to go back to a career tied to the grief of losing his good friend, so he quit.

One night in the depths of despair, Schemmel told his wife, Diane, he was about to lose it. She responded by telling him, "I get my strength from God," and then left the room.

In the ensuing moments, Schemmel had a realization that there was more to a relationship with God than just going to church on Sunday and offering emergency prayers as a troubled plane plummeted toward destruction. Right there, he prayed for God to change him, saying, "God, for the first time in my life I admit that I've been defeated. Please come into my life and help me because I can't do it on my own. Just come into my life. Please."

With a sense of hope and purpose restored over the ensuing weeks, Schemmel once again sought a job in basketball. Within two months he was hired by the NBA's Minnesota Timberwolves as their radio play-by-play announcer. Soon after, the same job opened up with the Denver Nuggets, and Schemmel was headed back to the city he and his wife loved.

He is, of course, flying again, almost weekly accompanying the Nuggets on their travel schedule. But now, more than a decade after his brush with death, Schemmel has overcome the once constant fear and flashbacks, and seen that even in that experience, there was blessing.

"The real reconciliation of the tragedy and the miracle that was United 232 happened for me exactly ten months after the crash, in the dim light of a bedroom as I sat slumped in a chair," says Schemmel. "It was when Diane spoke the words that were my turning point. The real reconciliation of Flight 232 was giving my life to God."

David Robinson

It is a classic example of David versus Goliath.

In this case, the David is David Robinson, the magnificent seven-foot-one-inch center for the San Antonio Spurs.

The Goliath is the huge bundle of expectations Robinson has faced ever since he came into the NBA in 1989.

No matter what Robinson accomplished over his first nine years in the league, it seemed his Goliath would not go away. What Robinson needed was a rock.

It's not as if Robinson had been a mediocre performer. In fact, he had been nothing short of phenomenal. In his first season, he was named NBA Rookie of the Year and helped the Spurs to one of the biggest single year turnarounds in pro basketball history. Without him in the 1988–89 season, the Spurs went 21-61. The following season, Robinson's first, they improved to 56-26, won the Midwest Division, and immediately became a title contender and one of the most feared teams in the NBA.

Robinson won a scoring championship in 1994. He was selected as the league's MVP in 1995. He led the league in rebounds in 1991; in blocked shots in 1992—the same year he was named the NBA's Defensive Player of the Year. In 1996, as part of the NBA's fiftieth anniversary celebration, Robinson was named one of the fifty greatest players in league history.

He became a fixture on the U.S. Olympic team, headlining efforts in 1988 in Seoul, Korea, 1992 in Barcelona, Spain, and 1996 in Atlanta, Georgia. He was the first male to be selected to three Olympic basketball teams and became the leading scorer and rebounder in U.S. Olympic history.

In San Antonio, his Spurs teams won an average of fifty-five games over his first seven seasons and won their division four times. But until 1999, there was still one thing Robinson had not accomplished, and it became the one thing he was known for. In his eight NBA seasons, David Robinson had not won a championship, and the critics wanted to know why.

The lingering doubt the media drummed up had implications to Robinson's heart. They were quick to label him "soft," telling the world he may be a fine player, but he obviously wasn't tough enough to win a title. The comparisons came to the game's other greats—Jabbar, Russell, Chamberlain, Malone, Olajuwon, West, Bird, Magic, and Jordan—all who won world championships.

What the media conveniently failed to remember, however, was that Chamberlain and West had each other, along with Elgin Baylor. Jabbar and Magic were also together, joined by James Worthy. Russell had Bob Cousy. Malone had Ralph Sampson. Olajuwon had a bevy of great outside shooters. Bird had Kevin McHale and Robert Parrish. Even Jordan had Scottie Pippen.

Robinson had Greg Anderson and Vinny Del Negro.

Actually, the Spurs did have some of what they needed to be a winner. There was underrated point guard Avery Johnson, Robinson's best friend on the team, and Sean Elliott, who could be counted on to knock down a key shot. And there were other elements of a team that could win, but they needed an offensive presence—a scorer—to take the heat off Robinson in order to become a championship team.

Until 1997, that is. That year, the Spurs won the lottery—NBA draft style—and found the missing piece to their championship puzzle. With the first selection in the draft that year, San Antonio selected collegiate Player-of-the-Year Tim Duncan, who many now consider the most complete player in the pro game.

The seven-foot Duncan gave the Spurs twin towers and gave the opposition twin headaches. He gave the Spurs a player opponents had to be concerned about and strategize against—both offensively and defensively. No longer could Houston, L. A., Utah, or Portland merely double-team Robinson in the playoffs and force someone else to beat them. Now, in that same situation, Duncan would do just that.

Robinson finally had his sidekick. But an unusual thing happened. Robinson stepped aside and let Duncan become the Spurs go-to guy. The rookie was the team's Jordan, Bird, or Magic. Robinson willingly played the Pippen, McHale, Worthy role. The megastar gave up the mega. He relinquished the glamour, the shots, and the celebrity for the good of the team. He played defense, blocked shots, battled toe-to-toe with the league's bullies, and grabbed the offensive garbage. Not only did he do it, and do it well, he did it without complaint.

Just two years earlier Robinson had signed the richest contract in pro sports history. Now he was playing second fiddle? It was like Pavarotti singing second tenor. Hemmingway ghost-writing a first-timer's novel. Bogart getting second billing. It was one of the most remarkable things ever seen in sport. And it paid off.

The Spurs, centering their offense around second-year player Duncan, brought the NBA title to the city of the Alamo in 1999 by defeating the New York Knicks.

Finally, David's Goliath had come down. And it happened because Robinson had become a David in every aspect of character the name possesses. He simply did what he clearly saw as being the right thing to do.

"How many superstars would've done it?" asks Spurs coach Gregg Popovich. "Not many."

"In today's NBA?" echoed teammate Sean Elliott. "I'd say none."

"I guess I just figured winning was more important than anything else I could do for the team," Robinson said.

Excuse me? For the *team?*

Most athletes deal with such a move with a scowl and vitriolic outbursts. Robinson responded with a smile and a helping hand. He immediately embraced Duncan.

His approach was exactly what you would hope to see from a true sportsman, which Robinson clearly is. He plunged into a two-year process of self-denial that put the Spurs in position to win the 1999 NBA title.

Robinson devoted himself, on and off the court, to mentoring Duncan and making him the best possible player. He was determined to fit himself in around Duncan's game. In effect, Robinson would pick up Duncan's crumbs, collecting his garbage and getting the ball every now and then. The go-to guy would become the go-from guy.

"We go out there, and we feel a great amount of trust for each other," said Robinson. "We believe in each other, and it's gotten to the point that every game is under our control. I love to give him assists. It's almost like if I give him the ball, it's automatic he's going to score."

"It wasn't a painless thing," Elliott said. "David had to make some adjustments. But near the end of the season, I saw it coming together."

Soft.

Unfortunately, the Admiral has had the S-word hung around his neck since 1995, when the top-seeded Spurs lost to the Houston Rockets in the Western Conference finals. The word had shown up with his name in the same sentence so often in newspaper columns, interviews, or highlight lead-ins, it seemed as if Robinson had taken it on as a hyphenated surname. *David Robinson-Soft.* That no one could or would define "soft" made the undertones even more cruel.

Slap your wife and/or girlfriend, sire a handful of children illegitimately, choke your coach, punch a fan in a bar, or spit on reporters, and you won't carry the tag *soft*. But preach abstinence, stay committed to your wife, practice hard, give to the needy, be a good dad, share your faith, and speak in complete sentences, *but don't win an NBA title* and see what happens. They'll call you *soft*.

"Here's a guy that gave $5 million [to a school]," said former teammate Doc Rivers, now coach of the Orlando Magic. "Nobody ever writes about that. Now, if he'd stolen $5 million . . . . "

"You don't win a rebounding award or a defensive player-of-the-year award in this league and be soft," says Popovich.

The problem for Robinson is that he is such a graceful athlete, that even when he is working hard, he appears placid—his tongue doesn't hang out, he doesn't yell at teammates or officials. He exhibits self-control on and off the court. That and the fact that he is a Christian tend to make him misunderstood.

Soft?

Tell me that a seven-foot-one, 250-pounder with a 32-inch waist, who is cut like a Greek statue and runs the court like a sprinter, then bangs it out inside with the likes of Shaq, Olajuwon, Mourning, and Ewing is not tough?

"It's very physical; there're big bodies out there all the time," says Robinson. "It makes it very tough mentally and physically because you know you can't go out there and have a mediocre night. So you have to be tough. You have to be tough-minded and you have to be tough physically. Physically because you have got 300-pound guys banging on you, and mentally because the pressure is there every night to perform.

"I'm not friends with anybody on the court. As a matter of fact, I don't even like guys on the court. You have to understand, it's your team against their team. It's me or them; only one of us can survive."

That sounds quite a bit like Bill Russell.

Robinson was supposed to be Russell with a better shot, which he has proven to be. He is a great defensive player and phenomenal shot blocker, who up until 1999 had been asked to carry the load offensively as well. Perhaps no one player in NBA history had ever been asked to carry as much of a burden for his team.

For the first time, in 1999, Robinson was asked to play like Bill Russell. And the Spurs won the title, compiling one of the finest seasons in NBA history.

Robinson's character was also seen during the 1995 season, when his contract was about to end. Spurs owner Peter Holt would have been faced with an open bidding war after the 1996–97 season to keep his star, who was highly coveted by a number of teams, including the well-heeled Lakers.

Instead of going for the big bucks on the open market, Robinson made sure Holt didn't face such a financial crisis, agreeing to a well-below market value contract of $66 million for six years late in 1995. The contract enabled the Spurs to have salary cap room to survive, and eventually sign Duncan.

It's hard to imagine another star player who is not only less infatuated with himself than Robinson, but also less in love with his money.

In 1997, Robinson and his wife, Valerie, announced a $5 million gift to establish the Carver Academy at San Antonio's Carver Center, a multicultural and multiethnic community center and arts presenter. It is still believed to be the largest onetime donation by an NBA player, perhaps any athlete.

"We've tried to meet people's needs in San Antonio on a basic level," Robinson says. "But we wanted to do more. The Carver has had a great impact on this community for one hundred years. And it is a big part of the black community, which meant a lot to us. . . . I'm not going to run this school. We will hire people to do that. We will emphasize discipline, life applications, morality, and academics. There will be no toleration of drugs, smoking, alcohol, or lack of respect. This is all part of God's plan for me and my family. . . . I have a heart that wants to serve and bless. That is what I am."

But it's not necessarily what he has always been.

In fact, Robinson really never even thought about a career in basketball until he was nearly finished at the U.S. Naval Academy. He grew up playing classical piano and jazz saxophone instead of pick-up basketball games at the neighborhood court. As an elementary school student, he was enrolled in programs for gifted students. In junior high, he took college-level computer classes and built his own big-screen TV from a kit. Baseball was his favorite sport, although he played most others, except basketball. His first experience on a basketball team came in his senior year in high school. After scoring a blistering 1,320 on the SAT college entrance exam (out of a possible 1,600), Robinson went to the academy as a six-foot-six-inch, 175-pound future sailor studying engineering and mathematics.

As a freshman at Navy, he averaged 7 points and 4 rebounds per game, and seemed uncomfortable on the court and not terribly interested in the game. But over the next four years he grew seven inches, and the game seemed to be made for him. What else does a graceful seven-foot-one-inch athlete do?

As a senior, Robinson became the top college player in the nation and was the first pick in the 1987 draft. After graduating with a degree in mathematics, he fulfilled his two-year service commitment to the navy prior to joining the Spurs.

Once in the NBA, where he thought he had it all, Robinson realized he didn't. The money, the fame, the NBA lifestyle didn't satisfy. He felt empty.

"I knew something was missing—I just didn't know what it was," Robinson explains. "I kept thinking about how up and down my life was. It seemed that every time I did something, I had to do it again—or do something even better. We'd start a new season, and I'd have to re-prove myself over and over again. It was never enough."

Then in 1991, a pastor by the name of Greg Ball was visiting the Spurs locker room. He told Robinson he wanted to talk to him about God. Robinson had some questions about "this Christian stuff," as he called it, so he agreed to meet with Ball.

The conversation that was supposed to last fifteen minutes ended up stretching to five hours.

Ball asked Robinson some pointed questions about how much he loved God, how much he read the Bible, how much time he spent praying, whether Robinson gave one day of his week to honor God. By the time the dialogue was finished, Robinson was challenged.

"I realized that I was like a mouse running around in a little cage, you know," says Robinson. "And I was running and you know what? I was doing great, running really fast; I mean, I'm winning everybody, you know; I'm making a lot of money. That's what I went to school for, you know. I'm doing great; I live in a nice apartment. I drive a nice car; I'm doing great. But, I realized at that point that the rest of my life I'd have been running, and what I wanted to accomplish, I don't know. I don't even know. I mean, whatever they told me I needed to accomplish I would have tried to accomplish.

"I thought I had everything. I mean, you are making millions of dollars a year, you have houses, cars, you have everything you think you want. And then all of a sudden I realized that God had given me everything; he had given me all this. But never once had I stopped and said thank you, Lord. Thank you, God, for giving me what I had.

"It made me realize that I really didn't love God," says Robinson. "You can say all you want to say, but if your actions don't back it up, then it means nothing. I realized that day that God had given me so much, and I had never so much as thanked him. I could see his love for me, what he had done for me, how he had stood by me, and how he had been calling out to me. My heart just broke.

"So that day I just cried. I said, 'Lord, I am so sorry; I am so, so sorry. I didn't realize I was being like a spoiled brat. I thank you for everything you've given me. I mean, you blessed me beyond hope, beyond comprehension. And I just want to give it all right back to you. And from this day forth I just want to learn about you; I want to walk with you; I want to hold your hand; I want to love you like I say I love you.' And man, he turned my life around 180 degrees. He turned my mentality around 180 degrees. And he gave me a joy and an ability to enjoy what I had that I didn't have before. . . . my whole world just opened up."

Finally, David found his rock.

"I can't overstate how important my faith has been to me as an athlete and as a person," Robinson says. "It's helped me deal with so many things, including matters of ego and pride. . . . I'm blessed that God has given me the ability to just enjoy the victories."

Understatement of his own accomplishments and an understanding of what is most important to him—these are hallmarks of David Robinson's character, no better exemplified than in his selfless act in taking the Spurs to the title. While the sportsworld stood and watched in awe, Robinson himself was nonplused.

David found his Rock. Goliath is dead. Character lives. The good guy is a winner—and an extraordinary human being.

HEART OF A CHAMPION™

Heart of a Champion™ Foundation

The Heart of a Champion Foundation is a unique educational support non-profit organization dedicated to the purpose of actively promoting virtues, values, and character qualities through sports-related programs and events in the educational environment that will influence and stimulate young people to integrate these values into their own lives and consistently demonstrate them in their schools, homes, and communities. This purpose is achieved through the creation, distribution, and promotion of high-quality interactive media materials and activities designed for young people ages five to eighteen.

You can find more information concerning the Heart of a Champion Foundation at:

heartofachampion.org or heartofachampion.net

Or write to: Heart of a Champion Foundation,

P.O. Box 740126, Dallas, Texas 75374-0126

Heart of a Champion™ Products

Heart of a Champion products are created by VisionQuest Communications Group, a leader in the production and promotion of virtuous and inspirational sports material. A wide variety of book, video, and gift items are available under the Heart of a Champion brand name. Heart of a Champion programs can be found on television, radio, and the Internet. Look for the Heart of a Champion logo on a product or program as an indication that it will inform, encourage, motivate, inspire, and re-inforce positive values while providing high-quality entertainment.

NOTES

Much of the material in this book was gathered in interviews conducted by Steve Riach and VisionQuest Communications for a variety of its television, radio, and video programs. Extensive files on each athlete have been maintained by VisionQuest for many years that contain various clippings and other reference material. Also consulted have been specific websites of the professional leagues, teams, and in some instances, the athletes themselves. In addition, the authors have specifically referenced information contained in the following authored articles and books listed below. Dates and titles are listed when known.

Chapter 1, Excellence

Randy Johnson: Phil Rogers, *Chicago Tribune*; Jim Street, *The Sporting News*, 1994; Tom Verducci, *Sports Illustrated*

Kevin Malone: Victor Lee, *Sports Spectrum*, 1999; Robert Kuwada, *Orange County Register*, 29 September 1999

Ritchie McKay: Victor Lee, *Sports Spectrum*, 1997; Kellie Anderson, *Sports Illustrated*, 1999

Dr. James Naismith: *Sports Illustrated* Editorial Projects Department, 1999

Nolan Ryan: T. R. Sullivan, *Fort Worth Star Telegram*; Talmadge Boston, Texas Rangers Game Program

Alex Rodriguez: Gerry Callahan, "The Fairest of Them All," *Sports Illustrated*; Pete Williams, "Alex the Great," *USA Baseball Weekly*, 1996; Mel Antonen, "Rodriguez's Bat Explodes on Scene," *USA Today*, 22 May 1996; Jeff Miller, "Great Expectations," Greater Results, *The Sporting 1997 Yearbook*; Bob Finnigan, "Alex Rodriguez: Missing Dad," *Seattle Times*, 22 March 1998; Tyler Kepner, "Alex Rodriguez's Talent Has No Boundaries," *Seattle Post-Intelligencer*; Florangela Davila, "Alex the Great," *Seattle Times*, 23 March 1997; "Amazing A-Rod," *USA Today Baseball Weekly*, 1997; Bob Finnigan, "A-Rod's Short Road to Stardom," *Seattle Times*, 13 March 1997; Michael Knisley, "All A-Rod, All the Time," *The Sporting News*, 28 June 1999

Chapter 2, Overcoming Adversity

Paul Azinger: Steve Hershey, *USA Today*

Mark Brunell: Steve Hershey, *USA Today*, 1998; Paul Attner, *The Sporting News*; Ken Walker, *Manpower* magazine

Tony Jones and Mark Schlereth: Allen Palmieri, *Sports Spectrum*, 1998

Jerry LeVias: Ken Stephens, *Dallas Morning News*; Whit Canning, *Fort Worth Star Telegram*

Dan Reeves: Jill Leiber, *USA Today*, 1999

Michelle Akers: David Smale, "Redirection," *Sharing the Victory*; Michelle Akers and Judith Nelson, "Full Cup," *Sports Spectrum*, September 1999; Michael Bamberger, "Dream Come True," *Sports Illustrated*; Kelly Whiteside, "World Beater," *Sports Illustrated*; Tom Felten, "The Golden Boot," *Sports Spectrum*, June 1996; Grant Wuhl, "Purple Heart," *Sports Illustrated*

Chapter 3, Leadership

Brad Smith: Terry Hill, Nashville, Tenn.; Bobbie Barker, *Sports Spectrum*, 1998

J. C. Watts: Michael Towle, *Fort Worth Star Telegram*

Bobby Bowden: Tim Layden, "No Quit in This Soldier," *Sports Illustrated*; Larry Guest, "Seminoles Chief a Master Recruiter," *The Sporting News*, 26 February 1990; David H. Carroll, "Saint Bobby," *The Sporting News College Football Yearbook*, 1993; David H. Carroll, "Champion," *Sharing the Victory*; Ken Walker, "The Wit and Wisdom of Bobby Bowden," *Sports Spectrum*, October 1993; Thomas J. Wheatley, "College Football's First Family," *Lindy's Football Annual*, 1992; David Caldwell, "FSU's Bowden Finds Time to Stay on Top of Coaching," *Dallas Morning News*

Chapter 4, Discipline

Orel Hershisher: Paul Attner, *The Sporting News*, 1988; Jerry Crasnik, *Sports Spectrum*, 1992; Steve Wulf, *Sports Illustrated*

Cade McNown: Jeff Arnold, *Sports Spectrum*, 1999

Scott Simpson: James Dodson, "Waiting His Turn," *Golf* magazine, September 1995

Aeneas Williams: Austin Murphy, *Sports Illustrated*

Cris Carter: Don Banks, "Catching a Falling Star," *The Sporting News*, 25 May 1998; Curt Brown, "Once Cut, Now a Cut Above," *The Sporting News Pro Football Yearbook*, 1995; Jeffri Chadiha, "Time Trial," *Sports Illustrated*; "Amazing Grace," *Beckett Profiles*, 1996; Will Greer, "A Receiver Who Gives," *Sharing the Victory*, December 1997; David Moriah, "Great Catch," *Sports Spectrum*, October 1995; Paul Attner, "As Great As He Wants to Be," *The Sporting News*, 16 November 1998; Richard Hofer, "Catching Up," *Sports Illustrated*

Chapter 5, Commitment

Jennifer Azzi, Rithie Bolton Holifield: Oscar Dixon, *Sports Spectrum*; Roxanne Robbins, *AIA* magazine; Ken Baker, "True Believers," *Women's Sports and Fitness*, 1998

Dennis Byrd: *Sports Spectrum*, 1994

Chad Hennings: Steve Landsdale, *Fort Worth Child*, 1995; John Weber and Jim Gibbs, *Sports Spectrum*, 1997; Jill Leiber, 1997

Eric Liddell: Steve Howell, *AIA* magazine

Dot Richardson: Paul Pringle, Copley News Service

Jason Taylor: Carolyn White, *USA Today*; Albert Dickson, *The Sporting News*, 1997

Jean Driscoll: Jennie Chandler, "Free Wheelin'," *Sports Spectrum*, November 1997; Fred Kroner, "Awards Keep Piling Up for Driscoll," *Champaign News-Gazette*, 9 June

1997; Jill Lieber, "Paralympian Simply Aims to Be the Best," *USA Today*, 22 August 1996; Rod Handley, "Overcoming Pain and Fear," *Sharing the Victory*

Chapter 6, Teamwork

Scott Brosius: Mike Umlandt, *Sports Spectrum*, 1999

Annett Buckner Davis and Jenny Johnson Jordan: David Leon Moore, "Beach Volleyball Players Have Faith in One Another," *USA Today*, 7 October 1999

Bob Christian: Furman Bisher, *Atlanta Journal Constitution*; Paul Newberry, *Associated Press-Gwinnett Daily Press*, 1998

Tom Hammonds: Geri Meachem, *Sports Spectrum*, 1996

Joe Gibbs: Lee Spencer, "Still Running the Team," *The Sporting News*, 27 December 1999

Chapter 7, Priorities

Laurie Brower: *Sports Spectrum*, August 1996

Tim Burke: "Leaving Baseball for the Kids," Family Research Council; Focus on the Family *Citizen* magazine, 18 October 1993; Richard Demak, An All-Star Father; "Major League Dad," Word Publishing, 1994

Jeff King: "Diamond Gems," *Sports Spectrum*, 1998

Bernhard Langer: *Arizona Republic*, 1994; Sam Wollwine, *Sports Spectrum*, 1996; Sam Wollwine, *Sports Spectrum*, 1992; Rick Reilly, *Sports Illustrated*

Johnny Oates: Evan Grant, *Dallas Morning News*; Phil Rogers, *Dallas Morning News*; Barry Horn, *Dallas Morning News*

Branch Rickey: Kevin Sherrington, *Dallas Morning News*, April 1997

Chris Spielman: Dick Shaap, "A Tale of Two Comebacks," *Parade* magazine, 12 September 1999; Dennis Dillon, "The Heart of Cleveland," *The Sporting News*, 26 July 1999

Darrell Waltrip: Ed Hinton, *Sports Illustrated*; *Sports Spectrum*, 1993; *Sports Spectrum*, 1995

Cynthia Cooper: Johnette Howard, "Comet's Tale," *Sports Illustrated*; Kelli Anderson, "Coop de Grace," *Sports Illustrated*; Oscar Dixon, "Greatest Role: Playing in Pain," *USA Today*, 2 September 1999; Alexander Wulf, "Won for All," *Sports Illustrated*

Chapter 8, Success

Jackie Joyner Kersee: Cathey Harasta, *Dallas Morning News*; Cigna Advertising Feature; "A Kind of Grace," *Black Elegance*, October 1997; Judith P. Josephson, *Children's Digest*, March 1994; Frank Deford, "Jackie, Oh!", *Newsweek*, 10 June 1996

Pete Maravich: Phil Berger, *Sports Illustrated*; Carolyn White, *USA Today*, 1988; Skip Bayless, *Virginia Pilot*, 1985; *The Sporting News*, 1988; Steve Jacobsen, *The Ledger Star*, 1988

Bruce Mathews: *The Sporting News*, 1997; Randy Weiler, *Sports Spectrum*, 1997

Gene Stallings: Bob St. John, *Dallas Morning News*; Debbie Becker, *USA Today*, 1997; Allen Palmieri, *Sports Spectrum*, 1993

John Naber: Chris Woehr

Jeff Gordon: Victor Lee, "Team Gordon," *Sports Spectrum*, NASCAR 1997; Andy Johnston, "Jeff Gordon," *Sports Spectrum*, Racing 2000; "Jeff Gordon, NASCAR Special," *Sports Illustrated*, 1998; Steve Goldberg, "Smile, You're a Winner," *Time*, 15 June 1998; Beth Tuschak, "Young Driver Gives Changes a Jump Start," *USA Today*; Liz Clarke, "New Force Drives Racing," *USA Today*, 29 January 1998; Kevin Sherington, "In the Driver's Seat," *Dallas Morning News*, 30 March 1997; Liz Clarke, "Gordon Rules NASCAR," *USA*

Today, 3 July 1997; John Sturbin, "Gordon Deserves Rousing Round of Cheers," *Ft. Worth Star-Telegram*; Steve Ballard, "Gordon: Victim of His Success," *USA Today*; Marcia Smith, "Gordon's Popularity Comes with a Price," *Dallas Morning News*; Skip Wood, "Gordon: Great or Grating?," *USA Today*; Mark Whicker, "Jeff Gordon Is the New Kid in Town," *Orange County Register*; Shav Glick, "A Veteran Champion at Only 24," *Los Angeles Times*; Kevin Lyons, "You're Friendly Neighborhood Superstar Is a Regular Jeff," *Ft. Worth Star-Telegram*

Chapter 9, Conviction

Justin Armour: Ken Durham, *Sports Spectrum*, 1994
Terry Blocker: Kevin Hunter, *Sports Spectrum*, 1995
Mark Dewey: Robb Bentz, *Sports Spectrum*
Reggie White: David Caldwell, *Dallas Morning News*, 1997; Roman Gabriel III, *Sports Spectrum*, 1999
Danny Wuerffel: *USA Today* Staff Reports
AC Green: Norm Frauenheim, "Green On a Mission—On and Off the Court," *Arizona Republic*, 24 October 1993; David DuPree, "A.C. Green: NBA Iron Man," *USA Today*, 20 November 1997; Michael Farber, "Iron Man," *Sports Illustrated*

Chapter 10, Sacrifice

John Amaechi: Erik Brady, *USA Today*, March 2000
Coy Bacon: Ken Walker, *Sports Spectrum*, 1992
Carl Erskine: Tom Felton, *Sports Spectrum*, 1994; Hill Horlacher, *AIA* magazine
Tom Landry: Tom Landry Tribute, *Dallas Morning News*, 1999; Gill Lebretton, *Fort Worth Star Telegram*
John Wetteland: *Campus Life* magazine, July 1997
Betsy King: Karen Rudolph Drollinger, "Back in the Swing of Things," *Sports Spectrum*, March 1993; Karen Foulke, "Betsy King: Around the World," *Sports Spectrum*, August 1994; John Garrity, "In a World of Her Own," *Sports Illustrated*; Bill Huffman, "Course of Action Builds Hope," *Arizona Republic*, 8 October 1993; Jerry Potter, "LPGA 10 Give a Week to Poor," *USA Today*, 19 October 1989; John Dodderidge, "Living Her Faith Daily," *Sharing the Victory*; Shelly Smith, "Inside Golf," *Sports Illustrated*; Bill Huffman, "King's Reserved Roots Branch Off into Golf," *Arizona Republic*, 18 March 1993; Richard Sowers, "Golf Queen King Is LPGA's Ace," *The Sporting News*, 30 October 1989; Jerry Potter, "Past Gives King Peace about Future," *USA Today*; Betsy King, "Betsy's Story of Her Road to the Top," *Links Letter*, January 1985; Mike Sandrolini, "Working Class King," *Sports Spectrum*, 1995

Chapter 11, Perseverance

John Stephen Akhwari: International Olympic Committee Information, *USA Today*
Avery Johnson: Greg Boeck; Brad Townsend, *Dallas Morning News*
Tom Lehman: Phil Rogers, *Dallas Morning News*; Rick Reilly, *Sports Illustrated*
Jackie Robinson: William Nack, *Sports Illustrated*
Paul Wylie: E. M. Swift, *Sports Illustrated*; Dave Brannon, *Sports Spectrum*, 1992; Roxanne Robbins, *Sports Spectrum*, 1997
Kurt Warner: Jill Lieber, "Rams' Warner Armed with Love," *USA Today*, 26 January 2000; Michael Silver, "Holy Smokes," *Sports Illustrated*, 18 October 1999; Michael Silver, "The Greatest," *Sports Illustrated*; Curtis Bunn, "Kurt Warner," *Atlanta Journal*

Constitution; Furman Bisher, "Warner's Unlikely Story Not Over Yet," *Atlanta Journal Constitution;* Gary Horton, "Breaking Down the Rams' Kurt Warner," *The Sporting News,* 1 November 1999; Gordon Forbes, "Warner Makes Big Jump But Keeps Passing Tests," *USA Today,* 30 November 1999; Kevin Lyons, "Rags To Riches," *Ft. Worth Star-Telegram*

Chapter 12, Faith

Ron Brown: "I Can: Ron Brown's Search for Success," Cross Training Publishing, 1992

Irving Fryar: *Sports Illustrated;* John B. Colsain Jr. *Sports Spectrum,* 1997

Barbara Nicklaus: Victor Lee, *Sports Spectrum*

Joe Girardi: Geri Meacham, *Sports Spectrum,* 1997

Jerry Schemmel: *Sports Spectrum,* 1997

David Robinson: Leigh Montville, "Trials of David," *Sports Illustrated,* 29 April 1996; Rick Reilly, "Spur of the Moment," *Sports Illustrated;* Frank Clancy, "Twin Engines," *The Sporting News,* 15 December 1997; Christin Ditchfield, "Tall Order," *Sports Spectrum,* March 1999; David Robinson with Phil Taylor, "Mission Accomplished," *Sports Illustrated;* Paul Attner, "A Gift For Giving," *The Sporting News,* 2 August 1999; Mark Whicker, "Spurs' David Robinson: He's Simply Admirable," *Orange County Register,* 18 June 1999; Douglas S. Looney, "Mr. Robinson Shares His Neighborhood," *Christian Science Monitor,* 25 June 1999; Sam Smith, "When Looking at David Robinson, Remember Bill Russell," *Chicago Tribune,* 15 June 1999; Kevin O'Keefe, "David Robinson Demonstrates That Class Still Matters in Sports," *San Antonio Business Journal,* 11 June 1999

PHOTO CREDITS